CURING INFERTILITY:
THE INCREDIBLE HUNYUAN BREAKTHROUGH

Become Pregnant and Healthy with Ancient Chinese Medicine

YARON SEIDMAN D.A.O.M.

"Not only will this book deepen your understanding of Chinese medicine, but also provide you with valuable insights of our close relationship with nature."

—TAIKEN JO, T.C.M.,
Director of ACURA Acupuncture Clinic, Tokyo, Japan

"Doctor Seidman truly understands what the classics were about and has shown us all the secrets to a long life and never ending health."

—ANDREW ORR,
Doctor of Traditional Chinese Medicine, Brisbane, Australia

"Dr. Seidman has reinvigorated the backbone of Chinese Medicine and applied it to modern reproductive medicine in an intriguing marriage of East and West."

—Z'EV ROSENBERG, L. AC.,
Chair, Department of Herbal Medicine, Pacific College of Oriental Medicine

"Yaron Seidman's book on treating infertility with Chinese medicine is an excellent example for the clinical power of the classical approach. Insightful, practical, clinically useful."

—HEINER FRUEHAUF, PH.D.
Founding Professor, School of Classical Chinese Medicine, National College of Natural Medicine, Portland, Oregon

"Dr. Seidman makes an important contribution to the body of knowledge on how Traditional Chinese Medicine offers women a natural and effective pathway to fertility."

—JOANNA ZHAO, L.AC.
Academic Dean & Clinical Director, Five Branches University San Jose, California

"Yaron Seidman's work is recognized as a significant adjunct to conventional infertility treatment programs. Women need to be aware such alternatives exist."

—EDWARD JACOBSON, MD FACOG
Greenwich Gynecology & Wellness, LLC Greenwich, Connecticut

For my mother and father, who by making the correct choices in life, taught me the traditional values necessary to lead my children down a path toward health, well-being and fulfillment.

NOTE: Every effort has been made to ensure that the information contained in this book is complete and accurate. However, neither the publisher nor the author is engaged in rendering professional advice or services to the individual reader. Neither the author nor the publisher shall be liable or responsible for any loss, injury, or damage allegedly arising from any information or suggestion in this book.

LTM Books
352 Seventh Avenue
New York, NY 10001
LTM Books is an imprint of LifeTime Media, Inc.

Visit our website at **www.lifetimemedia.com** or **www.ltmbooks.com**

Neither LifeTime Media nor any of its goods or services are in any way affiliated with, associated with, sponsored by or approved by Lifetime networks, Lifetime television, or Lifetime Entertainment Services.

ISBN: 978-0-9823975-1-0

Library of Congress Number: 2009942436

All LTM Books and LifeTime Media titles are available for special promotions, premiums, and bulk purchase. For more information, please contact the manager of our sales department at 212-631-7524 or sales@lifetimemedia.com

Distributed to the trade by Perseus Book Group
To order books for the trade call 1-800-343-4499
Printed in the United States of America
10.9.8.7.6.5.4.3.2.1

Design: Christina Freyss
Edited by: Scott Fields

TABLE OF CONTENTS

· · · · · · · · · · · · · · · · · · ·

上古之人其知道

FOREWORD

. . . .

The treatment of infertility has, like most aspects of modern medicine, become a "high-tech" process. Acronyms such as IVF (in-vitro fertilization), ICSI (intracytoplasmic sperm injection) and PGD (pre-implantation genetic diagnosis) have become familiar terms to most couples undergoing infertility treatment. In most areas of medicine, these high-tech advances are major strides in the conquest of disease. With infertility, these advances have also made treatment a cold, clinical process rather then the natural process that most couples hoped conceiving a child would be.

The first IVF baby was born in 1978 and the process became clinically available as of the mid 1980's. Prior to that, reproductive endocrinologists using proven techniques helped many infertile couples achieve pregnancy. Although some of those techniques were certainly clinical, such as surgery to correct pelvic problems, many were more natural, involving natural hormone treatments, tracking of the menstrual cycle and properly timed intercourse. Most of these techniques are still available today but have fallen by the wayside in the contemporary approach of high tech infertility treatments.

This clinicalization of infertility treatment has also extended into the realm of traditional Chinese medicine, a discipline where the personal touch has always been held sacred. As of recently, certain ancient Chinese techniques have, because of peer-reviewed research, been accepted by Western infertility medicine. Most notably, IVF pregnancy rates have been shown to improve with acupuncture. Many current practitioners of traditional Chinese medicine have geared their practices toward these findings and learn only those aspects of eastern techniques that relate directly to IVF or other Western treatments. They do not study or learn many of the ancient Chinese remedies and treatments that have for thousands of years helped couples conceive.

In this book, Yaron Seidman explores in depth this loss of traditional techniques of infertility treatment that appears to dominate both traditional Chinese medicine and Western medicine today. He also discusses alternatives to the contemporary approach to infertility treatment.

He proposes an innovative combination of the best of non-invasive western reproductive medicine with the best of traditional Chinese medicine backed-up by modern high tech treatments if necessary. The majority of infertile couples would undoubtedly prefer this combination of natural techniques verses going directly to drugs, injections and plastic cups.

KAROL CHACHO, M.D.
BOARD CERTIFIED INFERTILITY SPECIALIST
AND REPRODUCTIVE ENDOCRINOLOGIST

PREFACE

· · · · · · · · · · · · · · · · · · ·

The "science of time" which we call Chinese medicine preceded modern science by at least 3000 years. In Curing Infertility: The Incredible Hunyuan Breakthrough, we will travel the path of this ancient discipline step by step to discover its genius. Primarily intended for infertility patients, the book is also aimed at Modern Chinese medical practitioners, most of whom lack any training in the classical ways.

To truly grasp the essence of Ancient Chinese medicine, we must leave modern thinking patterns behind. If it is viewed from the perspective of Western medicine, the discipline's meaning and great value will be missed entirely. If it is approached with an open mind, an amazing world will open.

AUTHOR'S WORD

· · · · · · · · · · · · · · · · · · · ·

I took fertility drugs at the beginning of this IVF cycle, as instructed by my reproductive endocrinologist. The doctor harvested 14 perfectly healthy eggs, out of which 12 fertilized. We did genetic testing to determine which embryos were the best quality. The doctor transferred three of these best quality embryos… and then we waited anxiously until the scheduled blood test just to find out that the pregnancy didn't take.

This story and others are commonplace at my Hunyuan Centers in Connecticut. We see women who repeatedly try In Vitro Fertilization and fail to conceive. In most cases, the doctor cannot explain what went wrong. Everything was "going according to plan" and yet in the end, nothing happened.

As the founder of the Hunyuan Method, my main concern is with the patient's health. I know from experience that when a woman is truly healthy, she can conceive and maintain a pregnancy naturally without artificial help.

As of yet, general knowledge of healthy natural conception is at best unsatisfactory. The average fertility patient is told to try "naturally" for six to 12 months, and if unsuccessful, to immediately proceed to drugs, invasive tests, and/or surgical procedures.

Sometimes treatment is recommended after just one month of trying naturally. Yet, the side effects of these treatments are many and the success rate is low.

Becoming truly healthy before attempting to conceive naturally optimizes a woman's chances for conception and will often prevent endless expensive fertility treatments. We have all experienced illness and disease when our bodies simply don't work as well. Optimum health is not only important for the mother's reproductive capacity and safety; it is also significant when it comes to the baby's development.

In the world of modern fertility treatments, health is often ignored. Stimulating the ovaries with drugs, or removing fibroids and fallopian tubes, does not make a woman healthy. Removal of eggs for fertilization, followed by replacement in the uterus, does not make a woman healthy. In fact, side effects I have seen in my patients taking fertility medications include hot flashes, abdominal distension, cysts, menstrual irregularities, elevated FSH levels, emotional breakdowns, back pain, heart palpitations and insomnia.

If you are at all familiar with Chinese medicine, the method to attain fertility presented here will no doubt seem very foreign. It is different from what most Chinese medicine doctors practice today. It explains "Health" from a "Hunyuan Method" perspective. "Hunyuan" is my term for Classical Chinese medicine, developed by the ancients, which is now practiced by very few. In this discipline, the doctor's first calling is to educate and inform his patients on how to stay healthy. It is different from, and often completely contradictory to, "Modern Chinese medicine," which, like Western medicine, is more concerned with treating symptoms.

Although I do not believe in taking most pharmaceutical drugs, I have a great admiration for Western medicine. Primarily occupied with symptoms and their instant elimination, Western medicine does so with great conviction and success. When a drug is intended to stimulate the ovaries, for example, it does so without hesitation.

On the other hand, my admiration for Classical Chinese medicine rises out of its swiftness in eliminating the *root* cause of an illness. I can think of endless examples to support this notion, but one which I will share involves a 42-year-old patient with a sinus infection which lasted for three months. She took three rounds of strong antibiotics, and although her symptoms lessened after each round, the symptoms continued to return within one to two days. When she came to see me, she complained of exhaustion, relentless headaches and constant coughing-up of green phlegm. I composed a Classical Chinese medicine formula made out of three herbs. When she returned the following week, she reported that after drinking the first cup of herbal tea, her head cleared within two hours, and by the next morning, her symptoms were gone. Two months later, the patient conceived naturally and at the time of this writing is eight months pregnant with no complications.

Modern Chinese medicine does not favor herbal formulas. Instead, the use of acupuncture is more common for treating infertility cases. Although modern studies suggest that placing acupuncture needles in a few predetermined points can improve IVF success rates, these treatments are not nearly as effective as the Classical Chinese herbal formulas.

"Health" is a relative concept. Although we may not be in optimum health, we feel healthy because we tend to compare ourselves to others who are less healthy. I will explain in this book what "health" should and shouldn't look like, and how to improve, remedy and preserve it. Most importantly I will show how improving your health can help become pregnant.

Statistics show that 14 percent of all couples in the US suffer from infertility. This translates to millions and millions of people, and hundreds of millions of dollars spent on infertility treatments. It is my hope that this book will allow the reader to make a better, or at least a more informed, choice as to what course of action to take with fertility treatments. Hopefully, the reader will realize that sometimes the fastest way is not necessarily the easiest way or the right way.

The one comment I hear most often from my patients is "I wish I had known about you earlier." What would happen if women with infertility issues turned to the Hunyuan method before turning to Western medicine? Although there's no definitive answer to this question, I am certain that thousands of couples who are childless would know the joy of parenting.

YARON SEIDMAN L.AC., D.A.O.M.
GREENWICH, CONNECTICUT

上古之人其知道
者法於陰陽和於
術數食飲有節起
居有常不妄作勞

1

GIVE THE ANCIENTS
A CHANCE

Salad causes cancer was something I was once surprised to hear during a lecture by a well-known nutritionist. Of course, she wasn't referring to the vegetables in the salad, but to the chemical-laden dressings most Americans pour on top of them. The lesson: lack of knowledge is the cause of the disease.

The same is true with infertility. With the right knowledge, infertility can often be avoided. Without the right knowledge, infertility will prevail.

The Yellow Emperor Inner Classics, the 2500-year-old book which forms the core essence of Chinese medicine, states in an opening paragraph of the first of two volumes: *The sages knew how to live in harmony with nature. They lived to be 100 years old but their bodies never declined and they seemed to be as if they were only 50 years old.*

The methods of these sages, transmitted over generations, provide a stark contrast to today's prevailing notion that new is better than old when it comes to the practice of medicine. We cling to the false belief that we are always increasing in general intelligence, and that previous generations knew less than us.

I am convinced that this worship of the new and "advanced" is a main contributor to many of the diseases we suffer from today. It is certainly a major cause for infertility, a condition which wasn't all that much of a problem when medical procedures were far less complicated. Modern science gives us a new set of rules that can result in more disease and illness, and more people living on drugs. Many pharmaceuticals are known to cause debilitating side effects and long-term deterioration. I often hear statements such as *This drug will take care of your cholesterol, but it might lead to a liver problem in the future.* With fertility drug treatments there is also a marked deterioration in the patient's health. An increased number of women are subject to infertility, miscarriages and /or pregnancy complications.

Originally, I accepted the theory that the present infertility boom was caused by the trend toward women focusing on their careers before having a family. However, after treating hundreds and hundreds of infertility patients, I am certain this is not the only cause, and perhaps not even the most important. In fact, many of my patients are in their twenties, and statistics show that women are now experiencing infertility at a younger age than previously.

GIVING UP MODERN PREJUDICES

To understand Classical Chinese medicine, the reader must attempt to remain non-judgmental, at least until completing the book, in order to avoid distraction by modern prejudice. The reader must be able to think beyond both Western medical science, and modern Chinese medical science, to see the flaws in those systems, and to see how these two disciplines have robbed Chinese medicine of its essence.

THE HIGH AND THE LOW

In ancient China, an individual's health was more precious than a thousand gold bars. It was precious because it was thought that human life was created out of the interaction between heaven and earth. Furthermore, the harmonization of heaven and earth was thought to equal the prolonging of one's health. It was felt that with healthy people living long lives, the natural cycle of birth and rebirth would go on forever, exactly like heaven and earth go on forever, birthing and rebirthing day after day and year after year.

The Chinese culture has spawned many brilliant physicians over its thousands of years of history. One such physician was Zhang Ji from the Second Century A.D. In the early years of his practice, he warned a Duke that if he neglected to take a particular herbal formula, he would lose his eyebrows in 20 years and subsequently die a terrible death. The Duke, a doctor himself, laughed it off, unable to believe in a diagnosis 20 years in advance. Nevertheless, 20 years later, the Duke's eyebrows fell off, and within three months he fell ill and died in great pain.

Zhang Ji's reputation grew until he was famous far and wide.

Adopting the pen name Zhang Zhongjing, he wrote **Shang Han Za Bing Lun,** considered one of the four classics of Chinese medicine for the past 2000 years and providing a foundation for the discipline.

Zhang Zhongjing and other physicians like him were centuries ahead of their time. They can be likened to Albert Einstein, whose theories about space and black holes in the universe still evade comprehension by many scientists today. Zhang and other ancient geniuses established the rules for harmonizing the body with nature, paving the way for long life and health. As healers, they were dedicated to the long-term benefit of the patient, and when they prescribed herbs, it was to heal for a lifetime, hence Zhang's ability to see his patient's condition 20 years ahead. Because of this long term view, Zhang is referred to in Chinese medicine as a "High Practitioner."

Unfortunately, this principle can be difficult to follow. Understanding the impact of one's actions for many years to come is not an easy feat. This gave birth to the "low-level practitioner," who was occupied with short term success in alleviating symptoms. As **The Yellow Emperor** describes it in the first volume, **Plain Questions,** a low level practitioner treats disease with a standard formula, while high level practitioners treat disease by analyzing the situation and then coming up with an appropriate solution.

High practitioners, in another classical description, always act in three stages. The first is the "Careful Heart" stage, where the practitioner must carefully consider the root cause of the problem and what should be done about it. In the second stage, referred to as "Big Gallbladder," the practitioner must be courageous and unafraid to do the right thing for the patient. In the third stage, or "Fast Hand," the physician must act quickly.

BRINGING BACK THE TRUE CHINESE MEDICINE

The popularity of acupuncture has long been increasing in the Western world, largely because practitioners and acupuncture schools have made an effort to integrate into mainstream Western medicine. While this is very encouraging on some levels, it also pushes the practice of acupuncture toward the Western medicine model of treating symptoms, and away from the Chinese medicine concern with long-lasting health benefits.

This is particularly true when it comes to treatments for infertility. Most acupuncture practitioners, embracing Western medicine's endocrinology related issues, give up traditional Chinese principles to follow the mainstream model of health. Unfortunately, this means that traditional Chinese medicine is all but extinct.

Ironically, in Zhang Zhongjing's time, a similar situation had developed. In the introduction to **Shang Han Lun,** Zhang writes: *I always admired the diagnosis and skills of the talented doctors of the past. It is strange that the doctors today are not cautious with medicine and herbs and their research of the herbal prescriptions is not thorough… They pursue on their tiptoes glory and power, their service is for fame and profit alone. They worship the tail end of the discipline and they forget about its essence. They magnify the outer shell and forget about the inner core. If the skin is not there, how can the body hair be at peace?*

Doctors everywhere are losing their heads and can't reach enlightenment, Zhang continues. *They do not cherish 'life' as if it were a benign affair, so how can they talk about fame and power?... Their diagnosis can only be partial and they can't see the entire picture. This is called viewing the patient through a peephole.*

Zhang believed that to be truly effective, practitioners had to be immersed in the classics until it was part of their being. He also explained that to love the body, and to honestly help patients, the practitioner must first learn about himself.

BELIEVING IN THE PATIENT AND HER BODY

When Western doctors fail with IVF treatments, they are prone to blaming the patient, generally because she is "too old," whether that means she's 30 or 46. When my patients fail to become pregnant with the Hunyuan Method, I view it as my failure.

It is of utmost importance to have total faith in the patient and her body. Western medicine believes that if an organ or body function fails, it cannot recover by itself and needs intervention, such as with IVF. Chinese medicine always believes that the patient's body *can* recover its functions on its own.

This difference in perspective lies in our different approach to thinking about the future. In Western thought, when the future is uncertain, most people believe that the outcome will be negative. This engenders a sense of safety in that Westerners already know something bad is going to happen, and thus cannot be surprised by it. In Asia, and especially in China, the approach has been quite different. The Chinese feel content over whatever the future brings, that nature is on their side, and that if they follow nature, the future will always be bright.

In Western medicine, if there is any question about a patient's condition and the doctor has to decide if the patient is ill or healthy, the tendency is to opt for illness. If the choice is to medicate or not, the decision will usually be to medicate. This is because it is "better" to pronounce someone ill and be wrong than to pronounce someone "well" and be wrong. It is believed that prescribing medication that is not necessary will simply be wasteful, but not harmful.

Extended to the world of infertility treatments, Western doctors start with the assumption that the woman has little chance of becoming pregnant. Expectations are lowered so if the patient does become pregnant, the doctor becomes a hero. In Chinese medicine, it is believed that only nature can decide who is fertile and who is not, and if the patient is healthy and in tune with nature, there's a good chance pregnancy will occur. Doctors cannot make it happen.

My experience shows that believing in nature always leads to a brighter future. Many patients in my practice have experienced it firsthand. They believed in their own fertility and they became pregnant naturally.

When a patient comes to see me, it isn't necessary for me to shatter her dreams and cause her to sink into despair, fearing the future. I encourage her and boost her confidence because it feels good to be treated with Chinese medicine. After every acupuncture session the patient feels invigorated. After every week of herbs, the patient feels more vital. If nothing else, excellent health is always achieved.

Infertility patients seeking help from Chinese medicine should seek out a practitioner specializing in Classical Chinese medicine. Patients seeking help via Western medicine should visit a reproductive endocrinologist. Combining Western medicine with acupuncture by a Modern Chinese medicine practitioner, or doing IVF with a Western doctor specializing in acupuncture, should be avoided. The disciplines simply do not mix. Western medicine can help if you use the right specialist RE, and Chinese medicine can help if you use a classically trained practitioner specializing in infertility.

Many women have become pregnant with the Hunyuan Method despite the fact that their Western doctor has assured them there was no possible way to become pregnant naturally because of their age. As **The Yellow Emperor** says: *The ones who live by nature, their body will be as if they are half their age and for those who live in contradiction to nature their body will be as if they are twice their age.*

Certainly age counts, but so does health, as well as what you eat, how you sleep, how much stress you endure, and what chemicals and drugs you are consuming.

It is time for each patient to become individually enlightened I believe that many 'infertile' couples will succeed naturally if only they will give themselves the chance. Patients must not let themselves be discouraged into IVF.

WESTERN MEDICINE – THE GOOD AND THE UGLY

In the past 100 years, Western medicine has made enormous progress, today's technology and equipment for advanced surgery and diagnosis indeed remarkable. However, along with success and advance there are some pitfalls as well. Sometimes power and conviction lead to a "my-way-or-the-highway" attitude.

Jerome Groopman, a cancer specialist, delivers a sharp and coherent critique of medicine's mistaken direction. In his book **How Doctors Think** he writes that approximately 15 percent of diagnoses are inaccurate, and that in medical schools, students are rarely taught to ask how an error could have taken place, let alone how it might be avoided in the future.

Most Western doctors are unaware of their mistakes. Even if patients remain unwell, no systematic effort is made to find out where doctors may have gone wrong. This is partly because most doctors believe there is no alternative to the treatment they have prescribed.

DRUGS AND POLITICS

In a recent survey of over 1,600 American physicians, nine out of ten reported a relationship with a pharmaceutical company. The benefits they received ranged from drug samples to tickets for sporting events, speaking honorariums, and money in exchange for persuading patients to join a clinical trial. The pressure of increasingly aggressive marketing tactics by the pharmaceutical companies only adds to a climate of endless misunderstanding. Most doctors receive information about new drugs directly from pharmaceutical representatives. Rarely do they personally investigate what is known about a drug. This dependency on biased information leaves doctors improperly equipped to make balanced judgments about which drugs to prescribe and when.

Congress recently expressed concern over the FDA drug approval process. In February 2007, the House Committee on Energy and Commerce's Subcommittee on Oversight and Investigation held a hearing in response to recent regulatory failures that allowed potentially harmful drugs on the market such as Merck's Vioxx. Hearing witnesses testified that the FDA drug approval process is subject to industry influence and that agency managers sacrifice sound science in the name of expeditious approval. One clinical researcher accused Aventis

Pharmaceuticals of complicity in a fraudulent clinical research project which the company had sponsored.

We have all witnessed the great number of medications recalled by the FDA over the years, and even more where warnings have been issued. When it comes to fertility drugs, some medications prescribed by Western doctors are not approved by the FDA for fertility treatment. It is therefore imperative that infertility patients about to begin drug therapy research the short and long term safety of the medication they will be taking. In my opinion, if no studies can be found that guarantee the safety of a particular medication, then it must be considered unsafe.

WESTERN ATTITUDE TOWARD EASTERN TREATMENT

It is ironic that many doctors in mainstream medicine believe that pharmaceuticals offer a real cure for disease, and that Chinese medicine offers only placebos.

In fact, studies for decades have shown that Western medicine often heals via placebo effect, even if this is not necessarily admitted by Western doctors. For example, back in the 1950's, a procedure called Internal Mammary Ligation was widely used for angina pectoris. In 1955, a Seattle cardiologist performed real and fake operations on his patients, discovering that patients with the fake ligation surgery had similar benefits to the patients with the real surgery.

In another example from 1993, orthopedic surgeon J. B. Moseley conducted a study with 180 arthroscopic surgery patients who had arthritic infliction of the knee. With the approximately 60 patients in Group 1, three incisions in the knee were made, scopes inserted, cartilage removed, correction of the soft tissue was performed, and finally, 10 liters of saline wash was administered. In Group 2, all procedures were repeated, except that no cartilage was removed. In Group 3, the placebo group, the patients were given anesthesia and the operation lasted the same length of time, but no scopes were inserted and no cartilage was removed.

Amazingly, the placebo group reported the same marked recovery and improvement in walking as did the other groups. Dr Nelda Wray, a co-author of the Moseley study said: *The fact that the effectiveness of arthroscopic lavage and debridement in patients with osteoarthritis of the knee is no greater than that of the placebo surgery makes us question whether the $1 billion spent on these procedures might be put to better use.*

MODERN CHINESE MEDICINE: TOO WESTERN FOR ITS OWN GOOD

Recently, I was introduced to another acupuncturist who specializes in administering acupuncture in conjunction with IVF treatments. Although she would prefer to prescribe herbs as well, Western medical doctors did not allow for that, causing her to come to the conclusion that the acupuncture treatment was effective on its own. "Does it matter what way the patient gets pregnant?" she asked me. "We only want to get them pregnant."

I believe that it does matter. Achieving good health, becoming pregnant, and giving birth to a healthy baby is preferable to simply becoming pregnant. Unfortunately, many practitioners don't understand the difference, and many actually believe that it is impossible for an infertility patient to become pregnant using Chinese medicine without IVF. This is, again, I believe largely a result of ignorance of Chinese medicine classics by many practitioners. According to **The Yellow Emperor**, women can get pregnant until the age of 49, and if they are following the **Dao**, even older.

I believe that Chinese medicine practitioners should practice true Chinese medicine. Working in conjunction with each other, we can move closer to Western medicine.

THE WISDOM OF THE ANCIENTS

For generations, the human species created dietary habits to fit into their environment and resources. Certain foods lead to survival while others did not. Each culture developed a somewhat different diet according to their climate, traditions, resources and needs. For example, dairy products were widely used in European cultures but hardly used in eastern Asian cultures. Therefore, dairy products might be very beneficial for people with European ancestry, while for those with eastern Asian roots, they might be harmful. To truly know the correct foods we should be consuming, we must take into consideration the season, our location on the planet, as well as our ancestry.

Unfortunately, modern society has moved away from this wisdom. Although we believe we live healthier lives than previous generations, we find ourselves debilitated by more illness. The public is under constant bombardment by an overwhelming degree of misinformation about what is healthy and what is not, leading to tremendous confusion.

When patients first come to me, I often hear statements such as: *My grandmother used to cook with lard (fat), ate a lot of butter and lived to be 95. She was never sick and she had five kids. I am eating 'healthy'– a lot of salad and fat free dairy – and I can't get pregnant.*

From a fertility standpoint, in many ways the grandmother's diet is better than her grand-daughter's. Most patients I treat come to me absolutely convinced that they are eating very healthily, when in fact their diets are very poor, at least for achieving pregnancy.

SHELF LIFE – MORE IMPORTANT THAN HUMAN LIFE

Enemy #1, of course, is the processed food manufactured by huge corporations looking at their own bottom line rather than the public's best interest. Shelf life becomes more important than human life, and lowering the cost of production is more important than keeping the ingredients healthy. Chemicals are added to preserve freshness and the public doesn't seem to care about what that means when it comes to their bodies.

The centralized production of food is also anathema to good health. In order to move from production to distribution center, which can be 2000 miles away, food must be processed to last as long as possible. Glitches and accidents in manufacturing can impact an entire nation, as evidenced by the e-coli outbreak resulting from centralized spinach distribution. Even the word "organic" no longer has the same meaning. More health conscious individuals are purchasing food grown locally in their area.

(NOT SO) NATURAL SUPPLEMENTS

Millions of Americans spend billions of dollars per year on dietary supplements, believing that they cannot get all the vitamins they need from the food they purchase. Although it is true that many of today's supermarkets offer only processed, modified, centralized and depleted food, it is incorrect to assume that supplements will be a substitute for healthy food. They will never replace milk, meat, fresh fruits and vegetables or clean air and water. Supplements are not natural. They were not made by nature. One will not find a multi-vitamin pill growing on a tree.

I rely on the ancient wisdom for my health. My mother didn't take pills, nor did my grandmother or my great-grandmother, and it goes back like this for endless generations. Why should I break this tradition by taking supplements?

Despite the excessive use of supplements, the American public has purchased over the past several decades, we are burdened with an increase in debilitating diseases such as cancer, heart disease, diabetes, asthma, allergies and infertility. Is this progress?

I believe we need to get our vitamins from the proper food – the food our forefathers ate – that is not found on a supermarket shelf.

Once a month I drive out to a farm in rural Connecticut to purchase a monthly supply of chicken for my family. The product is not certified organic, but in the farmer's words, is simply "raised the way the Lord intended". When I visit local farms to purchase chicken, milk, meat and produce, I feel reassured that I am taking proper care of my family by providing them with excellent food, while also supporting the farmers who make that possible.

Flowing with nature is far preferable to conquering it. Genuinely healthy food heals people and makes them fertile. Depleted food and supplements do not.

LIFE STYLE – A CRUCIAL COMPONENT IN FERTILITY

The Chinese medicine classics emphasize the need to understand Yin and Yang to stay in balance by not doing too much or too little, as well as to follow the Dao, which means to follow the harmony of nature. The three primary areas where modern society does not follow the Dao, and does not take into account the principles of Yin and Yang, are in work, sleep and stimulation.

The most acute problem of our modern lifestyle is our excessive work schedule. According to Chinese medicine guidelines, one should wake up at sunrise, plow his field through the early morning hours and then sit under the tree and rest for the remainder of the day.

Today's work habits are considerably different. Our bodies are exhausted day in and day out. **The Yellow Emperor – Plain Questions** says that to bear children, the kidneys must be full of energy, and when we work too hard or too long, our kidneys are depleted of that energy.

Patients often tell me that they start the day at 7 AM and finish work at 9 or 10 PM. Sometimes, when we are wrapped up in our work, we feel energized. We must understand, however, that the hard work is not what is creating the energy. Our bodies are extracting the extra energy from our kidneys.

Modern fertility drugs exhaust the body further. Working hard and using fertility drugs simultaneously is tantamount to the body pulling in two different directions. Sometimes the situation is even more difficult because the cost of the fertility drugs requires us to work even harder. Under such circumstances, the kidney's Yang energy is drained.

If you hope to become pregnant, the first step is to work less and spend more relaxing time in nature. This is following the Dao of nature.

With the invention of electricity and light, our sleeping habits have gradually changed. **The Yellow Emperor** classic describes in detail how to harmonize with nature by following the patterns of the sun, hence sleeping more in winter and less in summer. When the body follows the harmony of nature, infertility will not set in before the age of 49. But if one works constantly and routinely stays up until 2 AM, the body will not have the chance it needs to do its job.

Our five senses are constantly barraged by the noise and pollution of urban environments, contributing an extra dose. When we're in nature, our sensory organs experience a slow down. Everything around us – trees, mountains, rivers – have been in the same place for centuries, with the quality of air fresh, and only the leaves moving in the breeze. This causes the kidney energy to remain at full capacity with no danger of depletion.

THE "BIBLE" OF CLASSICAL CHINESE MEDICINE

The Chinese developed one of the earliest civilizations on the planet, with examples of highly-developed, complex writings dating back to the late Shang Period (circa 1200 BC). The Oracle Bone Inscriptions found at the site of the last Shang capital near present-day Anyang in the Henan Province are written in a language similar to classical Chinese.

Chinese legend tells us that 5000 years ago, circa 3000 BC, two medical figures became prominent. The first, Shen Nong, (the farmer deity), was reported to have tasted 100 herbs in a single day, and to have discovered 70 definite toxins. The second figure, Fu Xi, is said to have drawn the eight trigrams and created the nine needles of acupuncture.

The Xia Dynasty (approx. 21st c BC. to 16th c BC), and Shang Dynasty (16th c BC to 11th c BC), saw great advances in the development of farming, alcohol brewing, silk weaving, astronomy/astrology, and the calendar. Archaeologically excavated records of divination from the Shang Dynasty, in the form of carvings on tortoise shells and animal bones (oracle bones), show references to eye ailments, headaches, abdominal ailments, intestinal bugs, and many other illnesses. At that time, therapeutic plants were already in use for treating disease.

In the Western Zhou Dynasty (11th c BC to 771 BC) royal doctors specialized in diet, disease, sores, and animal care. The number of frequently used medicinal substances at that time exceeded 100, consisting of herbs, minerals and animal material.

The Spring and Autumn Warring States Period and the Eastern Zhou Dynasty (770 BC-221 BC), produced all types of scholastic ideology and reached a high level of sophistication. The most important work of all began with a dialogue between **The Yellow Emperor**, a legendary monarch whose reign extended from 2497- 2398 BCE, and his medical advisors, the chief advisor being Qibo. From there, the dialogue continued for another 500 years, becoming a book with two volumes, **Plain Questions** and **Miraculous Pivots**, the authorship usually attributed to the Yellow Emperor even though he was long deceased. Today's version of the book comes from 762 AD, after well-respected scholar Wang Bing spent 12 years reorganizing the classic into 81 chapters.

The book **The Yellow Emperor** systematized and consolidated ancient medical experience and theory into one medical work. Using the philosophical ideologies of Yin, Yang and the Five Elements, it demonstrates that the human body is an organic whole, and its health and illness is intimately connected to the natural environment.

The Yellow Emperor deals with anatomy, physiology, and treatment, and beyond medicine, it presents moral, idealistic and spiritual considerations. It describes five **Zang** organs, which are **Yin** related. These are the liver, heart, spleen, lungs, and kidneys. The other six **Fu** organs are related to the **Yang** principle. These are the bladder, gallbladder, stomach, small and large intestines, and the triple burner, which is not an organ, but rather relates to the energy and water pathways of the body. Two other significant concepts mentioned are meridians, which are 12 energy channels, and Qi (pronounced Chee), which is the energy that flows through the meridians.

The Yellow Emperor departs from the old shamanistic viewpoint that illness is caused by unearthly influences, and instead it argues that it comes from emotions, environment, lifestyle, age and heredity factors. To maintain optimum health, one must be aware that the world is composed of diverse forces and principles, such as Yin and Yang, Qi (energy) and the five elements, and that an equilibrium between these components must be kept. It states that if longevity is well-preserved and kidney energy kept full, women will conceive naturally until the age of 49, and men until the age of 64, *when the essence of heaven and earth dries out*. The classic goes onto state that it is possible to bear children at an even older age if the body is kept in perfect shape.

OTHER TEXTS ADD WISDOM OVER THE YEARS

Following The **Yellow Emperor,** the second most important classic is **Shennong Bencaojing** (Classic of Herbal Medicine). The word bencao translates to "essential herb." Written between the 1st and 2nd Century BC, it is considered to be the first comprehensive Chinese pharmacopoeia reference, and lists a total of 365 medicinals from which 252 were of plant source, 67 from animals, and 46 from minerals. Each medicine was divided into one of three categories. The superior class included 120 medicines considered to be non-toxic and to contain invigorating effects to preserve vitality or prolong life. The second class included average medicines of which 120 were listed. Medicines in this category were used to prevent illness and restore the individual's vitality. The third class included 125 inferior medicines considered to be toxic and were specifically used for therapeutic purposes to treat diseases.

During the eastern Han Dynasty, prominent physician Zhang Zhongjing, also known as Zhang Ji (150-219 AD) lifted Chinese medicine to new heights when he authored **Shanghan Zabinglun** (Treatise on Cold and Miscellaneous Illnesses). Containing six parts that correspond to the six spheres of energy, it deals with the treatment of many febrile conditions, and is significant because it discusses diagnosis and treatment methods based on an assessment of the symptoms of different pathological conditions. For the next 1000 years (until the Jin-Yuan Dynasties of 1200 AD) all of Chinese medicine mainstream was based entirely on **The Yellow Emperor** and the **Shang Hanlun**, with famous scholars contributing to its development through the centuries.

In 1237, during the Song Dynasty, Chen Ziming became the first physician to devote an entire work to women's health and gynecology with **The Complete Compendium of Gynecological Prescriptions.** This began a new trend of specialization in the field of gynecology and obstetrics.

During the Jin-Yuan period, from 1127-1368, the northern Jin tribes and the Mongolians took control of much of China, and many progressive cultural changes resulted. This new thinking impacted medicine. Four new schools of thought emerged, presenting new ideas of understanding life and health. A new interpretation of **The Yellow Emperor** began to emerge.

The four new schools of thought, referred to as "the Schools of the Jin-Yuan" gave rise to two opposing branches of Chinese medicine. The one branch believed in the older ways of The **Yellow Emperor** in terms of harmonizing the six spheres and preserving the Yang. It believed that the ways of the sages in researching health were accurate. The other branch questioned conventional wisdom. These beliefs lead to the Modern school of Chinese medicine. Ultimately, China's internal weaknesses gave into western influence. Medical doctors associated with the church played a major role. An increasing number of medical schools, run jointly by Chinese and Western doctors, were established, and many western medical books were translated. A new generation of doctors saw a wealth of knowledge in Western medicine.

To those who wished to modernize China, Chinese medicine became a symbol of the old, backward ways of doing things. Government officials began calling for the abolition of Chinese medicine. A legislative proposal entitled **A Case for the Abolishment of the Old Medicine to Thoroughly Eliminate Public Health Obstacles,** by Yu Ai and Wang Qizang, suggested that important Chinese medicine principles, such as the Yin Yang theory and the five elements, were not based on reality and therefore fraudulent. On February 26, 1929, the proposal was passed, by the first legislative session of the Central Ministry of Public Health, severely limiting the practice of Chinese medicine and prohibiting the establishment of Chinese medicine schools. Even Mao Zedong instructed his army in 1942 to uproot all "shamanic beliefs and superstitions". Like his nationalist adversaries, he thought of Chinese medicine doctors as no better than "circus entertainers, snake oil salesman or street hawkers." [1] In 1953, however, Mao reversed course and claimed it as a national treasure.

THE DISCIPLINE CONTINUES TO EVOLVE

Despite the emphasis on Modern Chinese medicine, the Ancient tradition has been kept alive from the 1600's through present day by loyal practitioners, including Dr. Lu Chong Han of the Huo Shen School, and his apprentice, Liu Lihong. In 2003 Liu Lihong published his work **Si Kao Zhongyi** (Reflecting on Chinese medicine), which has had an impact unparalleled in the last 100 years, sparking renewed interest amongst numerous practitioners in the classics. I have been fortunate to study with Dr. Liu.

Liu Lihong quoted the sages: *A good doctor can treat a patient and he can also heal the entire country*. His work is his testimony.

1 Chinese Medicine In Crisis: Science, Politics, And The Making Of "TCM" /Heiner Fruehauf

HUNYUAN METHOD FOR FERTILITY

I established the Hunyuan method in 2002 after returning from a long visit with Professor Liu Lihong in Beijing. I was deeply influenced by his infinite understanding of the Chinese medicine classics. Even though I had been researching the classics for many years, I was overcome by his passion and devotion to this art, and I felt Zhang Zhongjing's wisdom emanating from Dr. Liu's teachings. In the following months, putting his teachings into action, I saw a dramatic increase in successes in my fertility practice.

"Hunyuan" translates to "inborn ability". It is the inborn ability of the Yang to transform into Yin and the inborn ability of the Yin to transform into Yang. It is the ability of the six spheres to interact with each other in order to create life. It is the inborn ability of a woman to bear children and be fertile.

It is with great humility that I put the Hunyuan Method and my name on the same page as the great scholars of Chinese medicine previously mentioned. I can only hope that my research will enable me to come closer to the wisdom of these great scholars.

Jessica had tried everything: IUIs, IVFs and even Chinese medicine but nothing worked. Yaron Seidman says that after Jessica's friend became pregnant with the help of the Hunyuan Method, she grew curious. Yaron says that at first she was skeptical, but after learning the difference between ancient and modern Chinese medicine, she decided to give ancient Chinese medicine a try. She conceived within three months. Jessica says that when she took the herbal formulas of the ancient method, it felt so different than the other modern formulas had before. She says that she felt so energetic and alive almost immediately, not to mention that it helped her conceive too.

2

UNDERSTANDING CHINESE MEDICINE

Over many centuries, Chinese physicians explored the influence on health from physical phenomenon, including six specific weather conditions: cold, dryness, dampness, wind, heat, and extreme heat. They also observed, like Albert Einstein, the relationship of causes to our health from non-physical phenomenon on a meta-scientific level. They focused on the existence of energetical relationships between man and the universe which are not simply felt or seen. As with Einstein's rejection by the scientific community in his earlier years, there has been great rejection of meta-science during various periods of Chinese history.

In the first 1500 years of Chinese medicine's development, meta-science was dominant, with ancient meta-science concepts such as Yin and Yang and the five elements taking shape. However, during the Jin Yuan dynasties this trend changed and new theories came into place. New physicians like Zhu Danxi began explaining phenomenon from a scientific standpoint. Although at the time it was considered great progress, I view it as a complete regression.

It is important to return to a meta-science understanding of Chinese medicine. It is impossible to create effective herbal formulas and acupuncture protocols without this perspective. Although Modern Chinese medicine, like Western medicine, can often relieve symptoms, it works contrary to the Chinese medicine rule of curing the root of the illness.

As emphasized previously, to understand the classical Chinese medicine, all Western-oriented thought pathways and biases must be put to the side. Once we have an open mind, we need to learn a bit about the Chinese language.

In our modern world, the main form of communication is with words, which we use either in talking or writing. However, in the classical Chinese environment, words were only one form of communication and considered the lowest form. Partly because of the need to save space on bamboo scrolls with limited surface area, the Chinese were forced to develop a method of communication that was spare in words but deep in meaning. They turned to the use of shapes and forms that were simultaneously capable of delivering multiple meanings in multiple levels of sophistication. The whole Chinese written system, in fact, was developed as pictures rather than alphabetic letters.

It is beneficial to study the characters that comprise the term "Chinese medicine," because these characters embody the meaning of the discipline itself. The two characters are "Zhong" and "Yi."

ZHONG YI ZHONG YI

"Zhong", the character on the left, has two meanings. China in Chinese is "Zhong Guo" or "the country of Zhong." The character also translates to "center," meaning this is the medicine of the center of all things.

If we break apart the Zhong character we will be left with two parts. The first part is a human mouth, representing a human being, and the second part is a line, representing a line drawn from heaven to earth. Therefore, drawing a line from heaven to earth and passing it through a human being results in what is called "center."

"Zhong," or "center" is the energy from heaven and earth that passes through and is exchanged within the human body. When we say the medicine of Zhong, we mean the medicine that solves difficulties arising from a disharmony of heaven and earth within our bodies.

Let's look at the character "Yi", meaning "medicine:"

The different elements are (from left to right): a case, arrows, the sound of arrows hitting the target, and a wine vessel. The case is for the arrows, standing for the tools that the doctor uses to treat illness. The tools must be "sharp" and able to hit a target from afar. The wine vessel symbolizes the vessel that contains the medicine.

The "Zhong" character and the "Yi" character combine to stand for the healing, or target, action the doctor takes to treat illness. The target in this case is the heaven and earth energies that exchange within our bodies. The heaven and earth energies are the Yin and Yang.

MEDICINE OF "TIME"

Chinese medicine at its core explores one thing and one thing only: Time. This is very different than Modern Chinese medicine and Western medicine, which explore "space."

The sages realized the unity of things. Everything in our world can be pulled back into unison under one concept. **The Yellow Emperor** explains: *As to exploring Yin and Yang, you can take ten and make it a hundred, you can take a thousand and make it ten thousand, and you can separate it in that manner endlessly. However, in pulling it back together, it is only one Yin and Yang.*

'Time" is what allows us to understand this unity. In Chinese medicine, the concept of "time" goes far beyond how we conceive of it today. To grasp it, we must gradually recalibrate our thinking process to match that of the sages.

The Yellow Emperor explains: *The ancient sages knew the Dao, they followed Yin and Yang, they harmonized with the ancient arts and numbers, their diet had rules, their sleeping and living habits were regulated, and they didn't labor for nothing. Their bodies united with their spirit, they fulfilled their heavenly years, lived to be a hundred and then they departed.*

The progression from conception, to birth, childhood, adulthood and then into decline and death, represents one single line of time. **The Yellow Emperor** calls it the "heavenly years." The genius of the ancient sages is to know the meaning of this 'stretch of time,' the true meaning of life.

Life, as is time, is intangible. You can't grasp it, box it, shape it, calculate it. However, you can know its Dao, or the laws and rules that compose it. **The Yellow Emperor** explains that the rules of life or the rules of "Time" involve following Yin and Yang.

When one understands the rules of Yin and Yang, then lifestyle, diet, sleeping and work all change accordingly. When we understand the stretch of time we call life, or the stretch of life we call time, there is no other truth. The material world becomes invisible, a new realm of time opening up before us. Time, or the "heavenly years" is the only thing that matters.

Entering this Chinese medicine world, we find nothing more precious than time, and nothing more precious than our life. We do not own our life nor do we own the stretch of time we are allocated by heaven. However, it is our responsibility as humans to live our heavenly years to their fullest extent. Thus it is our responsibility to understand life and how to keep it going all the way to the end. We have to know the Dao. We have to understand Yin and Yang.

In reality, "Time" goes far beyond our lifetime. It extends to the heavenly years of our children, grand children and endless generations thereafter. That "The sages knew the Dao of heavenly years" explains that they understood the significance of not only their own lives, but rather the heavenly years for billions of people over many thousands of years to come.

Although we have made great progress in science and technology, this signifies an advance solely in "space", and has concurrently brought about a retreat in our understanding of "time." In China in particular, the exploration in the direction of "space" had a significant boost from Communism during the Twentieth Century when Chinese medicine was viewed as feudal and archaic. It was also seen as full of "secrets", because the traditional way of learning Chinese medicine was by discipleship: a student following his teacher for many years in order to grasp the essence of the medicine and to be enlightened into the understanding of life and time. In 1950, the new communist government and Mao Zedong claimed to initiate a new kind of medicine with no secrets, which would be open to everyone to learn with great ease. The result was that every deep and difficult aspect of understanding the sages, classics, and "time" were omitted. The ancient ways of research into time and life was prohibited. Thus Chinese medicine, while using ancient vocabulary, became Western in thinking. Endless scientific research proved Chinese medicine to be baseless, and of course it is baseless within the context of scientific research. Life was no longer the focus, but rather disease was the target, in the very same way that Western medicine operates today.

Only now does it look as if science will stop its endless pursuit of matter and space and unfold gradually again into the exploration of time and life. In November of 2008, Einstein's celebrated formula e=mc2 was finally corroborated 103 years after he first published it. Laurent Lelloch, a scientist of France's Center for Theoretical Physics, using some of the world's mightiest supercomputers, has set down the calculations for estimating the mass of protons and neutrons, the particles at the nucleus of atoms.

This study involved computations "envisioning space and time as a part of a four-dimensional crystal lattice structures." From this we can see that a theory computed by Einstein's "inner vision" could only be proven 103 years later, and only after including time and space computations and not "space" computations alone.

When modern science uses "time", the world of energy opens up. This is why there is a renaissance in China and around the world of classical Chinese medicine and research into "time" and "life". Doctors, layman, or mathematicians are all beginning to ponder these questions of life once more. People are starting to ask such questions as: "Is this drug really good for me, are pesticides on food safe, should I move to a place where there is cleaner air?"

Where is this stream of new consciousness coming from? Why have organic foods regained popularity? It is because people have begun to think, even though on a subconscious level, about the concept of life and time. In fact, the moves to eliminate global warming means that without even knowing it, people are going back to the "Dao."

INTRODUCING YIN AND YANG

The concept of time, as discovered by the sages, had different patterns representing different aspects of Yin and Yang. When a patient is sick or infertile, the practitioner's job is to identify which pattern of Yin and Yang is not working properly. This is called differentiation of syndromes. This differentiation is very difficult to see and requires the practitioner to be enlightened in the concept of "time."

Differentiation of syndromes is not similar to differentiation of disease. For example, if the patient has a headache in the forehead, modern Chinese medicine teaches that it is a stomach problem, because the stomach meridian reaches to this area. This diagnosis does not require enlightenment. As Mao Zedong claimed: *Every uneducated person can learn it and learn it fast.*

The analysis of the same headache from the classical Chinese medicine perspective is taken much further. It is a stretch of time, and not just an organ or a meridian, and must be dealt with in this way. As a headache on the stomach meridian, it is part of the Yang Ming sphere which belongs to the autumn, and its energy is descending. The skill of Chinese medicine is not in the "modernized and scientific" differentiation of symptoms, but rather the differentiation of life syndromes we call Yin and Yang.

If you train your brain in classical thinking then the treatment of infertility takes an entirely different shape. It is no longer the treatment of symptoms such as blood deficiency, kidney Yang deficiency or even worse, Western medicine symptoms such as Polycystic Ovary Syndrome (PCOS), high Follicle Stimulating Hormone (FSH), or endometriosis of which the cause is forever "unknown."

Rather, it is about "time." It's about the practitioner's ability to ensure not only a pregnancy, but more importantly, enable the mother, the baby, and the baby's offspring for generations, to fulfill their heavenly years. For this reason, the treatment of infertility with classical Chinese medicine is of such great importance; one pregnancy and birth affects so many who will come later.

The treatment of infertility via Western or Modern Chinese medicine is not really concerned with future generations. In fact, a study lead by Dr Laura A. Schieve found that 6.5 percent of singleton babies born after fertility treatments that went to term weighed less than 5 lbs., 8 ounces. In the general population only 2.5 percent of babies delivered at term had weights this low. Another Australian study showed that the incidence of birth defects in babies conceived by IVF and ICSI (intracytoplasmic sperm injection) was 9 percent as compared to only 4.2 percent in the general population. Dr Allen A. Mitchell, an epidemiologist at the Boston University School of Public Health suggested that infertile couples who are contemplating fertility treatments such as IVF should be told about these studies.

Chinese medicine realizes the truth in staying healthy, and the importance of health for our future generations. Studies are not necessary to convince our common sense. We trust our common sense naturally. Understanding time means to understand health. Understanding health means that future generations will thrive.

TIME AND 24 QI

The Yellow Emperor states: *He who well understands heaven will know man's life. He who well understands the ancient times will know its modern day's implications. He who well understands Qi will know its significance for any living matter.*

Throughout this book we will learn about heaven, ancient times and Qi. The more we know about these three, the more we will understand infertility and how to become fertile.

Qi is the invisible force that gives us life which we call "life-force.'" As we just discussed in the previous chapter, "life" is the stretch of time from conception until death. **The Yellow Emperor**, in its quest for understanding time and life, states the following: *Five days is one Hou (time unit), while three Hou is one Qi.* Therefore, one Qi is equal to one-half of a month, and we have 24 Qi every year.

Each Qi corresponds to a phase of the moon, and there are two phases per month. The first phase, one Qi long, extends during the time the moon is born until it grows full; the second phase begins with a full moon and progresses until the moon is gone.

The Yellow Emperor states: *The knowledgeable person sees the unity in things, while the dull minded sees the differences.* The sages of old chose a path of unification and the basic understanding that everything under heaven follows the rules of life.

The 24 Qi help us understand these rules of life. They make the big Qi of heaven more accessible here on earth. We realize that this big Qi, including the sun, earth and moon, as well as day and night and the four seasons, all move in a circular motion. The 24 Qi also govern lifespan, helping to segment the beginning, growth, and decline and end phases.

The sun's movement determines the 24 Qi, or segments, of the year. Aside from rising in the east and setting in the west every day, the sun travels north during the spring and south during the fall (in the northern hemisphere). In midsummer the sun is directly above our head and as north as it can get, so the temperatures are the hottest. In midwinter the sun is as south as it can get in an oblique angle toward us, so the temperatures are very cold. A similar situation occurs during a 24-hour cycle. The sun rises toward us in a sharp angle and the temperatures cool. During midday, the sun is directly over our head, the temperature at its peak. It then sets in a sharp angle toward us, the temperatures cooling down again.

For the study of Qi, we must take the ancient's perspective that the sun circulates around us. It shines at us from the left, top and right and then it travels through a zone where we can't see it. When we face south, sunrise is to our left and sunset is to our right.

The moon waxes and wanes 12 times in a year, absorbing the sun's energy and reflecting the sun's light. However, every month the sun is in a different angle toward the earth, and during the course of a year, the sun moves in two opposite directions, north and south, creating two halves of the year; a birth and growth half, and a decline and storage half. In the spring and summer there is an increase in heat, while in the fall and winter there is a decrease of heat.

EACH OF THE 24 QI OCCUPIES A HALF MOON CYCLE, THE SAGES ATTRIBUTING NAMES TO DESCRIBE FUNCTION:

1. XIA ZHI — summer extreme
2. XIAO SHU — slight heat
3. DA SHU — big heat
4. LI QIU — fall begins
5. CHU SHU — heat enters
6. BAI LU — white dew
7. QIU FEN — fall's split
8. HAN LU — cold dew
9. SHUANG JIANG — frost descends
10. LI DONG — winter begins
11. XIAO XUE — slight snow
12. DA XUE — heavy snow
13. DONG ZHI — winter extreme
14. XIAO HAN — slight cold
15. DA HAN — great cold
16. LI CHUN — spring begins
17. YU SHUI — water rain
18. JING ZHE — hibernation startles
19. CHUN FEN — spring's split
20. QING MING — obvious clear
21. GU YU — grain rain
22. LI XIA — summer begins
23. XIAO MAN — small fullness
24. MANG ZHONG — grain fullness

Two kinds of Qi (energy) govern our life, **Ming** and **Xing**. Ming, our original Yang energy which comes from our parents, determines the heavenly years we have to live. Xing is the Yang energy which comes to us from heaven and the sun, helping us to live our lives to the fullest. All living matter, including animals, trees and rocks, has a Ming, or internal fire, as well as a Xing, or external source of fire. The Earth itself has two kinds of fire, one emanating from the sun, and the other from the planet's core. Xing and Ming cannot exist without each other. For any life form to take place, we need these two kinds of "fire."

The 24 Qi describe first and foremost the relationship of the sun to our earth. In the northern hemisphere, when the sun is at its most northern point, its angle to earth is almost perpendicular and the temperatures are at their warmest. The Yang energy from the sun hits the earth's surface in the most direct way, causing the absorption ability, or Yin aspect, of the earth to decrease. As a result, the heat stays above the ground surface. In autumn, when the sun is moving toward the south, its light is less intense, and hence the ability of earth's Yin to absorb the Yang energy is increased. The sun's Yang energy gradually goes underground.

In winter, when the sun's intensity is weakest, the Yin energy is the strongest, the sun's Yang penetrating deep into the earth to warm what the sages called "the underground water". Going into spring, the sun travels back north, resulting in the Yin's decreased ability to absorb and the Yang's gradual re-emergence onto the earth's surface, life springing out. As the sun reaches the north point, the summer is at full bloom again.

During winter and nighttime, the Yang energy goes into extreme storage inside the earth. This storage allows the Ming fire in the center core of the earth to survive. It also allows the Ming fire in the center of human beings to survive as well. The sun on the surface gives life, but the sun under the surface gives life too, just in a different way.

In our modern analytical eyes, the sun ceases to impact us when it disappears under the earth and night falls. In reality, it does impact us – we just don't view it in this way because we are not accustomed to seeing the invisible. The sun's disappearance is what allows the moon to be visible, the moon reflecting the sunlight onto us as we sleep, helping to keep us alive during sleep. Concurrently, the sun nourishes the Ming fire in the center core of the earth. During the day, it warms up the exterior and during the night, it warms up the interior. The same happens with seasonal changes when the sun travels north and south. In summer the sun warms up the exterior, while in winter it warms up the interior.

This theory is not yet within the scope of modern science, but with new research, things are changing rapidly. Only recently, scientists have discovered 'Flux Transfer Events, or FTE's, which are essentially portals through which particles can flow. Space physicist David Sibeck of the Goddard Space Flight Center explains about FTE's: *Ten years ago I was pretty sure they didn't exist, but now the evidence is incontrovertible.*

FTEs form when the Earth's magnetic field presses against the sun's magnetic field. Approximately every eight minutes, the two fields briefly merge or "reconnect," forming a portal through which particles can flow. The portal takes the form of a magnetic cylinder about as wide as Earth. The seasons, as well as north and south directions, play a role. Space physicist Jimmy Raeder of the University of New Hampshire, on the website physorg.com, explains that the cylindrical portals tend to form above Earth's equator and then roll over Earth's winter pole. In December, FTEs roll over the North Pole. In July they roll over the South Pole, where it is winter.

Even though the scientific understanding of the connection between earth and sun is still in its infancy, we can see that the thinking process is moving closer to the ancient's perspective.

THE 24 QI

1. XIA ZHI (summer extreme) – Sun arrives at northern point, or summer solstice. The weather is hot.

2. XIAO SHU (slight heat) – First half of the moon following the arrival of the summer extreme, thus the heat above earth's surface is aggravating.

3. DA SHU (big heat) – Second half of the moon following summer extreme. Heat above the surface at most extreme.

The sages explaining Yin and Yang noted that the heat must arrive at its most extreme before reversing into cooling mode.

4. LI QIU (autumn begins) – Sun moves southwards, Yang energy begins its descent toward earth.

5. CHU SHU (heat enters) – Yang energy first penetrates the earth's surface.

6. BAI LU (white dew) – Yang energy partially penetrates earth's surface, although more heat still above the surface than below.

Dew descends in early morning and possibly in late evening.

7. QIU FEN (fall's split) – Equal distribution of heat above and underground.

8. HAN LU (cold dew) – Heat underground more intense than above ground, the Yin now strong enough to pull most of Yang's energy underground. Temperatures above ground are cold, the morning dew feeling cold to the touch.

9. SHUANG JIANG (frost descends) – Yin intensifies, most of Yang now under earth's surface.

Cave dwellers in northwestern China feel at this time that the underground is turning warm. The morning dew freezes into frost.

10. LI DONG (winter begins) – The Yang sinks into the underground water or center core of the earth.

11. XIAO XUE (slight snow) – The water begins to melt underground as more and more Yang and heat enter. Water above ground descends upon earth with no Yang, as snow.

12. DA XUE (heavy snow) – An increase in momentum from the previous step, The Yang completely sunken into the underground water and the core of the earth. The underground water is the melted lava and hot springs coming from the center of the earth. The sun's Yang is supporting Ming.

13. DONG ZHI (winter extreme) – Arrival of the sun to its southernmost point.

14. XIAO HAN (slight cold) – The first half of the moon following the arrival of the sun in the south. The Yang is stuck inside and doesn't want to come out. The temperatures above ground are freezing cold.

15. DA HAN (great cold) – The second half of the moon following the sun's arrival in the south. The Yang storage underground reaches its extreme, while the temperatures above ground reach their extreme freezing point.

16. LI CHUN (spring begins) – As the sun increases its angle with the earth, the pull of the Yin decreases. The Yang energy gradually exits the underground water, beginning its rising motion unto the earth's surface. Temperatures above ground experience a slight warm up.

17. YU SHUI (water rain) – Yang reaches the surface, rivers and lakes thawing and flowing again.

18. JING ZHE (hibernation startles) – Yang is still more underground than above aground, startling the hibernating insects underground, signaling the plants, insects, animals and humans that the spring is about to take full force and it is time to come out.

19. CHUN FEN (spring's split) – The Yang energy is equally distributed above and below ground.

20. QING MING (obvious clear) – Most Yang is above ground, the temperatures warm and the leaves back on the trees. It is called 'obvious clear' because we can see the full bloom of spring with our naked eyes.

21. GU YU (grain rain) – The Yang energy is completely above the ground's surface. The Yin forces are completely diminished. Due to sufficient Yang, the grains begin to grow. Enough Yang in the above ground water is called 'rain'. No Yang in the same water is called snow. Rain and snow signify the different position of the Yang above or underground.

22. LI XIA (summer begins) – The temperatures above ground are turning hot, as there is no Yin. The Yang floats above the earth's surface.

23. **XIAO MAN** (small fullness) – The grains on the ear begin to fill up. The temperature above ground is even hotter and the fruits and grains begin the process of ripening.

24. **MANG ZHONG** (grain fullness) – The Yang energy above ground is enough to cause grains and fruits to ripen, flavors at their climax.

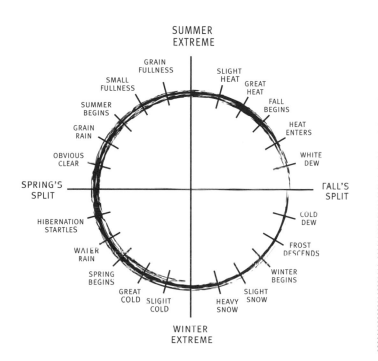

The sun's Yang is now floating above the surface and supporting Xing. It then moves back into position 1, the summer extreme. This is called the circular motion of the heaven's big Qi.

24 QI, HEALTH AND FERTILITY

After we wake up from a good night's sleep, we feel stronger and recharged. Our life force has grown stronger.

The same is true of the Yang energy when it disappears from our sight during the night, and during the fall and winter. In both instances the visible sun and Yang go underground. The ancients saw the sun, and Yang, at this time as performing a nourishing, "keeping life" mission.

The four seasons play a greater role in preserving life. When the sun travels to the south and Yang energy enters underground in fall and winter, the life force is considerably nurtured, allowing a rebirth and a flourishing during spring and summer. From the perspective of the sages of Chinese medicine, nature has rules with which it has commanded itself in order to preserve its own life.

Of the 81 chapters in **The Yellow Emperor**, the second chapter, "The Great Treatise of Harmonizing the Four Seasons with Qi and Spirit" is extraordinarily significant. Spirit in this context is a human being or a living entity on earth. The spirit is coming from heaven down into the living entity.

Harmonizing the four seasons and the 24 Qi with our spirit and with our life is crucial for our survival, health and fertility. This chapter states that: *The Yin and Yang of the four seasons are the root and foundation of the myriad things. Because it is the root, the sage nurtured the Yang in the spring and summer and he nurtured the Yin in the fall and winter. He followed the root of life so he could join the realm of birth and growth of the myriad things. If he would resist this root he will punish his own foundation and damage his own 'Truth'. Thus the four seasons and Yin and Yang are the beginning and end of the myriad things. They are the foundation of life and death. If you resist it, disaster will come, but if you follow it, disease will never rise. This is called Dao.*

For the enlightened sage of old, there was no need for medicine. He knew how to adjust his own rhythm to the rhythm of the four seasons and the 24 Qi, thus preventing any and all diseases from taking hold of his body. When we harmonize with the 24 Qi and the four seasons, it is the same. No disease can arise, including infertility.

Chapter 2 goes onto explain that the sage who walked the path of Dao found order, and those who didn't walk it, found chaos. In other words, by walking the path of Dao, the sage found health instead of disease. Rather than attempting to apply order to chaos, **The Yellow Emperor** explains, he did all he could to prevent chaos from forming.

Today we talk about preventative medicine, however we have no clue as to the root of life. We follow patterns of convenience under the false pretense that our life is an isolated unit, and that we can remedy it irrespective of nature, the four seasons or the 24 Qi. This is why illness often overtakes us, even though we eat "right," pop supplements, and turn to promising drugs.

We are supposed to be impressed that today's life span is near 80, up from 45 at the turn of the Twentieth Century. However, 2000 years ago, with zero use of drugs, life expectancy for those who followed the Dao was 100. The root of our life is within the circular motion of nature. If we truly understand this notion, we can bring ourselves to the state of being where "disease will never rise," and where women will maintain their fertility until the age of 49.

The second chapter of The **Yellow Emperor** continues by explaining how to follow the Dao in a practical way. We are urged to *nurture the Yang in the spring and summer and nurture the Yin in the fall and winter.* When we nurture Yin and Yang, we reach harmony with the four seasons. The tool we need to accomplish this task is the 24 Qi, which tells us how to harmonize with the four seasons at any point in time. **The Yellow Emperor** describes the different state of affairs in each season. In spring, the Yang gives birth to flowers and plants. In the summer, the Yang hovers above the surface, the tops of the trees full of life. Rarely do we look at the bottom of the tree trunk. In the autumn, however, when the leaves fall, we look downward at the earth's surface. The pulling down action of the earth is manifesting, the Yang "agitated."

The surface is where the exchange of heaven and earth occurs. It is the axis point between energies, or the **Qi Jiao** (Energy Exchange).

To understand this "agitation" of Yang in fall, we must compare the winter to the summer. The Emperor says that in summer, when the Yang is high above ground, the tops of the trees blossoming, the Yang is fully consumed. The sages called this *glorifying of the exterior and diminishing of the interior*. When the exterior flourishes, the interior dwindles. Thus the Yang in the fall becomes agitated, desperate to go back home to winter where it can sleep undisturbed while it recharges. If it doesn't come down, it will die.

The Emperor then goes onto explain the optimal sleep habits we need to adopt in order to harmonize with the four seasons. In the spring and summer, we nourish the Yang by going to bed after dark and rising before dawn. In the fall and winter, we nourish the Yin, going to bed early. In the fall, we wake-up early as well, but in the winter, we rise after dawn.

In spring and summer, when the Yang is above ground, we must help it accomplish its task. We go to bed late and wake up very early. This harmonizes our body with the Yang opening movement around us. We need little sleep because nature needs little sleep.

It is often difficult to fall asleep in hot weather. When we use air conditioning, we fall asleep earlier, because it is re-creating this condition of winter. However, this artificial re-creation of natural environments is risky, the Emperor warns, because *the sage followed the root of life so he could join the realm of birth and growth of the myriad things. If he would resist this root he will punish his own foundation and damage his own "Truth."* Faking winter in the middle of summer is resisting the root.

I have previously mentioned Xing and Ming. Xing is the daily life we are living and Ming is the heavenly years that we have in storage. The life that we live every day is precious, however the life we have remaining to live is not less precious. When the Yang stores itself underground undisturbed to recharge, we are recharging our Ming, or our allocated heavenly years. In the Chinese text, The Emperor explains that we need to wake up late in winter and chose the character **Wan** to describe this action.

The character as a whole carries the meaning "to be late." However, the left component translates to "sun," while the right side translates "to escape." In

WAN

35

winter, the sage will stay in bed until the sun "escapes" from underneath the earth, where it is charging our Ming heavenly years.

Again, it is important to remember that the actions we take not only affect our time here, but also affect those who will come later.

眞

ZHEN

The character Zhen, which means "truth," is used to describe a human being. It also translates to "a newcomer among the immortals." The Emperor warns that if you resist this root then you will not only harm your foundation (meaning your life), you will also harm your immortal life (meaning all your future generations).

This kind of long-term vision and wisdom is practically non-existent in our modern world. The most we usually think about is one generation down to our children. Speaking for myself, I know little about my grandfather. I only know the name of his father and some stories about his life, and I don't even know the name of my grandfather's grandfather.

I see my responsibility as getting back to this root the sages treasured so much. I must harmonize with nature so that children five generations down the line from me will have the life that I am having today.

The Yellow Emperor describes some of the daily actions needed to harmonize with nature:

SPRING: Nourish the 'Yang' by engaging in physical exercise, encouraging the stored energy below ground to emerge onto the surface of our body.

SUMMER: Because the Yang energy is above ground, we stay outside. We cannot get enough sun – we are insatiable. Any outdoor activity will cause our Yang to float to the surface and thus be synchronized with nature.

AUTUMN: We act as a rooster, which is bursting with energy in the morning but retires early in the afternoon. Full vigorous physical activity should be done early in the morning.

WINTER: We must pattern ourselves after the sunlight, sleeping more to restore our energy and limiting physical activity.

In this second chapter of **The Yellow Emperor**, we might note that only in winter is there something we "must" do.

"Must" in Chinese is written as **Bi**, which is the character **Xin** (heart) with an extra oblique

BI   XIN

line crossing it. We use the word heart to describe our heart's wishes. However, the word "must" signals that we must do what is needed, regardless of what our wishes might be. Therefore, the oblique line turns "heart" into the opposite of heart.

The Yellow Emperor uses the word "must" in winter because the storage of Yang in this season has to do with our life expectancy, or Ming. In the other three seasons the wrong actions will impact our daily energy, or Xing. We may become ill, lethargic, or unproductive, but the impact on our life span will be minimal. In winter, if we do not act in the way that we must, and instead follow our heart's desires, then our Ming – our lifespan –will be shortened.

Thus the sage realized the importance of following sunlight in winter. He was to sleep longer hours during the winter, and also to keep physical activity to a minimum because the warming effects of the sunlight in winter are minimal. He was to be like the winter sunlight – mellow and subdued. His physical movements were to be slower and more contained.

In each season, we interact with a different state of energy, which means that in each season we must have a different state of mind. Maintaining the correct mindset is just as important as maintaining a physical regiment.

In spring, our intentions and ambitions rise. We interact more with nature and society. In summer, our ambitions are in the extreme. We project outwards, admiring our surroundings, interacting with them. In fall, the energy returns downward to the earth's surface, and our ambitions retract. We harmonize with nature by calming our spirit, drawing it back into our body. In winter, our ambitions and desires are withdrawn into a place where they are well hidden.

Of course, all of this stands in sharp contrast to our modern life, where we are constantly striving and never withdrawing or resting. We have lost our rhythm with nature.

When an infertility patient turns to storage and withdrawal during the winter, the chances of achieving conception in spring are greatly increased. This is called the Dao of nourishing "storage." When one reflects the spring in this way, it is referred to as the Dao of nourishing "birth." When one reflects the summer in this way, it is called the Dao of nourishing "growth." When one reflects the fall in this way, it is called the Dao of nourishing "gather."

If we don't allow our body and mind to follow the energy transformations in each season, there are consequences. The second chapter explains: *If spring is resisted, the liver will be harmed, and as a result, the summer is cold and growth will be scarce. If summer is resisted, the heart will be harmed, and as a result the autumn 'gather' energy will decrease and one will suffer fever and chills. Additionally, if summer is not followed, one will become severely ill in winter. If one resists autumn, the lungs will be harmed, and in winter storage will be scarce. If winter is resisted, the kidneys will be harmed, resulting in impotence and faint in the spring when 'birth' will be scarce.*

JUE

Let's focus on the winter and summer. The character for faint is **Jue**, which means "in one's dwelling there is obstruction and shortness of breath." Both impotence and faint, or shortness of breath, signify that there is an inability to reproduce. Also, **The Yellow Emperor** says that if summer is resisted, we will not only suffer "fever and chills" in the fall, we will become severely ill in winter.

Although **The Yellow Emperor** chooses summer's disharmony as a potential cause for a severe illness in winter, the truth is that resisting any of the three seasons will cause a severe illness in winter. And severe illness in winter means that there will be no ability to reproduce in spring.

As mentioned previously, our modern climate controlled environments can make it difficult to be in tune with nature. If we heat up our homes in midwinter, we are not creating summer, we are creating an artificial summer. We are heating our home with oil, gas, or coal, all of which are extracted from the depths of the earth, which **The Yellow Emperor** refers to as "underground water." Because our artificial summer is derived from storage, the more storage we use in winter, the less we have to give birth in the spring.

Yet, **The Yellow Emperor** tells us that in winter we must *expel the cold, then naturally it is warm, do not allow Qi to leak from the skin, bring the Qi urgently into containment.* **The Yellow Emperor** realizes the obvious – that in winter we must keep ourselves warm to keep ourselves alive. However, it cautions us that we cannot allow the warmth to leak from the house, and we must contain the heat so that we do not become too warm. We cannot sweat, or be outgoing in our ambitions, because if we are, we will disconnect with nature, and suffer impotence and faint in the spring.

DUO

Interestingly, the character used to describe "containment" is **Duo** , which in its original form meant "a bird who wants to fly but a hand grasping it down." This means that in winter we naturally want to behave as if it were summer, but we need a conscious act containing this desire in order to fit it into the storage energy of winter. This is called "bringing the Qi urgently into containment."

From the perspective of the Classical Chinese medicine, leading a "healthy lifestyle" does not mean going to the gym or eating a "healthy" granola bar. It means that we need to understand nature. Since we are part of nature and not independent entities as modern society may lead us to believe, we must harmonize with it. If we do so, we will fulfill our heavenly years, and women will have the ability to become pregnant until the age of 49.

SEPARATION VS. UNIFICATION

Our modern concept of time is linear. Today is today and tomorrow is tomorrow. Today and tomorrow cannot be the same thing. It is what we've learned since childhood as separation and differentiation. We as westerners believe that when we separate and differentiate, we can tell right from wrong and good from bad.

In Chinese history and culture, the main driving factor is unification and harmony. Instead of saying "this is good and this is bad, let's avoid the bad," the Chinese ancients asked "This is good and this is bad. How can we harmonize them together and make them work?" Instead of differentiating between today and tomorrow, the ancient sages tried to unify today and tomorrow. They tried to unify this year and next year. They were looking for the similarity in patterns instead of the difference. Or at least they were looking for the similarity in patterns so they could understand the difference between them.

THE ZODIAC SIGNS

The Chinese sages used a system of 12 zodiac signs, referred to as "the 12 earthly branches," to draw parallels in assimilating the time concept of today and tomorrow. While the 24 Qi explain how to break down Yin and Yang into pieces, the 12 zodiac sign show you how to unify the entire time concept into one. They also created ten "heavenly stems," a system of ten zodiac signs to describe heaven's energy.

The 12 earthly branches are: **Zi, Chou, Yin, Mao, Chen, Si, Wu, Wei, Shen, You, Xu** and **Hai.** In each energy cycle, whether it is a daily, monthly, or yearly cycle, there is equivalence. A daily cycle is midnight to morning, morning to noon to the afternoon and back to midnight again. A yearly cycle is spring, summer, fall and winter. A monthly cycle is the empty moon, growing moon, full moon and decreasing moon. From an energetical point of view, the daily, monthly and yearly cycles are all the same. They all have the storage, birth, growth and decline phases.

The sages used the 12 branches to describe the similarity in these cycles. "Zi," for example, represents the state of hidden Yang energy, when it is least visible. It describes midnight, middle of winter and an empty moon. From any particular energy cycle, Zi is where the Yang energy is least exposed or least visible. We call this phase "the storage of Yang." The earthly branch "Wu" describes Noon, middle of summer and full moon, the time where the Yang energy is most warming and most lighting.

The following is a chart of the earthly branches describing the unification of "Time:"

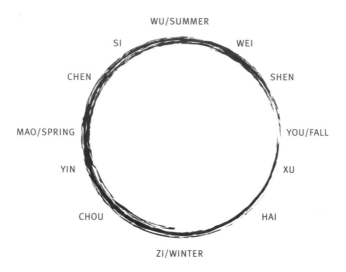

THE CHANGES SYSTEM

Energy changing is the root of life. It is why we are on this planet, why we have plants and animals, oceans and land masses. The ancients realized that change, or Yi, is what makes the difference between life and death. But what is changing and how?

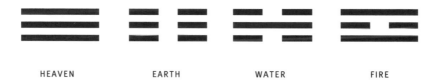

Because these questions are difficult to answer, the Chinese sages developed the Yi, or "Changes," system as something of an addendum to the Chinese characters. It is a system of images we call trigrams, or "Gua," which are composed of three lines: either solid lines or broken lines. Solid lines represent Yang energy, while broken lines represent Yin energy.

By describing Heaven and Earth with the trigrams, the sages set the foundations for Chinese medicine development. "Heaven" is described with three solid lines, meaning that heaven is a pure Yang energy phenomenon, with no Yin energy involved. Earth, on the other hand, is described with three broken lines. This indicates that earth is a pure Yin phenomenon.

To describe the "Yi," a before and after state are referenced, "Xian Tian", or Pre-Heaven, and "Hou Tian," or Post-Heaven. The "before" is before there was life, and the "after" is after there was life on earth. To understand life, health and fertility we need to understand what happened in this change.

The Chinese classics describe life as an interaction between heaven and earth, or an interaction between Yang and Yin. If there is no interaction between heaven and earth, or no interaction between Yang and Yin, there is no life. In order to describe this interaction, the sages used water and fire trigrams. The water trigram has two Yin lines on the top and bottom, with one Yang line between. The fire trigram has two Yang lines on the top and bottom with one Yin line in the middle .

Because both are essential, the ancients considered water and fire to be the basis for all life on earth. For life to be created, the Yin and Yang must be in relationship, and to do this they must exchange their essence. The Yang essence is the middle solid line of the heaven trigram , while the Yin essence is the middle broken line of the earth trigram . This is also referred to as the Yang within Yin and the Yin within Yang. When the middle Yang line of heaven reaches the middle of the earth trigram it creates the water trigram and when the middle Yin line of the earth trigram reaches the heaven trigram it creates the fire trigram .

The ancients described the importance of water and fire to our lives in more than one way. They created a sequence of eight trigrams to portray the pre-heaven state and a different sequence of the same eight trigrams portraying for the post-heaven state. (See illustration below)

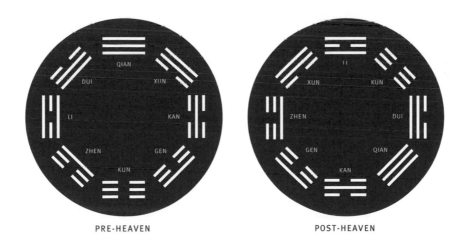

PRE-HEAVEN   POST-HEAVEN

The illustration explains the different relationships of the trigrams before and after life was created. We can see in the pre-heaven trigrams that the positions of north and south are occupied by heaven and earth. After the trigrams have changed to the post-heaven condition, these north and south positions are occupied by water and fire respectively. This explains that in pre life, the heaven and earth are pure Yin and pure Yang, and after life is created, they must be water and fire.

It should be noted that some of the eight trigrams in the illustrations are more important than others when it comes to the creation of life. The important trigrams, including water and fire, are always found in north, south, east and west, reminding us of the importance of water and fire in our lives. The four less important trigrams were placed in the four corners, namely southeast, northeast, southwest and northwest.

Heaven and earth means the entire universe and all the life that is in it. When the Yang essence is exchanged with the Yin essence, water and fire are created, and therefore life is created. This is exactly what happens between husband and wife in conception.

THREE YIN AND THREE YANG

The key to healing is to understand Yin and Yang. The most significant breakthrough of the sages in the Yin and Yang arena was the dividing of the Yin and the Yang into six spheres, or segments – three segments of Yang and three segments of Yin:

TAI YANG (great Yang)
YANG MING (bright Yang)
SHAO YANG (lesser Yang)

TAI YIN (great Yin)
SHAO YIN (lesser Yin)
JUE YIN (extinct Yin)

To understand three Yin and three Yang we have to go back to nature, where the most pronounced Yin and Yang cycle is that of the seasons. In the following illustration, please note that "South" is at the top because in Chinese culture and history, all maps display south at the top.

The spring belongs to the east and the fall belongs to the west. The east is where the sun rises and that is where the energy rises. The east energy is like the spring energy, where the plants are springing upward and the energy is rising. The west is where the sun sets and the energy descends. The energy of the fall is descending when the leaves are falling back to the ground.

The energy of the universe has four stages. Spring is about birth, summer about openness/growth, fall about retraction, and winter about storage.

In the past 500 to 700 years, some Chinese medicine practitioners with limited understanding of the ancient ways, and therefore limited understanding into the depth of Yin and Yang, began to categorize the four seasons in a logical way that distorted the course of Chinese

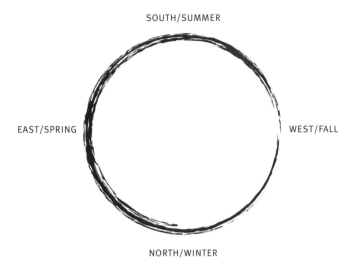

SOUTH/SUMMER

EAST/SPRING   WEST/FALL

NORTH/WINTER

medicine history. They claimed that because spring and summer are about opening up, they represent the Yang energy in nature, while fall and winter represent the Yin energy because they are about retracting and storing. This divided Yin and Yang into two halves, the feminine and the masculine. As Western philosophies were introduced into China about 400 years ago, this concept became even more widespread. Today, this idea is taught in acupuncture schools worldwide as the root of Chinese medicine, it is what I was initially taught. However, after spending countless hours learning classical Chinese, and researching the Chinese medicine classics, I now believe that this is not the case. Yin and Yang must be understood on a deeper level in order for treatment to be more effective.

OPEN, CLOSE AND PIVOT

The mechanisms behind these six spheres that make the Yin and Yang energies work are "opening," "closing," and "pivot." These movements act in succession, and together guarantee that life will go on without interruption.

The pivot is where the opening and closing actually takes place. It transforms the action of the energy, motivating the transition of the seasons. A door can be used as a metaphor. It needs a hinge to transform the static state of an unmovable slab of wood into a dynamic state of opening and closing. It transforms the door from a pre-heaven state into a post-heaven state. The two pivots are "Shao Yang" and "Shao Yin."

THE TAI YANG PHASE

The **Tai Yang phase** is the first phase of the energy transformation and is referred to as the birth of Yang energy. Tai Yang has several meanings in the Chinese language. It is called "Greater Yang" and is also the Chinese name for the sun, as well as for dawn as seen from the top of a mountain. It is the representation of birth and the representation of life. As long as there is expansion of energy, it is a time of "Tai Yang."

Understanding physical matter is a much simpler process than understanding the energetical process of life. Physical process can be examined and observed under a microscope. With energy, or at least life-force energy, comprehension requires a depth of thinking. The deeper the thought, the more life is understood. When you understand life, you understand illness and are able to restore health. You are able to understand infertility and restore fertility.

In this process of gaining depth, we will describe the Tai Yang from different angles. By combining all of these angles, we will understand Tai Yang in a variety of ways simultaneously.

The first angle is the birth concept. It is where the Yang (or great Yang or Tai Yang) is first born at midnight, or the time of Zi, in the middle of winter or when there is no moon. It stretches until Wu, which is noon or the middle of summer or full moon. It represents the time stretching from the moment we are conceived to our adulthood or mid-years. In other words, it is the first half of all life as we know it, which is why Zhang Zhongjing dedicates half of his life work to Tai Yang.

The second angle to take in understanding Tai Yang is to look at its energetical qualities. **The Yellow Emperor** describes these as "cold" and as "water."

My teacher, Professor Liu Lihong, describes in his book "Si Kao Zhong Yi" the importance of water. Without water, there is no life. What is the relationship between water, cold and the Tai Yang? Liu Lihong explained the Tai Yang as the opening up of energy. What happens to water when the energy opens up or warms up? It evaporates skyward, or heavenward, where the cold atmosphere (cold energy) forces it back down to earth in the form of rain. When **The Yellow Emperor** describes Tai Yang as cold and water, he is referring to this phenomenon of water circulation that allows life on earth.

The third path to take in understanding Tai Yang is to relate it to the two organs that compose the Tai Yang sphere in the body – the bladder and small intestines. These two organs, in the Chinese medical system, are the organs responsible for water metabolism. The small intestines digest the water and the bladder controls the excretion of excess water. If the water metabolism is impaired, it is mainly because the Tai Yang system has a problem.

An impaired water metabolism affects our fertility. Part of the Tai Yang phenomenon is to help the water be distributed throughout the body in a proper and adequate way, areas with too much water sent to areas in need.

This stands in contrast to today's understanding of drinking and hydration. The trend today is to drink as much as possible in order to keep hydrated. Growing up, I don't recall seeing anybody walking with a water bottle on the street, but today it seems that a water bottle is part of everyday existence. When we constantly drink water, however, the Tai Yang organs are engaged in an excessive fashion. The bladder and small intestine are under extreme stress. On the other hand, some people don't have time to drink even if they are thirsty, and this will cause a different set of problems. For normal Tai Yang water metabolism, we should strive for balance in drinking water. There is no such thing as one size fits all so each individual must find her own balance.

The fourth way to understand Tai Yang is to study the two meridians that compose the Tai Yang sphere: the bladder meridian, which is the most important, and the small intestine meridian. The bladder meridian starts at the inner cantus of the eye, runs along the top of the head and down the center of the back along both sides of the spine. It continues to flow down the posterior side of both legs until it reaches the lateral side of both little toes. It is the longest meridian, and the only one out of the 12 that is distributed exclusively on the posterior (back) side of our body.

The Yellow Emperor states that the reason the Tai Yang relates to the entire posterior side of our body is that in ancient times, when people plowed the fields, their front side faced the earth, or Yin energy, while their back side faced the sun, or Yang energy.

When the Tai Yang is obstructed, the Yang energy cannot open up. If the Yang energy is only partially present when spring arrives, the flowers will seem poor and tired. It would be the same for people if the Yang energy did not open far enough when we wake up in the morning. We would feel lethargic and tired.

Because Tai Yang represents the sun, a warming force and source of light, we find it more difficult to wake-up in colder weather. This is why the Yellow Emperor recommends less sleep in the summer. When the body encounters a burst of cold energy, such as when walking into a very cold air-conditioned office in the middle of summer, the opening of the Yang is obstructed. This can result in chills or catching a cold. We may experience a headache or stiff neck because the bladder meridian, running along the neck and head, is obstructed. We feel chills because the Yang energy can't open up to warm the body.

To remedy this obstruction, we must use warm herbs, such as cinnamon and Ma Huang. These herbs can be ingested until minor perspiration appears. In other words, the best way to recover from a cold is to help the Yang expand, but to stop before sweating begins. As Zhongjing writes, *If the patient sweats like dripping water, he will never recover* because the Yang will become deficient. The body seeks harmony and balance; opening too much will cause profuse perspiration. The Yang will lose strength, the ailment becoming stronger.

The Yellow Emperor notes that the Tai Yang enters and exits the body through the center of the chest. When we take Western medication for the common cold, many people experience the cold moving into the chest and then turning into a lingering cough. In this, we have not solved the obstruction of the Yang mechanism, we have simply pushed it a layer deeper. The enter and exit mechanism has been obstructed. Using cold herbs to treat the common cold causes the same results.

If warm herbs are not used, then ingesting a hot rice soup and lying down beneath blankets to rest should clear out the cold within a day or two. If you do not rest, keep warm, and drink warm soups, then the cold will move into the chest, obstructing the Yang and developing into a far worse situation such as a sinus infection. It will then be difficult to avoid western drugs. Every action that we do to help preserve the Yang will help us become closer to fertility.

Tai Yang, like all six spheres, has a root, a manifestation and a center. The root of Tai Yang is cold, because it starts at Zi, or midnight/midwinter, the coldest time. The manifestation is hot because the Yang is the opening of the hot energy until it reaches Wu – noon/ mid-summer. The center of Tai Yang, where it connects to the internal body, is the Shao Yin sphere.

The Shao Yin is where all fertility happens. When the Tai Yang is obstructed, the Shao Yin suffers the consequences. In today's modern medicine of separating and differentiating one disease from another, the common cold is completely inconsequential to fertility. In Chinese medicine of unification and harmony, when the Yang mechanism is obstructed, the Shao Yin and fertility will suffer. Problems with the Yang mechanism are of course not only a consequence of the common cold but also to a variety of factors and situations that impact the Tai Yang channel. If this channel is kept open, the chances for fertility will greatly appreciate.

It is important to avoid overstimulation of the Tai Yang. Although it may feel like we are stimulating the Yang energy, when we go to a party and stay out late, but this can lead to exhausting the energy. The extra stimulation that we all experience from work, TV, or driving a car, as well as exposure to cold foods and cold drugs, causes our Yang energy to become more deficient. Additionally, practices like Qi Gong and meditation, which were used in the past in China to keep the Yang intact, are no longer in widespread use.

To achieve fertility, it is important to begin modifying behavior and customs. For example, when you want an iced drink, try and do without it.

A fifth aspect of the Tai Yang is the time when the energy is best open to a remedy for any imbalance. With Tai Yang, it includes the three months of summer on the lunar calendar, as well as 9 AM until 3 PM, when the Yang energy is at its most open state.

THE YANG MING PHASE

The Yang Ming phase is the part of the Yang mechanism responsible for the closing down of the energy. It prevents the Yang from staying open forever. It has a protective action in preserving the Yang, ensuring its retraction into a storage phase. Farmers are well aware of the fact that if the winter is warm, the growing season the following year will be poor. Not sleeping well at night or long enough at night causes our energy level to be weak the following day.

The Yang Ming sphere occupies the time from Wu until Zi, from noon until midnight, and from the mid-summer, when the Yang energy is at its most open, until the mid-winter, when it is completely stored. It is the part of our life from adulthood to death.

As for its energetical qualities, The Yellow Emperor describes Yang Ming as "Dry" and as "Metal."

There are two different types of dryness, a real dryness and an apparent dryness. Liu Lihong uses the example of wet laundry. What happens to wet laundry when you put it in the dryer? The laundry becomes dry. But what happens to the water? It evaporates and transitions to a different place. If the dryer is in a closed laundry room, you'll see the steam on the windows or the walls. The same is true when we boil water. It evaporates until there is no water left in the pot and the pot is dry.

This is one kind of dryness – local or apparent dryness. It is the result of the transformation of water from one state into a different state.

As for a true dryness of water, let's look at what happens to water in the dead of winter when the weather is freezing. The water becomes solid as ice. A block of ice cannot be poured into a cup. But if we add Yang energy to it, such as heat, the ice will melt and become water again. The dryness of water without Yang energy is a true dryness of water.

When the Yellow Emperor describes the Yang Ming as dry, he refers to true dryness and not apparent dryness. He refers to the state where the Yang energy is moving into storage. The inborn ability of Yang Ming is to transform the Yang energy in the water into storage.

Why is the Yang Ming quality similar to the metal quality? It is because the metal is heavy and descending. It's an element that belongs to the autumn, and in a daily cycle, to the afternoon and evening hours. It belongs to the time of Shen, You and Xu, when the energy is at its strongest descent.

The third concept of Yang Ming is in relation to the organs of the body, specifically the stomach and large intestines, two organs that break down and expel the food we eat. These are both downward actions. The food's energy and nutrients come from heaven. We extract all the Yang energy from what we eat and drink so our life can continue. We allow all the turbid Yin and substance of the food to descend and be expelled as feces.

The fourth angle to take when approaching Yang Ming is its meridians. The large intestine meridian, which starts at the index finger, runs along the medial side of the arm and reaches the face from both sides at the nose. The stomach meridian, which starts at the face, runs downward along the front of the body until it reaches the tip of the second toe.

The Yang Ming meridians cover the entire front, or anterior, side of our body. Between the Tai Yang and Yang Ming, all of the Yang energy circulates up the back and down the front of the body. If both channels are working properly, we will feel energized and vital, and our health will be maintained.

The fifth concept of Yang Ming is the unlocking time from Shen until Xu. In the yearly cycle, these are the three fall months of the lunar calendar. In the daily cycle, it represents from 3 PM until 9 PM, when the descending Yang energy is at its most potent action.

When the Yang Ming becomes obstructed, the stomach and large intestines are full, bringing on possible constipation. The obstruction can occur from eating oily, greasy food that creates local heat. It can also be created by unnatural foods, such as modern processed food, artificial sweeteners, coloring, preservatives, or soft drinks. Common symptoms associated with constipation are shortness of breath, as well as insomnia due to the Yang's inability to go into storage at night. When the body can expel all unnecessary materials, a healthy state of Yang energy can be maintained. If the Yang cannot go into storage at night, it will bring on difficulty in sleeping.

The Yang Ming does not become obstructed with real dryness, when the Yang in the water is closing (cooling) into a storage phase. With an apparent, or local, dryness, the bowels become dry and constipated. Zhongjing describes the symptoms associated with this pattern as heavy perspiration, a rise in temperature, a red face, and an intense, surging pulse. Heavy perspiration is the result of the body fluids evaporating out of the body like the wet laundry in the dryer. Feeling hot, as well as having a red face and an overactive pulse, is all signs of too much heat or the inability of the Yang to cool down. This will cause the Yang Ming to become dry and constipated, obstructing the Yang Ming downward cooling movement.

The Yellow Emperor suggests that the Yang Ming should be remedied from its center, which is Tai Yin "Damp" and "Earth." We should use moistening or dampness, or as Zhongjing suggests, a clearing of the heat, with the use of purgatives and cold herbs. He also warns that as soon as the bowels restore their function, purgatives must immediately be stopped. This is because purgative and cold herbs damage the Yang energy, and with that, the life force. It is only a temporary localized heat that needs to be cleared so the Yang Ming can descend.

It should be noted that not all constipation is a Yang Ming issue, and other forms of the condition are not accompanied by perspiration, hot feelings, or having a red face. This constipation is generally Yang deficiency related and belongs in the Shao Yin sphere. In Ancient China, one could only use purgatives if it was a Yang Ming related problem and only for a short period of time. If it was a Yang deficiency constipation issue, the Yang energy has to be strengthened, not purged.

With regard to the insomnia symptom associated with the Yang Ming obstruction, sleep medication will not solve the problem, as it deals solely with the symptom and not with the cause. Instead of the Yang energy closing down, it is scattered as it is with anesthesia. It may seem like a peaceful sleep, but it is a completely different state of energy. When one awakens from anesthesia, the Yang energy is completely exhausted, not rejuvenated. When insomnia is caused by a Yang Ming obstruction, removing this obstruction will bring on sleep.

THE SHAO YANG PHASE

Shao Yang is described metaphorically by **The Yellow Emperor** as a pivot. It is the door hinge that allows the opening and closing of the Yang energy. We can see the Yang energy expression in its different phases of birth, growth, retraction and storage – the growth of the plants coming out of the earth, the leaves budding from the tree branches – but we cannot see the energy itself. It is like the seed of a plant, so small that if we drop it to the ground, we may not be able to find it again, but if we stick it in the ground, it may sprout a huge tree. The energy and potency – the Yang – is invisible, yet it is there.

The energy without the seed, or without the Yin matter, will not work, nor will the seed without its energy. It is only when the seed and its energy are combined that we can get this life effect. It is only when the heaven's pure Yang has some Yin substance within that we get this fire that is characteristic of Shao Yang. It is the pivot that allows the Tai Yang and Yang Ming to continue and circulate. It is the force and quality that allows the Yang mechanism to repeatedly open and close without exhaustion.

In the Chinese earliest Daoist work **Dao De Jing** the author Lao Zi writes: *Dao gives birth to one. One gives birth to two. Two give birth to three. Three give birth to the ten thousand things.* When we have two actions, such as opening and closing, it is not enough to make life happen, for there is no continuation. One cycle must open a new cycle, or we cannot call it life.

Let's take an apple tree for example. The tree grows and bears fruit. The apples ripen and fall to the ground. If the apples do not contain seeds, they will not give birth to other apple trees. This is what Lao Zi means by saying one gives birth to two, two give birth to three, and that the third element is what ensures the ten thousand things to flourish.

The Shao Yang sphere ensures the continuation of life. It ensures that when we go to sleep at night, we will wake up in the morning to a new day, and when our Yang energy is consumed during the day, we will retreat to sleep to recharge. It ensures this life cycle of Yang energy will continue until we reach a point in our lives when it will be time to stop. It also has a crucial relationship with our fertility, which is what insures a new generation, via its relationship with the Yin pivot, Shao Yin.

The second aspect of Shao Yang is its energetical qualities. **The Yellow Emperor** describes the Shao Yang as "Minister Fire".

What is the importance of fire in our lives? Electricity is a form of fire. Combustion in engines is a form of fire. We use fire for cooking. We use fire to keep warm in winter and to keep us cool in summer. We use fire to light the night and operate our computers. The use of fire is what separates us from the animal kingdom.

In the book of changes (Yi Jing), the trigram for heaven, **Qian** – is three Yang lines. It is pure Yang energy. At this state of energy there is still no life. The same is true with the earth trigram **Kun.** These are three broken Yin lines representing pure Yin substance without energy, and no life.

HEAVEN   EARTH   FIRE   WATER

Only when substance and energy meet – when earth and heaven meet – and exchange essence, is life formed.

The fire trigram, Li, has two solid Yang lines, one at the top and one at the bottom. In between the two Yang lines there is one broken Yin line. Fire is Yang energy above and it is Yang energy below, but embedded in the Yang energy is a Yin substance. Let's take for example the fire in engine combustion. The fire is fueled by gasoline. Without this substance, there is no fire. The same is true with cooking on the stove. The fire is there because gas is burning. When we burn a fire in a fireplace, there is wood within that allows this fire to burn.

In the water trigram, the pure Yin substance, represented by the upper and lower lines, receives energy from heaven, which is represented by the Yang line in the middle. This makes a lifeless substance into water. We have discussed previously that water becomes lifeless if we remove the Yang from it.

Shao Yang, the pivot of the Yang mechanism, is described as "Minister's Fire," while the pivot of the Yin mechanism, Shao Yin, is described as "Emperor's Fire." These two types of fire complement each other. A scholar from the Jin Yuan dynasties (1200 AD) Zhu Danxi, and his followers, in an effort to explain why we have disease, erroneously theorized that because we have one water and two fires, the Yin is always deficient, and the Yang is always in excess.

A minister in a government is an individual who is engaged on a daily basis with the details of running the country, and generally has direct contact with the citizens. An emperor, on the other hand, stays in the palace and has the function of overseeing the big picture.

The minister fire of the Shao Yang is the fire which is actively engaged with all the body's functions, and specifically with the opening and closing of the Yang energy. It is the fire that warms up the body. It is the fire that gives us the appropriate energy to wake up in the morning and go to sleep at night. It is the energy that allows us to hear, see, smell, drink, eat, walk, run, write, read, talk, and laugh. It is the physical fire that makes us function.

The third aspect of Shao Yang is its organs, the gallbladder and the Triple Burner. In Chinese medicine anatomy, these two organs are in a very special, often misunderstood category. The Chinese medicine anatomy contains eleven organs – Six **Fu Yang** organs and five **Zang Yin** organs. The Fu organs are hollow and allow movement of turbid matter to pass through. The stomach, small intestines, large intestines, bladder, triple burner and gallbladder fall into this category. The five Zang organs store essence and do not allow movement through them. The heart, lungs, kidneys, liver and spleen, are in the Zang family. The gallbladder is in a special category because it stores bile and releases it for digestion. It has the function of a Yang organ and of a Yin organ simultaneously. It is called an extraordinary organ.

San Jiao, or the triple burner, is unique in that it is the only "organ" in the Chinese medicine anatomy which is not a physical organ, but is pure function. Containing three "burners" that transmit the minister life's fire throughout the entire body, it also provides the passageway for body fluids to be distributed. The upper burner includes the lungs, heart and brain, and is the root of our spirit. The lower burner includes the kidneys and liver and is the root of our essence and substance. The middle burner, the root of our post-heaven life, includes the spleen and stomach, and is where the food and liquid come into our body, giving us the life force or the fire we need.

The fourth aspect of Shao Yang is its meridians, the triple burner meridian and the gallbladder meridian. The triple burner meridian starts at the ring finger, travels upward through the center of the arm between the Tai Yang and Yang Ming channels, then runs along the side of the neck and the side of the head. The gall bladder meridian runs along side of the head, down the side of the rib cage and side of the legs until reaching the fourth toe. When a person stands upright with arms relaxed at both sides of the body, both meridians run exactly on both sides of the body between the front, which is the Yang Ming channel, and the rear, the Tai Yang channel. The Shao Yang is the connecting factor between the opening upwards of Tai Yang and the closing downwards of the Yang Ming.

Nature designed each and every aspect of our body with a specific function. We need the Shao Yang pivot to make opening and closing work. We need this Yin matter within the Yang energy, or in other words we need this minister fire distributed on the side meridians of gall bladder and triple burner to make the Yang mechanism work.

It is on the sides because Yin matter goes downwards and Yang energy goes upwards. When tending to a campfire, we generally adjust the logs, or add more logs, from the side, because the fire flares upward and we'll be burned if we're above it. When we want to adjust the Yin "logs" that will cause the Yang fire to change, we have to do it from the side. We are not affected by the Yin or the Yang. This is the concept of the Shao Yang meridian distributed on both sides of the body.

The fifth aspect of Shao Yang is the time for unlocking, or remedying, which includes the times of Yin, Mao and Chen. These times make up the daily cycle from 3 AM until 9 AM, and represent the three months of spring in the Chinese lunar calendar. It is a time of "kindling warmth" as opposed to the summer's robust fire, very gentle warmth that spreads around in nature, causing plants to spring from the ground and birds to emerge.

The Yang energy of Shao Yang is a gentle fire that promotes growth and development. It is different then the pathological fire we have seen in the Yang Ming section that can cause dryness and constipation. The gall bladder releases bile which aids in digestion and is the warmth needed for metabolism. In Chinese medicine, the five flavors (bitter, sweet, pungent, salty and sour) belong to the five elements, the bitter taste belonging to fire. It is not a coincidence that bile is bitter and is stored in the gall bladder. It is the minister fire or the kindling warmth that is needed for our metabolism and it is achieved with the help of this bile.

The spring and the early morning hours possess this unique quality of light warmth. It is the energy in nature that promotes a healthy Shao Yang function, and is the reason Chinese medicine recommends consuming the day's main meal in the morning, a light meal at lunch and a small snack for dinner. The morning warmth is what aids the metabolism and digestion. Eating large dinners and small breakfasts will cause the Yang mechanism to suffer greatly, and is one reason why maintaining the wrong eating habits will cause disharmony even with a healthy diet.

When the Shao Yang becomes obstructed, the opening and closing will become obstructed like the rusted hinge of a door will make opening or closing difficult. The Shao Yang is, as discussed before, a third dimension helping the Tai Yang opening and the Yang Ming closing, and difficulties are expressed as a Tai Yang malfunction or a Yang Ming malfunction. For example, if the Shao Yang's kindling warmth (minister fire) is unable to assist in the Yang Ming's closing down, then local heat will accumulate in the Yang Ming, creating apparent dryness (the pathological dryness caused by local heat) in the bowels, resulting in constipation. This is described as a **bing bing**, or a mutual disease, of Shao Yang and Yang Ming.

An imbalance in the Shao Yang may cause a bitter taste in the mouth, a dry throat, and blurry eyes. Bitter is the flavor of fire, dryness the pathology caused by fire, and blurriness the result of flaring fire or pathological fire. Shao Yang problems are caused by fire: not a minister's or "kindling wood" fire, which is just warm enough to help metabolism but is not too hot to obstruct it.

As Liu Lihong explains, there are three organs that are most prone to opening and closing. The mouth opens and closes for Yang (talking) and for Yin (receiving and chewing food). The throat opens and closes for Yang (breathing) and for Yin (swallowing food, drinks and saliva). The eyes open and close for Yang (to catch light and vision) and for Yin (to allow Yin storage and tears). If the pivot or the hinge is obstructed, the opening and closing will suffer. The Yang energy is obstructed and the result is pathological heat or not enough warmth. The action needed is to harmonize.

Another main symptom of the Shao Yang disease is an alternating cold and hot feeling, frequently experienced after taking fertility drugs. Pre-menopause symptoms such as hot flashes can at times fall under this category as well. Other symptoms include pains along the sides of the body, or a headache on one side of the head, signaling an obstruction of the Shao Yang meridians, as well as decreased appetite and nausea due to need for the spleen energy to ascend and the needs of the stomach's energy to descend. The Shao Yang minister fire needs to harmonize this upward and downward separation.

Zhongjing's description of a decrease in appetite and nausea was "sitting quietly and not wishing to eat," which is a reference to the Yang mechanism connecting with the emotions. Energy disharmony can be brought about by emotions. Certainly, anxiety associated with the inability to conceive can have a negative effect on fertility.

Most body functions require harmonizing, and need the Shao Yang's minister fire to help. This includes the reproductive organs of both women and men. Shao Yang's root is fire (minister fire), its manifestation is hot as it harmonizes the Yang energy, and its center is Jue Yin, which will be discussed in a later section and includes the liver organ, a major player in fertility. The Shao Yang harmonizing function is closely related to the liver function of harmonizing and soothing the blood. This plays an important role in creating or preventing fertility and reproduction.

It is important to understand there is connectedness between all aspects of our energy, and that any action we take has an impact on our health and fertility. It is not only the ovaries or uterus lining problems that are related to fertility. What we eat, how we sleep, and how we medicate all impact different aspects of our energy.

THE TAI YIN PHASE

Before we begin our discussion of Tai Yin, which is the first phase of Yin, it is important that we analyze the Chinese characters of Yin and Yang. As previously discussed, each part of a character symbolizes a specific idea the Chinese sages wanted to express, and the combination of parts in each character also express ideas. The Yin and Yang characters are identical on the left, but different on the right.

YANG   YIN

The right section of the Yang character has three parts. The upper part is a sun in the sky. The middle part is the line under the sun, which represents the earth. The third part is the lines under the earth, which represent the sun rays of light and warmth. This character stands for the Yang energy, or the outdoors. When one goes outside into the sunshine, one feels the Yang energy. It is a life giving light and warmth.

The right section of the Yin character also has three parts. The upper part is the roof of a house. The middle part is a person sitting in the house. The bottom is the steam coming out of cooked rice or cooked food. The Yin character represents the Yin energy, which is indoors, and has to do with our physical body or with physical matter. The bottom represents the presence of energy which is hot in nature, but is not coming directly from the sun. It is coming from elements that were derived from the earth with the sun's help like rice, water and firewood.

When we compare both characters, we see that we are dealing with two different states of energy. In the Yang character, the sun rays go downwards, while in the Yin character the steam is going upwards. Yang has less matter and more energy, and gives us the force for life. Yin has more matter and less energy and gives us the energy associated with matter, which is needed for life as well. In Chinese medicine, physical matter which is living, such as body tissues, bones, and muscles, is in a state of condensed energy. It is not the same as the Yang energy that we cannot see. It is physical matter but it contains energy within.

Both Yin and Yang characters have a section on the left side representing a hill or a mound. The hill is where the earth is swollen like a pregnant woman, and is the place where the earth is growing closer to the heavens. It is a symbol of heaven and earth exchanging energies, and of life and future generations.

The hill to the left summarizes the characters of Yin and Yang. Whether it is physical living matter or invisible life's energy, both represent the exchange of heaven and earth, they are both living and are needed for life; and both are warm. The life force, whether it is outside or inside the body, is warm. The Yang energy and the Yin matter must all contain this warmth which is the root of life.

Cold is not Yin; rather, it is the absence of Yang energy. When the night is cold it is because the sun is absent, not because the moon is radiating cold toward the earth. To understand Yin and Yang, we have to understand this hot and cold concept. As noted, both pivots of the Yin and Yang (Shao Yin and Shao Yang) are fire; the Shao Yang is minister's fire and the Shao Yin is emperor's fire. This is exactly the description of the warmth within the Yang and the Yin.

When we reach the Tai Yin, or the Yin within Yin, we have reached the physical living organism. The Tai Yin is where physically living matter interacts with other physically living matter. For example, the living parts of food and drink (nutrients) interact with the Tai Yin spleen organ. Air that we breathe interacts with the Tai Yin lung organ. Water is the embodiment of the Yin state. It contains life because it has warmth, or Yang energy, within. The warmer the water, the more life there is. The Tai Yin anchors the Yang energy into the body. Without it, the Yang would float away.

The second aspect of Tai Yin is its energetical qualities, described by the Yellow Emperor

KUN

as "Damp" and "Earth." Earth, described in earlier chapters, is represented by the Kun trigram that contains three broken lines with no Yang energy within. This is the expression of solid matter. It symbolizes the body's tissues, such as the bones, flesh, skin and inner organs. All living things spring from the earth, so it has additional meaning. Earth is closely related to water and dampness. The ancient character for damp, Shi, is:

SHI   SHI

The character Shi has four parts. On the left side, the three lines represent water. At the top is the sun. In the middle is a character that represents mystery, and the character representing the earth is at the bottom. The entire character combination illustrates a situation where the sun is shining on the earth, and while it is doing so, something mysterious about the interaction causes the water to evaporate and become dampness.

The third aspect of Tai Yin is its organs – the spleen and the lungs. The spleen is responsible for receiving the Yang energy from food and drink. This is referred to as the root of the post-heaven energy – where we get our energy after we're born. When we choose the foods we eat, it is important to consider whether or not it contains Yang, or heaven energy. Natural food has heaven energy because it is produced by heaven and earth. When food is harvested, its natural instinct is to perish, because once it is removed from nature its Yin matter and Yang energy want to separate. Today, the food industry processes and packages food so that it can stay on the shelf for many months. It is sometimes difficult to say whether or not this packaged food is alive, but at best, it is not as alive as it could be. From a Tai Yin perspective, the recent trend toward consuming more locally grown, fresh food is very wise.

The lungs, like the spleen, are responsible for the post-heaven energy received into our body after we are born, as opposed to the energy we receive from our mother while in the womb. The lungs are responsible for taking the heaven's Yang from the air and inserting it into our body as we breathe. The spleen is receiving the Yang within Yin – it receives the Yang energy which is embedded in the food, while the lungs receive the Yang-within-Yang, the pure Yang energy in the air, which is completely invisible. Both Tai Yin organs receive the Yang energy in its different forms and then insert it into our body's physical matter.

The Tai Yin sphere is responsible for anchoring the Yang energy into physical matter. The spleen belongs to the earth element and the lungs belong to the metal element. The metal in its natural state is concealed within the earth, which means metal and earth are closely related.

Another function of the lungs, as described by **The Yellow Emperor**, is to rule the Qi (energy) and the Jie (points). The characters Qi and Jie can also mean time periods. One Jie is 15 days, and one Qi is 15 days. Together in Chinese, the words Jie Qi translates to the four seasons and their 24 Qi segments. The lungs control our ability to conform to the changing seasons and to benefit from each season's energy. They control and nourish the skin and body hair, because they regulate the Qi and the Jie, the interaction with the seasons changing around us.

The fourth aspect of Tai Yin is its meridians: the spleen meridian and the lungs meridian. When a person stands upright with both hands to the sides of the body, the Tai Yin meridians are distributed along the inside of the arms and legs (medial side). Their location on the body facilitates the job of the meridians, which is to bring the condensed Yang energy into the body tissues. They bring the Yang within Yin or the Yang within the matter into the body.

The fifth aspect of Tai Yin is the unlocking times, which are **Hai, Zi** and **Chou**. These times represent the three months of winter in the lunar calendar, and in the daily cycle they are from 9 PM until 3 AM.

In order to understand this fifth aspect thoroughly, it is important to understand the three Yin spheres, which are more closely related than the Yang spheres, and often interchangeable. In addition, the three Yin meridians can be difficult to separate. This is because the Yin mechanism, while still opening, closing, and pivoting, occurs inside the Yin material.

Hai, Zi and Chou are the times during the energy cycle where the Yang energy is in its most stored state – where it is the most invisible. During the dead of winter or the middle of the night, the Yang energy has not disappeared, it's in storage. When we are sleeping, we are in a living Yin state, the Yang energy having contracted but still residing within the body. This is why we naturally feel colder when we sleep and must cover ourselves with a blanket. In Chinese medicine, the time from 9:00 PM until midnight is when the body rejuvenates its blood (material). If we sleep at this time, our blood will be vigorous and many of our ailments solved, including fertility. The first thing that an infertility patient needs to consider is to change sleeping patterns. Going to bed at 9:00 PM for several months will greatly increase the chance of conception.

The time of Hai (9 PM-11 PM) is when the Yin is pure and the Yang is in complete storage. The time of Zi, one hour before midnight, is where the first Yang – the Tai Yang – is born. The Yang then grows during the time of Chou (1 AM-3 AM). Sleep is important because when the Yang rises within the Yin, it is similar to the steam elevating from cooked rice. It provides life inside the house – life inside our body. It is important to sleep at the right time so the body becomes harmonious with nature.

When we have an obstruction of the Tai Yin sphere, sleep is a remedy. Symptoms associated with this obstruction generally begin with the abdomen – the center of the body that belongs to the earth – feeling full or bloated, signaling that the Yang is not transforming the Yin harmoniously. When a woman feels bloated during the menses period, it is because the Tai Yin is not harmonious. When an infertility patient receives medication, the abrupt stimulation of Yang brings the Tai Yin into disharmony, often resulting in a bloated feeling. In Western medicine, this is referred to as a "side effect." In Chinese medicine, this phenomenon is a "disharmony."

Pain in the abdomen is the result of cold, which signifies the absence of Yang – where the Yang energy does not transform the Yin substance and (Yin) energy and the Yin becomes obstructed. Pain in Chinese is **Teng Tong.**

TENG TONG

The left character is 'Teng.' The section on the left of Teng represents a person lying on a bed, signifying disease. The right part in Teng is the character **Dong**, which is winter, when the Yang energy is stored, the weather is cold, and the Yin can't transform. On the right side of the 'Tong' character, is **Yong**, which signifies a path or a way. This embodies the meaning that if something is obstructed, it will become painful.

In our daily lives, when we drink cold drinks, eat cold foods, consume cold herbs and cold medications, this will lead to the obstruction of Tai Yin. Preserving the Yang energy of the spleen (Tai Yin) is the most important factor in the treatment of any disease.

In addition, in Tai Yin obstruction, the food will not stay down and the person will vomit, proving that a Tai Yin obstruction is caused by cold (Yang absence). The Yang cannot warm the earth and food metabolism stops.

THE SHAO YIN PHASE

Shao Yin is the pivot of the Yin mechanism, and is closely related to the Tai Yin, and could be said to be inseparable. When the character for dampness was discussed, the mysterious element within it was mentioned. With our analysis of the Shao Yin, we will attempt to unveil this mystery.

Water and earth, as well as water and fire, need the Yang energy in order to create life. The Shao Yin is the embodiment of this. The essence of the pure Yin (earth) and the pure Yang (heaven), the living Yin (water) and the living Yang (fire) is all within the Shao Yin. The interaction between heaven and earth in the body, and the way water and fire complement each other, are all functions of the Shao Yin, the Yin mechanism's pivot. The "mysterious" part of the character for dampness is related to the Shao Yin ability to orchestrate this harmony between Yin and Yang.

In Chinese medicine, a person's actions and events over a lifetime are all consequential to his or her Shao Yin sphere and reproductive ability. This includes long-time eating habits, sleeping habits, and the way in which ailments have been treated. It even includes how the individual's parents ate, slept, and treated ailments before they were born.

The second aspect of Shao Yin is its energetical qualities. **The Yellow Emperor** refers to the Shao Yin as "Emperor's fire." The leader or the emperor of a country is the figure that unites the entire country. The Emperor Fire in our body is the sphere that unifies the body and emotions. The reason for two kinds of fire in the six spheres is that the Shao Yang fire warms up the body, while the Shao Yin fire lights up the body. The emperor fire represents the brightness of the light.

The third aspect of Shao Yin is its organs, the kidneys and heart. The kidneys belong to the water element, while the heart belongs to the fire element. This represents the water and fire interaction within the body.

In the body, the heart is like the emperor. It is the organ that allows this unity in the body. **The Yellow Emperor** describes the heart as *the emperor where **Shen Ming** comes out*. Shen means "spirit/soul," while Ming translates to clear. Loosely translated, it means that the heart is where the spirit becomes clear.

The Yellow Emperor: Plain Questions describes the Shen/spirit as *The vast interaction of heaven and earth where the human spirit penetrates*. It also states: *Spirit in heaven is wind and in the earth it is wood, in heaven it is heat and in the earth it is fire, in heaven it is mist and in earth it is dirt (earth from the five elements), in heaven it is dryness and in earth it is metal, in heaven it is cold while in earth it is water*. This is the description of the five elements in nature as related to the spirit.

The spirit in heaven and earth represents the energetical qualities of each of the six spheres. The Tai Yang sphere is cold and water, the Jue Yin sphere is wind and wood, the Yang Ming is dryness and metal. Tai Yin is earth and mist. Only Shao Yang and Shao Yin unite into one category where one is heat and one is fire, which are the two aspects of the same fire – heat and light. Both statements of The Yellow Emperor describe the spirit as a pathway between heaven, earth, and man, or between Yin, Yang, and man. The spirit is the mechanism connecting us to heaven and earth. It is the mechanism and unifying factor that connects us to nature, allowing the Yang (heaven) and Yin (earth) to interact within our bodies.

MING

When the Yin and Yang separate at death it is said that the spirit has departed. So what does it mean that the spirit is clear? Let us look into the character **Ming**: The left side represents the sun; the right side represents the moon. These are the two most clearly distinguishable objects in the sky, and are visible due to their light.

The statement that the heart is where the spirit is clear means that the heart is where the spirit sees everything. The emperor fire is the light that is needed for the spirit to see what is happening in every part of the body. All ailments are caused by the spirit that is not clear because it is in the dark and cannot see.

Western medications such as pain relievers are actually a hindrance to solving the root problem of any physical issue because they remove the light from the spirit in order to relieve the symptoms. The emperor can no longer see what is happening in his kingdom. When it comes to infertility procedures, if a patient who undergoes IVF treatments doesn't feel side effects such as hot flashes, weight gain, or abdominal distension and bleeding, it is because the spirit is now clouded and medication side effects are masked. Therefore, the spirit is not clear and the emperor fire is not shining the light that it should.

The heart organ is the most important organ and contains the most important function in the body. Without it, the body cannot see and repair ailments, connect to natural surroundings, or connect to heaven and earth. The body's Yin and Yang energies are in chaos. In Chinese medicine, the heart fire combined with the kidney Yang is called "True Yang."

The kidneys belong to the water element. The water interacts with fire to create life. **The Yellow Emperor** states: *The kidneys are the officer of Qiang. It is where cleverness comes from.* The Emperor goes onto state that: *The kidneys control hibernation. They are the root of storage. They are the place of essence.*

QIANG

Qiang has two meanings. It translates to "rice worm," which resembles a male's penis, and is the Emperor's way of describing the kidneys' control of the reproductive organs (male and female). The second meaning of Qiang is strength. Let's look at the character **Qiang:** The left section represents a bow (as in bow and arrow). The right section features a worm at the bottom and a mouth on top, representing a worm with a big head. The bow, a symbol for true strength, is hard and soft at the same time. It has the strength of steel, yet it flexes when it is shot. The male genitalia can also be flexible and stiff, and this ability to transform is what **The Yellow Emperor** refers to as cleverness. That "the kidneys are the officer of Qiang" means that the kidneys, which belong to the water element, rule this quality of maintaining a hardness and softness simultaneously. This quality, however, cannot be separated from the heart.

The heart is where the spirit becomes clear and the kidneys control the hard and soft of the genitalia. These are the preliminary conditions for reproduction. When the male and female become intimate, the emotions are even. If male stimulation or anxiety is too great or too little, or there is a lack of desire, he will not experience erection. The same is true with female arousal. Too much and too little are both counterproductive. The heart is where the spirit resides and the emotions are kept in check. When the spirit is calm and the emotions content, or when there is love, the emperor fire can go down to the kidneys and warm up the kidneys' water. The kidneys' water will allow the Qiang to bend and straighten and reproduction to take place.

In contrast, IVF and timing ovulation, instead of warming the heart's emotions, is cooling the fire off. It separates the heart's fire from the kidney's water.

The Yellow Emperor states: *The kidneys control hibernation. They are the root of storage. They are the place of essence.* Hibernation, storage and essence are three layers of the same thing. Hibernation is when we sleep and recharge our energy for the next day. Storage is the storage of the Yang energy in the physical matter, or what we call Yin energy. Essence is the unification of energy into the matter forming one seed that can give life to another cycle. The Shao Yin is the sphere where we recharge our energy, it is the sphere where the energy stores in physical matter (Yin energy) and where the seed for a new life is created.

The kidneys belong to water. The water trigram has two broken lines and one solid line in between.

The essence in the water is the Yang energy (solid line). We call this "one true Yang." In Chinese medicine, this is the most precious substance/ energy of our lives. If one wastes it, one's life is wasted and future generations are wasted as well. Our goal with Chinese medicine is to restore this one true Yang. It is to restore the energy for the following generations.

Preserving hibernation is when we sleep well. Preserving the Yin energy includes not harming the Yang energy by following the guidelines of Tai Yang, Yang Ming, Shao Yang and Tai Yin. Preserving the essence is when we follow the guidelines of Shao Yin. We nourish the emperor's fire of the heart (emotions and clear state of mind) and keep the one true Yang of the kidneys.

Regarding the effects of steroid use, Liu Lihong maintains that it unleashes the true Yang in the kidneys, the body healing as if with a miracle. But the Yang is depleted – it is consumed. With hormone stimulation in fertility treatments, it is a similar situation in that the Yang in the kidneys becomes depleted. This depletion is antithetical to conception. As **The Yellow Emperor** said: *The Yin and Yang must harmonize. This will give birth to an offspring.* If the Yang is depleted and can't be harmonized with the Yin, this will cause infertility.

The fourth aspect of Shao Yin is its meridians of the kidneys and heart. When one stands upright with hands to the side, palms touching thighs and the feet close together, the Shao Yin meridians run along the inside of the body on the posterior side (the inside of the arms and legs but close to the back). The inside of the body is Yin and the posterior part is Yang, thus it is the Yang within the Yin. The heart and kidneys meridians start in concealed areas under the feet and under the arm pits, thus their origin is concealed in the pre-heaven. In other words, the Shao Yin energy comes from our parents, so we can't see its beginning.

The fifth aspect of Shao Yin is the unlocking time, which extends from Zi until Yin, from 11 PM until 5 AM, overlapping with the Tai Yin times of Zi and Chou. This explains the closeness between Shao Yin and Tai Yin, and therefore the closeness between the earth and the water.

The Shao Yin starts at Zi which is the birth of Yang. It is the one true Yang within the water – the Yang energy that gives life to the water. Chou and Yin are the growth of Yang into two and into three.

Lao Zi says: *One gives birth to two. Two give birth to three and three gives birth to the myriad things.* The Shao Yin progress of one, two and three is a full body of Yang within Yin. It is what we call an emperor fire. It is a full heaven trigram (three solid lines) within the Yin. It is the Yang within Yin.

Shao Yin is the embodiment of heaven and earth interacting within the body. It is the kidney water and heart fire in the body that act like the heaven and earth in nature. The Shao Yin, like the Shao Yang, is the pivot, and the pivot belongs to fire, the driving force behind the Yin and

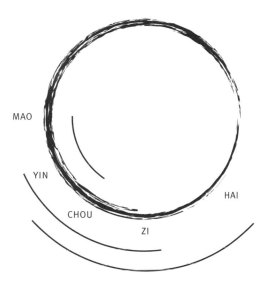

Yang. In the Yin mechanism, the fire is less warming then in the Yang mechanism, yet it is a full body of Yang within the Yin that drives the Yin mechanism into change. That is why the unlocking time of the Shao Yin is entirely within the Yang growth phase.

When the Shao Yin becomes obstructed, the pulse is thin and small, and the body wants to sleep but cannot. The heart feels irritable, urination is clear and frequent, and thirst is pronounced.

With regard to the heart feeling "irritable," it is important to analyze the Chinese character **Fan** (irritable). The left part represents fire while the right section represents a head. The fire or heat comes up to the head, bringing on irritability.

This fire needs to descend into the kidneys and not ascend to warm up the body. Ascending fire is the minister fire of Shao Yang, which moves the entire Yang mechanism. The Shao Yin fire is a descending fire connecting the emperor into the water, or as described previously, it is the "one true Yang" of the water. This is like the sunshine lighting downwards onto the earth. The sunlight is not lighting upwards. This is the pivot fire of the Yin mechanism – the energy that is imbedded in the physical matter. This is the rooting of the energy into the matter. When this fire doesn't root into the body, there are two main symptoms that arise: the person is very tired but is unable to fall asleep. The second symptom is internal irritability. These symptoms occur because the fire can't connect with the water.

This fire and water connection happens in the Shao Yin in the middle of the night while sleeping. In nature, it happens in the middle of winter when everything is hibernating. The emperor fire is resting in the water, which in Chinese medicine we refer to as "the dragon is resting in the water." In Chinese myth, the dragon is the mightiest creature that flies in the highest heavens and dives into the deepest seas. Its movement is agile and clever. The dragon in the water is this phenomenal Yang energy in the water that gives it life and recreates life over and over again.

While sleeping, the dragon or emperor fire descends into the water. This allows a restful sleep and vigorous energy the following day. During the day, an individual's spirit is visible, and if the spirit is lacking, the person looks tired and the light in his eyes is turned off. No vibrant spirit, or metaphorically speaking, no dragon, is showing itself. During the night while sleeping, the dragon goes to rest in the deep sea, or in the water, or the north, or in the kidneys (these are all synonyms from a Chinese medicine point of view). When we objectively consider the different states of mind during active day and sleeping night, the difference becomes clear.

Additional symptoms of the Shao Yin imbalance include frequent urination of clear urine. This has to do with the Yang's failure to warm up the kidneys. When Yang is too intense, the kidneys warming up too much, the urine turns yellow, but when Yang is lacking, the urine is clear. There is no heat in the urine.

The most important symptom in the Shao Yin is the thin and small pulse, which is again a problem of water and fire. Fire is the energy and water is the substance. The most "water-like" substance in the body is blood, as it fills the veins and arteries. If the blood (water) is missing, the pulse will be thin. This is in contrast to a full-bodied pulse where the blood is ample. A small pulse is a fire problem, or to be more accurate, an emperor fire problem. How is it an emperor fire problem?

First, let's consider the minister fire that must warm the body. When there is too much warmth, the pulse turns rapid and when there is lack of warmth (or cold) the pulse turns slow. This is because warmth and Yang accelerates the water, while cold slows it down.

Zhongjing, in his description of the pulse, does not mention a slow pulse, he describes it as thin and small. The pulse within our body is the embodiment of life. When someone faints, we check the pulse to find if he or she is alive.

The cycle of every heart beat in a pulse is similar to every day's cycle. It is similar to every year's cycle. Each pulse has a spring, summer, fall, and winter. There is a cyclical and repetitive movement to it. The winter is the water or the blood of the pulse. It is the Yin energy of the pulse. The spring, summer and fall are the Yang energy of the pulse. The Yang energy of the three seasons is long when compared to the winter season.

In each heartbeat, a long spring, summer and fall pulse should be felt. If the pulse is short it means that the Yang or emperor fire mechanism of the kidneys is in decline. It is the heart's spirit that harmonizes the seasons and the body. When a person's heart fire is healthy and the kidney's true Yang is strong, the pulse is long.

Infertility is to a large degree a Shao Yin problem. The emperor fire does not warm the kidney's true Yang. The spirit does not store in the essence. The energy does not root in the matter. The common symptoms that I encounter with most infertility patients are Shao Yin symptoms of Yang deficiency such as cold hands and feet, or a cold nose, while others feel hot flashes and night sweats. There is not enough warm (Yang) energy to warm you.

How can we understand hot flashes and night sweats as Yang deficiency? Zheng Qinan explains it as follows: *Yang deficiency has straight and odd symptoms. Straight symptoms are cold feet, cold hands, pale face etc. There are, however, odd symptoms like red face and feeling hot. This is because the water contains the pre-heaven Yang. When the Yang is deficient, the water overflows and carries the original Yang with it upwards. The original Yang (emperor fire) should go downwards to warm the water; however, when it is deficient it cannot go downwards and floats upwards instead. This will give rise to symptoms such as hot flashes and night sweats. When the true Yang is strong again, the Yang will root into the water and will not float upwards.*

In my practice, I recognize that hot flashes and night sweats of the Yang deficiency type can be alleviated rather quickly with very hot herbs. The worse the night sweats and hot flashes, the hotter the herbal formula needs to be. This is in order to save the Birthing Yang from separating. What is the main cause of infertility? The true Yang in the water is deficient and the emperor fire is too weak to descend.

In my experience, patients who have never used fertility drugs or birth control pills restore their true Yang and emperor fire rather quickly and easily. Patients who have used fertility drugs and birth control pills restore the water's true Yang with great difficulty.

Lack of true Yang explains why many IVF cycles fail, despite a successful embryo transfer. It also explains most "unexplained" infertility.

THE JUE YIN PHASE

Jue (diminished) Yin is the last sphere of the Yin mechanism. It is where the Tai Yin and Shao Yin come to an end, enabling the Yang to flourish. While the Tai Yin is true Yin and the Shao Yin is the Yang within the Yin, the Jue Yin is the Yin within the Yang. The closing of the Jue Yin finds itself entirely within the Yang realm.

When we compare the three Yin phases to fertility and reproduction, the Tai Yin is the creation of the sperm and egg, the Shao Yin is the conception and creation of a new life, and the Jue Yin is the development of the fetus within the mother. The Jue Yin is already a new life separated from the previous cycle (from the parents) yet it is still connected to the mother and not truly independent. It is only when the baby is born that the Jue Yin phase has completed its work and is an entirely independent new cycle.

The second aspect of Jue Yin is its energetical qualities. The Yellow Emperor describes the Jue Yin as "Wind and Wood." The character of **wind** is composed of two parts.

FENG   FENG

The outer encasing character is called "**Fan**" and its meaning is "altogether" or "all." The inner character is a worm, the same worm we had in the character Qiang in the previous Shao Yin discussion. Together the meaning is that the wind is giving birth to all types of worms. It is explained in **The Yellow Emperor** that the five "worms" represent all living animals, including humans.

CHONG

FAN

The character Chong (worm) has in the center a mouth with a vertical line in it. This represents a man or an animal. When we extend this line upwards, it is as to reach to the heavens, and downward to the earth. This represents the connection of all living things to heaven and earth. At the bottom there are two feet, signifying a human.

The character Fan (all) has two parts as well. The outer encasing suggests "containing everything" while inside there is the character Yi (one) that suggests unity. Combining all the different parts of the character **Feng** (wind), the meaning of wind suggests a unity of all living things between heaven and earth. According to Sinologist Bernhard Karlgren, an ancient variant of the same character was written with an inner picture of the sun instead of a worm.

FENG

This suggested in a similar way the unity under heaven. All life forms under heaven receive their life-force energy from the sun.

Indeed, the Chinese sages said "the wind is the messenger of heaven and earth." This meant that all living things, humans included, are the messengers of heaven and earth. Human beings in particular were considered the mirror of heaven and earth interaction. They are the embodiment of Yin and Yang and life. Jue Yin, being the life already created but not yet separated from its parent, is best described by wind. What is the quality that describes this fetal phase so well? It is wood.

Wood has several meanings. Let's look at the character **Mu** (wood).

The horizontal line is the earth and vertical line is a plant sprouting from the ground. The two oblique lines are the roots of the plant under the ground. This describes all life forms that spring from the earth, including humans and animals, as we are all nourished by the earth's pure Yin energy. In ancient China, there was no separation between man and nature.

MU

Wood is a quality that springs from the earth and rises toward the heavens. This is a quality that changes the egg and sperm into a baby. The Yellow Emperor describes the wood quality as "to bend and to straighten," or the ability to change from one state to another. The wood quality assists the male genitalia in becoming hard and soft when needed, and also explains the ability of the embryo to straighten from a very curled position into a fetus, and finally a baby. The character Mu (wood) also best describes the phase where the energy has roots in the Yin under the earth, but at the same time starts a new life in the Yang above the earth.

What is the connection between wind and wood? **The Yellow Emperor** says *the east gives birth to wind and the wind gives birth to wood.* The east, the wind, and the wood are three different layers of the same thing. The east is where the sun, or the Yang energy, rises or comes out of the earth. This Yang energy gives birth to wind, which represents all living things on earth. The living things (wind) give birth to wood, to reproduction, and ultimately, to the next generation. Wind and wood cannot be separated. Life and reproduction cannot be separated.

The Tai Yin and Shao Yin "come into extinction," as **The Yellow Emperor** says, by the birth of a new life, or by the wind giving birth to the wood. Jue Yin is important to solving infertility because it allows us to understand miscarriages and the health of the fetus.

The third aspect of Jue Yin is its organs, the liver and the pericardium, a double-walled sac that contains the heart and the roots of the great vessels. **The Yellow Emperor** calls the pericardium *the walls surrounding the emperor (heart)*. When pathological energy attacks the heart, the pericardium will receive it first to protect the emperor. In reality, the pericardium has a deeper meaning and we should look into it further. Why wasn't the pericardium separated from the heart in ancient times? It was very strange that there were 12 meridians including a pericardium meridian, but there was no pericardium organ. They were six Yin meridians, but only five Yin organs. What was the reason for this odd phenomenon?

To understand, let's look into the Chinese characters to find some clues. The character Xin Bao (pericardium) is composed of two characters.

XIN   BAO

The character on the left is heart (Xin) and the one on the right is a case or a sac (Bao). Combined, pericardium is the case surrounding the heart. From this initial assessment we can see that the heart and the pericardium (sac around the heart) are closely related. If we look further we can see that the character Bao (sac) on the right has two parts to it; an upper part and a lower part.

First look at the Chinese characters for all the Yin organs: spleen, lungs, kidneys, liver, and heart. Except for the heart, they all carry the flesh radical within the character, meaning that the character has something to do with the physical body or flesh.

FLESH   SPLEEN   LUNGS   KIDNEYS   LIVER   HEART

Why doesn't the heart character carry the flesh section? The heart is the emperor fire. It is the light that shines within the body, the organ that belongs to fire, and as such, can ascend to the heavens because it has very little physical matter, but is full of energy. Of the five elements, wood, metal, water, earth and fire, it is the only element able to ascend, while all the others descend because of their heavy physical matter and gravity which pull them down.

By ascending to heaven, fire can connect the earth material to the heaven's energy. The heart belongs to fire as well. It has the least matter and most energy. It is where our spirit dwells, and where our energy connects the earth to heaven. Yet, isn't there a physical blood pump we call the heart? In my opinion, this is the pericardium. The heart muscle and the heart sac make-up the pericardium. **Shan Zhong** is what **The Yellow Emperor** calls the physical organ of the heart (pericardium and heart muscle combined).

FLESH   SHAN   ZHONG

The character to the left is **Shan** (some pronounce it Dan) and the character to the right is **Zhong** (meaning "center"). Zhong contains a vertical line going through a mouth. This is again the idea of connecting heaven and earth within the person (the mouth is a person). When **The Yellow Emperor** says that the physical blood pump is Shan Zhong, his first meaning is that the blood pump has something to do with connecting heaven and earth, which is life.

The character Shan on the left has two parts. The first is **Rou** (flesh), indicating this is a Yin organ composed of physical matter. The right section of Shan is composed of a roof on the top, a double-walled structure in the middle, and a sun rising over the horizon at the bottom. The roof means that this entity is covering all the organs in the body. The double walled structure means that this entity is the most protected and revered in the entire body. The sun rising over the horizon means the birth of life, when a new cycle has started or when a baby has emerged from the womb. **The Yellow Emperor** is describing the pericardium/physical heart as the most important (roof), most protected (double walled) and beginning of life (sunrise over the horizon).

Furthermore, the pericardium (Xin Bao) has an additional meaning, which explains why the pericardium was originally not a separate entity from the heart. It will also help us understand why the pericardium is a Jue Yin, or the fetal part of the Yin. Examining the character **Bao** (sac):

XIN   BAO   BAO

The top part is Bao and it means to wrap around (drawn here separately on the left), while the bottom part is called Si and it means "fetus." Looking at the ancient character of Bao, one can see the fetus inside the belly.

ANCIENT BAO

So when we think about the heart "sac" (pericardium), we are focusing on a fetus. When a baby is not yet born, it is inseparable from its mother. The Jue Yin is the "extinction" of the Yin into a new life, "extinction" in this instance meaning new birth.

The Yellow Emperor says: *When the Yin reaches its highest peak , the Yang is born.* The cycle of Yin and Yang, or the cycle of life and birth, is happening all the time. It happens in a woman's life span when she gives birth to a child. It happens in a year's span, when winter gives birth to spring. It happens in the span of a day, when night gives birth to the morning, and it also happens within a heartbeat. When the heart beats once, it is a new life that was just born. It is a new push of blood and energy into our body. What happens when the heart stops beating? There is no birth; there is not another life in another beat, and no additional cycle of life. When we refer to the heart sac and the fetus in the sac, we mean the heart muscles pumping the blood and energy to allow us "life." It is a description of how our life is continuing. The pericardium is not a mere muscle like the muscles of the leg. It is the organ with which the spirit connects, where heaven and earth pump life into our body.

The Yellow Emperor goes further to describe the Shan Zhong (center of the chest/pericardium) as the *faithful minister* – the one who obeys the emperor without deviation. It is the faithful blood pump that never fails us.

The liver is analogized by **The Yellow Emperor** as the army general and the organ from which thinking and planning emerge. The liver functions are important for our life in the same way that an army general is important to the army. If the general thinks and plans strategically and thoroughly, his army will be victorious in a time of war.

As opposed to the other organs, which are necessary in a time of peace, the liver is necessary in a time of war within the body. A state of war exists when the Yin phase (storage) wants to transform into a Yang phase (expansion). In our daily life, a state of war exists every morning when we wake up, when sleep changes into awakening. In nature, a state of war exists when winter hibernation turns into spring's life and prosperity. The Yang energy wants to separate, but the Yin energy wants things to stay together. This war between the Yin wishes and the Yang wishes is called Jue Yin. The liver is the general who has to plan how to win this war. If the liver fails in planning this transition, the war will be lost, and the body will not awake. If the liver fails to plan, a baby will not be born. A pregnancy is a war over the baby's continued attachment to the mother or separating from her. If the liver function fails due to poor planning, and the baby separates too early, there will be a miscarriage. If the baby does not separate at term, a still birth will occur.

In Chinese history, the ultimate victory is to defeat the opponent before the war has even started. This is achieved with a well-planned strategy. In our daily life, a healthy liver delivers a well planned strategy for a seamless transition from Yin into Yang. If the liver is unhealthy, the planning will be poor, and a woman will have difficulty maintaining a pregnancy or having a healthy baby.

The Yellow Emperor states: *The liver harmonizes the tendons and ligaments, and its function is to straighten and bend.* The liver is concerned with the flexibility we have in our body, especially in the joints. The liver function allows us to bend forward and sideways, and to stretch and bend our arms, hands, fingers, and knees. We previously mentioned the wood element and its function to "straighten and bend" as related to the male genetalia. A poor diet, inadequate sleep, excessive stress, or the taking of medication, will damage the liver. The army's general can no longer plan effectively. Pregnancy will be harmed.

The Yellow Emperor goes on to state that: *When a person lies down, the liver receives the blood and the person's eyesight is clear. When the feet receive the blood, he can walk. When the hands receive the blood, he can grasp.* This refers to the all-important liver function of regulating the blood system in the body. This is different from blood circulation, but rather the harmony of Yin and Yang.

The color of blood is red, which belongs to the fire element, while the consistency of the blood is fluid, which belongs to the water element. Together they are life. When the blood reaches the feet, life has reached the feet, and the person can walk. When blood reaches the hands, life has reached the hands and a person can grasp. When the life-force, or the correct combination of Yin and Yang energy, reaches any particular part of the body, this part will function. Of course, this includes the uterus, ovaries and fallopian tubes. To achieve this harmony, we must first harmonize the liver.

The emperor's second statement also explains that when a person is lying down, the liver receives the blood and the person's eyesight is clear. The simple meaning here is that when a person is active, blood flows out of the liver to the body, and when the person is lying down, or resting, the excess blood in the body returns into the liver for storage.

As for clear eyesight, I don't believe **The Yellow Emperor** is referring to blood circulation here, but rather about life. For this discussion I would like to introduce another concept of ancient Chinese medicine: Jing and Wei.

Jing is the vertical line that connects heaven and earth, water and fire, and Yin and Yang. **Wei** is an additional aspect that connects all things among themselves – one human to another, an animal to another, a tree pollinating with another tree. With reference to the Jing and human beings, the person is standing upright with his head in the heaven and his feet on the ground. His spirit is connected to the heavens while his body is material and connected with the earth. The human being is composed of heaven and earth, and is a third unique phenomenon, which is heaven and earth combined. It is Yin and Yang combined, which is life.

With Wei, however, the person is lying down in the animalistic posture, the posture taken when a couple lies together to conceive a new life, or when a person goes to sleep trying to conceive a new life for the next day. What makes us different from animals is that instead of remaining in wei, we shift from Wei to Jing. This also shows a greater responsibility for human beings in this world, and why we are able to save or destroy it.

When the **The Yellow Emperor** states that the liver receives the blood when the person is lying down, he is referring to the Wei position. The liver is receiving the life force when the person is creating a new life. The liver is the army general and should plan how this will happen; in order to do so, however, the eyes must be clear. When the energy goes into the liver for procreation, the vision must be clear for the sperm to know which egg to visit, and the egg to know which sperm to receive.

The Yellow Emperor goes onto state that *all channels (meridians and blood vessels) belong to the eyes.* Many meridians go through or connect to the eyes; however, the eyes, able to tell good from bad, are related to all organs of the body. Any harm to the body (illness or injury) will make the eyes blurry, obstructing the liver's ability to harmonize the Yin and the Yang in order to create a new life. Pregnancy will be impossible to sustain. This is how the liver is related to the Jue Yin phase of creating a new life.

The fourth aspect of Jue Yin is the liver and pericardium meridians, running along the middle of the median side of our arms and legs. Standing upright with both palms attached to the sides of the thighs and with both feet close together, the Jue Yin meridian runs in the inside of the arms and legs in the middle (not leaning front or rear). They are parallel to the Shao Yang meridians in the sense that they run in the center of the arms and legs. What is interesting about the liver meridian is that it starts on top of the foot, which is Yang in nature, runs upwards through an area of the inner leg, which is Yin in nature, and terminates where it distributes close to the gall bladder Shao Yang meridian. It runs from Yang, through the deepest Yin and ends up at Yang.

The meridians of Jue Yin explain the connection of wind-wood and the minister fire, and how together they create life. **The Yellow Emperor** says that a fierce fire will consume the energy while mild warmth will nourish the energy. This is related to the ability of wind to create new life, which does not happen in either extreme heat or cold, but rather in comfortable warm spring weather. Without the warmth of the minister fire, the new life will not have the Yang energy needed to evolve itself.

The Yellow Emperor says that the Yang is born so the Yin can flourish. *Yang energy is like the relationship of the sun to heaven. If the sun loses its place in the heaven, life will stop and the greatness of life is gone. So when the sky is turning, the sun must shine. This is the reason that the Yang is above and protecting us from the outside.*

In this statement, the Emperor explains the importance of Yang energy as the source of life. In the body, even though the Yin is crucial for life, the Yang is the source of life. Waking up in the morning is the Yang energy. Creating a baby from an egg and sperm is Yang energy. **The Yellow Emperor** says that the Yang energy of our body is like the sun in the sky and is the reason why the Yang is above, protecting us from the outside. The sun in the sky is crucial for life in the same way that the Yang energy is crucial for life. The Yang is defending us from ailments and is nourishing life.

It is important to preserve Yang energy. The sun will never stop shining, but our Yang can be finished because we belong to the earth. The energy in our material is borrowed from heaven. If we preserve the Yang, we will live longer, healthier lives and be able to give this Yang "seed of life" to a new generation.

It is interesting to note that the liver meridian is circulating through the genitalia and the reproductive organs. Since one of Jue Yin's main functions is to allow a new life to develop, it makes perfect sense that the Jue Yin meridian will nourish the reproductive organs. The liver meridian has internal pathways that circulate to the crown of the head, which is the most Yang area of our body. This shows again the distribution of the liver function from the Yin to the Yang. Chinese medicine sees the Jue Yin and liver as the transformation of the old Yin to the new Yang.

The fifth aspect of Jue Yin is the unlocking time, from Chou through Yin and into Mao, which is from 1 AM until 7 AM. The character of **Chou** shows a hand that is tied down, **Yin** is two hands straightening an arrow, while **Mao** depicts the killing of an animal as a sacrifice.

The progress in the Jue Yin is explained by these three meanings. The first step of Jue Yin is tied to the previous Yin and cannot move into the new life. The second step is the army general planning and taking measures for moving into the new life. The third step is the extinction of the old cycle and the beginning of the new cycle. Killing an animal as a sacrifice means transforming the matter/flesh of the animal into heaven energy, which is different than eating the animal and descending it into the earth via a bowel movement. The action of sacrifice was viewed in ancient times as complete selflessness, required for giving up the old life or the old Yin and starting a new life with a new Yang.

The Yellow Emperor says that the Jue Yin is where the Yin is extinct and the Yang rising. The Yang refers to the center of Jue Yin, which is the warmth of Shao Yang that is rising. The times of Chou, Yin and Mao best describe the extinction of the night and the birth of the day. It best describes the extinction of winter and birth of spring. This is the best time to treat a Jue Yin ailment.

What happens when the Jue Yin becomes obstructed? **The Yellow Emperor** and Zhang Zhongjing both maintain that the wind is the root of the hundred diseases, which means all diseases. It is also, as previously explained, the process of creating a new life, which shows itself every morning when we wake up, with every new spring, with every heart beat, as well as when a woman becomes pregnant and gives birth. Wind is the process of the Yang energy emerging out of the Yin. When the Yang does not emerge out of the Yin properly, we can say that the wind has a problem, and this is what is referred to as *the wind gives rise to the hundred diseases.*

Zhongjing says that symptoms for a Jue Yin illness include **Xiao Ke** (thirst), hunger with no desire to eat, and vomiting of worms when one does eat, as well as a hot and painful heart, meaning a heart attack. He also says that if the patient purges downwards with cold herbs, there will be endless diarrhea.

These symptoms have confused many practitioners over the centuries, as they are confusing and infrequently observed. However, why did **The Yellow Emperor** say that the wind is the root of the hundred diseases? Shouldn't the wind, being the Jue Yin energy, give rise to ailments in the Tai Yin or Yang Ming spheres? It definitely should.

Zhongjing describes here a variety of sample symptoms giving rise to ailments of the other five spheres. Let's look at our circle again.

When these symptoms are analyzed, Zhongjing's assertion about "wind giving rise to the hundred diseases" is explained. The thirst, as Chen Xiuyuan said, is the Shao Yang fire, the center or the core of Jue Yin, and that the fire of Shao Yang is most needed by the Jue Yin to allow the Yang to grow and the Yin to become extinct. When the Shao Yang fire within the Jue Yin is too strong, the patient will become very thirsty.

The second symptom arises when the energy pounds against the heart, which becomes "hot and painful." When we set up the five Yin organs around the circle, the heart, or fire element is at the top, or in the south. This corresponds to noon, the time of Tai Yang. What Zhongjing means by this energy pounding against the heart is that the Jue Yin energy rushes upwards abnormally into the Tai Yang sphere. Remember that the Tai Yang opens up the Yang energy from the coldness of midnight until the warmth of midday, and that this opening must be gradual. The Tai Yang goes in and out through the chest. When this opening is abrupt, the Yang energy rushes toward the fire of midday – toward the Tai Yang or the heart or the south. In this case, the energy is pounding against the heart, resulting in a hot and painful heart.

TENG   TONG

Teng and **Tong**: The outer shell on both characters represents an illness. Teng has an inner component that represents winter, meaning that when there is cold obstructing the energy, there is pain. With Tong, the right component means "to pass through." When the energy cannot pass through; when it is obstructed, there is pain. So Teng and Tong are two kinds of pain derived from different causes. One is from cold and the other is from external accidental factors. Both are the result of an obstruction in energy flow.

Zhongjing uses the character Teng (cold pains) to indicate that the heart can become hot and painful. The Tai Yang manifestation is hot but its root is cold, and the Tai Yang energy is cold and water. However, the Tai Yang is the opening of the Yang mechanism and also deals with warmth. The one is the root while the other is the manifestation. The heart feels Teng (cold pains) and hot is a description of a Tai Yang illness. In this illness, the root and manifestation of the Tai Yang are impaired. If you go back to the Tai Yang discussion and look for the different illnesses that can rise from a Tai Yang disharmony, these are all included in the statement "the heart feels hot and (cold) pain."

The third symptom of the Jue Yin illness is the feeling of hunger without the desire to eat. This is a Yang Ming problem of constipation, derived from local heat that creates dryness in the bowels. The Yang Ming is composed of the stomach and large intestines. When there is heat in the stomach, the person is hungry and when there is heat in the large intestines, the person is constipated. If the abdomen feels full from constipation, there is no desire to put more food into the stomach, even if the stomach fire causes a hunger sensation. Zhongjing explains that when the wind cannot give birth to a new Yang, not only will the Tai Yang opening suffer, but the Yang Ming closing down will suffer. There will be adverse heat in the Yang Ming when it actually needs to cool down.

The fourth symptom Zhongjing describes is "eating will cause the patient to throw up worms." This is a Tai Yin problem. If you return to the Tai Yin discussion, you will find that one of the Tai Yin illnesses is "the food will not come down and the person will throw up." This is because the Yang energy does not warm the earth (spleen), causing a cold obstruction of the spleen. If food is ingested, it will be vomited out.

The fifth symptom is endless diarrhea, the result of purging the patient with cold herbs. This means that the true Yang of the kidneys is deficient when the Jue Yin is diseased. With the use of cold herbs to purge downwards, the Yang energy of the kidneys will collapse and the body will be unable to hold in the bowels. As noted, the Shao Yin is where the Yang is first born and grows into two Yang lines, then into three Yang lines, representing the full body of Yang, or the heaven trigram. The motion of growing and increasing Yang is upwards. Endless diarrhea means that the kidney Yang is not growing upwards, but is instead collapsing downwards. This is again a Shao Yin problem caused by the Jue Yin wind. The general cannot plan how to bring the Yang energy back and the war of life will be lost.

The wind is the root of the hundred diseases. If we can keep our wind healthy and unobstructed, all minor problems that come will be solved naturally by the body. There will be no need for over-the-counter, under-the-counter or behind-the-counter medications.

Our Yang energy goal is to harmonize with the surrounding nature so the Yin energy will not be affected. When the Yang energy fails or becomes exhausted, the Yin energy is impacted. The first line of Yin energy to be effected is the Tai Yin spleen, which is a simple problem. Strengthening the spleen will return the body to a healthy course. Beyond that, advancing pathology into the Shao Yin and Jue Yin is very difficult and complicated, and will normally happen with the very elderly, where energy has been exhausted and the body's defenses are absent or low. Then, pathological progression into the core of life can be present. What I find alarming is that so many young people today have Shao Yin and Jue Yin syndromes – chronic diseases such as heart problems, diabetes and cancer.

Most infertility patients are Tai Yin patients. Their bodies still work well at the core, yet something is missing which can easily be fixed. Other patients that I see, unfortunately, do belong to the Shao Yin-Jue Yin pattern of disharmony, generally due to the consumption of excessive Western medications. These compounds invade the core of life, or into what Chinese medicine calls "wind," and disharmonize it.

For thousands of years, while Chinese Philosophy has been about flowing with nature, the western philosophy has been about conquering nature. Most Western medications are xxx-blocker or xxx-antagonist etc. They attempt to interfere with body functions in order to create a new scenario, which is not what nature intended.

THE FIVE ELEMENTS

The theory of the five elements is at least 2500 years old and has set a foundation for understanding the universe and ourselves. Over the centuries, many physicians used it to perfect their healing skills. In the five elements, we can see the five species, five colors, five flavors, five emotions, five grains, etc… They are part of the six heavenly energies, and also present in the five earthly energies.

As stated previously, the five elements are wood, fire, earth, metal and water. There are two basic relationships between the elements: one is a generation relationship and the other a controlling one. **Sheng,** the generating relationship, describes the generation of one element from the other – the way wood gives birth to fire, fire gives birth to earth, earth gives birth to metal, metal gives birth to water and water gives birth to wood. It is a complete cycle of one element generating another over and over again.

With the second basic relationship, **Ke** the controlling relationship, the elements check each other to make certain they are in balance and not excessive. Wood controls earth, earth controls water, water controls fire, fire controls metal and metal controls wood again. This cycle is also endless.

There are, in addition, specific rules for the behavior of the elements – Sheng (over controlling), **Cheng** (adverse reaction) and **Fu** (revenge). These are abnormal actions of the elements defined by The Yellow Emperor.

When these control and generation cycles go out of balance, disease arises. For simplification purposes, let us refer to the elements as A, B, C, D and E. A gives birth to B, B gives birth to C, C gives birth to D, D gives birth to E and E gives birth to A. In the controlling cycle, A controls C, B controls D, C controls E, D controls A and E controls B. When A, for example, is over-controlling C, it is referred to as **Sheng** (victory). When C is adversely controlling A, we call this adverse control or **Cheng** (take advantage of). When A over controls C, then D is revenging by over controlling A and we call it **Fu** (revenge). These are the basic rules for disharmony in the controlling cycle. The more over-control there is, the more revenge there will be from D onto A.

The controlling Ke cycles and the generating Sheng cycles base themselves on the three Yin and three Yang. Tai Yang is cold and water. Yang Ming is metal and dryness. Tai Yin is earth and damp. Each element; wood, fire, earth, metal and water has its own use and its own life energy. The control and birth cycles of the five elements are the control and birth of these "life" energies. When we understand this principle, the application of Chinese medicine takes a different twist.

For example, when we discussed the earth element, we said that the earth is Tai Yin and its energy is damp. The Yang energy from heaven going into the earth to create the vapor of dampness is the principal way the earth comes 'alive.' At the same time, the earth itself is the opposite of life; the earth without Yang energy equals death. Earth plus damp will generate life, while earth with no damp will end life. This situation with the earth is of course true for the other four elements as well. When we understand this principle, we realize that the generating cycle of fire giving birth to earth, is actually fire generating the Yang mist of the earth, and when we talk about the wood controlling the earth, it is the wood that controls the Yin (dead earth aspect). The generation cycle and the control cycle act on different aspects of the earth.

Five emotions correspond to the five elements: anger, joy, pensiveness, grief and fear. Anger belongs to wood, joy to fire, pensiveness to earth, grief to metal and fear to water. Within the five elements there are two types of relationships. One relationship is a nourishing (generating or giving birth) relationship, while the other is a controlling relationship.

The nourishing relationship of the emotions is: anger nourishes joy, joy nourishes pensiveness, pensiveness nourishes grief, grief nourishes fear, and fear nourishes the anger again. The controlling relationships of the emotions are as follows: anger controls pensiveness, joy controls grief, pensiveness controls fear, grief controls anger, and fear controls joy.

In an emotional crisis, one must determine by observation if the emotion is in a deficient state or in an excessive state. When the emotion feels strong, the patient should sit or lie down for 10 minutes to conduct the observation. If the emotion is deficient in nature, then the patient should nourish its element, and if the emotion is excessive, then the patient should control its element. For example, if grief is excessive, the patient must attempt to control the grief by increasing the amount of joy in her life, joy being the controlling emotion for grief. Because grief belongs to metal and excessive metal will over-control wood, controlling the grief with joy will make certain that the wood element will not suffer a great loss.

However, if the grief observed is a deficient sadness, the earth must be nourished to solve the grief, because grief is weakening the metal itself. The element that nourishes grief is pensiveness. Pensiveness is earth and earth nourishes metal. The patient should add pensiveness or thinking into her life.

It is important to keep our emotions in balance. Prolonged imbalance of the emotions will deplete the body's energy and fertility will decrease.

IMPAIRED EMOTION	REMEDY
Excessive anger	SADNESS
Deficient anger	FEAR
Excessive joy	FEAR
Deficient joy	ANGER
Excessive thinking	ANGER
Deficient thinking	JOY
Excessive sadness	JOY
Deficient sadness	THINKING
Excessive fear	THINKING
Deficient fear	SADNESS

Inherently, emotions are neither good nor bad, they are natural. When they are out of balance, they can cause a disease, and when they're in balance, they can restore energy back to harmony. It is common to see a person who grieves for an extended period become ill, or even in extreme situations, die. It is important to understand the direction in which an emotion is going so we can work with it. When we know our emotions, we can remedy them.

Anger belongs to wood and its direction is upward. Anger can make us jump with clenched fists, our face becoming red as the overall energy rushes up. The power of anger is strong and intense and it has a lot of substance to it, just as does wood.

Joy is different. Its direction is also upwards, but its quality is light. When we laugh, we look up. The blood comes up to the face but the inside is hollow, or rather full of energy, with no material like fire. The fire flares upwards but it is mostly energy with no physical material.

Pensiveness is even. It is in the center and it is not going up or down. Our body feels balanced and in control in this state, and we can assess our situation.

Sadness is moving down. When we grieve, we lower our heads and look downward. We sit down or lie down in the fetal position. The center of sadness is solid-like metal. We may feel like there is a lump in our throat or our chest. It feels as if something is sitting on our shoulders and pushes us down. This is the quality of metal.

Fear is also about going down. When a person is startled, he can lose control of the urine and bowels. Instead of lying down, we want to go under the bed. There is no lump in the throat or chest, but rather the knees buckle and we may feel on the verge of collapsing. The energy is fluid like water, not solid like metal. Water simply finds any way it can to flow downwards, the urine flowing without control. Everything just wants to melt down.

We need all of our emotions to stay healthy, but we must guard against emotions controlling our lives and/or impairing our health. When a relative or dear friend has died, it is good to grieve. The metal heaviness of grief is bringing you closer to the earth and helps you control the excessive anxiety coming from the liver (wood), as well as helping nourish the deficient fear coming from the kidneys (water). However it is not good to have the emotions in excess for a long time. **The Yellow Emperor** describes excessive emotion as follows: *Anger causes the Qi to ascend, happiness causes the Qi to weaken, sadness causes the Qi to dissolve, fear causes the Qi to descend, startling causes the Qi to be chaotic and pensiveness causes the Qi to become a knot.*

How do we know if an emotion is excessive or deficient? Excessive emotion will go with its direction, while deficient emotion will go against its direction. For anger, an excess means jumping up in anger, deficient means sitting down and clenching your teeth in anger. If the anger contains excessive wood, you flare up, and if the energy is deficient in wood, you can't flare up. With joy, excess means laughing out loud and looking upwards as you laugh, and deficient joy is laughing while looking down and covering your mouth as you laugh. For pensiveness, excess may be an inability to stop talking in order to tell other people your thoughts, and a deficiency means thinking inwardly and not sharing your constant stream of thoughts with anyone. For sadness, excess is curling in bed and crying, deficiency is to suppress the tears and feel like you can fight it, when in fact you can't. Fear excess means wanting to curl under the bed and to never come out, while fear deficiency may be a tendency to be easily startled.

When trying to balance our emotions, we need to look for the positive in each emotion. If one is angry over an IFV failure, instead of blaming the doctor or wanting to punch a hole in the wall, sit down, close your eyes and think "I am so sad I didn't get pregnant. It is no one's fault. I am just sad." The anger will dissolve quickly and the spleen and stomach will remain undamaged. Anger is wood and wood controls earth. Stomach and spleen are earth. If the liver's anger overbears on the spleen and stomach, these two organs will become sick, very likely producing a stomach ulcer.

From my experience, at least 80% of infertility patients suffer kidney Yang deficiency. The emotion of the kidneys is fear. Because the emotion is excessively out of balance, the kidneys are deficient. Giving the patient hope belongs to pensiveness. The pensiveness will control excess fear and the kidneys can recover. This is why patients who are given hope sometimes become pregnant without any treatment at all.

One must have a grieving process in place when beginning a journey toward pregnancy. Fear will harm the kidneys and anger will harm the liver. When the kidneys and liver cannot function well, infertility will follow. At the same time, grief belongs to metal/lungs, and metal nourishes water/kidneys. Thus controlled and balanced grief will help the patient strengthen the kidneys and get closer to fertility. Fear and anger are the enemies of fertility while joy, pensiveness and grief are its friends.

3

CHINESE MEDICINE
AND FERTILITY

Part of my inspiration to write this book comes from two particular patients, one from Chicago and the other from Hawaii, who share a common story which is not unlike many stories I have experienced in the past. The patient from Chicago is 44 and the patient from Hawaii is 45. Both contacted me in early 2007. Both initially felt the Hunyuan method was too good to be true, that time was of the essence, and that more drastic measures such as IVF were needed. Both women turned away form the Hunyuan approach and went with conventional medicine. The Chicago patient tried four IVF cycles, while the Hawaiian patient tried five. Neither woman became pregnant. In early 2008, they both came back to the Hunyuan Method. Both conceived naturally, one after two months of herbal sessions, and one after five months.

Stories like these are painful for me. These women did not have to go through the IVF treatments. They did not have to spend their entire savings. They came to me first but weren't convinced I could help them. This wasn't because I didn't share success stories or because the Hunyuan method didn't make sense to them. It was because they couldn't ultimately go with a method that does not have the endorsement of the trillion dollar modern medicine machine.

It has been 20 years since I began to study Chinese medicine, and ten years since I began my research into Chinese medicine classics. This research has shed light on how to solve difficult ailments and how to grasp health. It is important to study the classics because they are the culmination of thousands of years of experience. It is not like modern "evidence based" Western medicine, where a conclusion about a certain therapy is made within a year or two. It has been tested over many generations.

Four famous scholars who have spent their lifetimes researching the Chinese medicine classics are Chen Xiuyuan (18th century), Zheng Qinan (19th century), Lu Chonghan and Liu Lihong (modern day). They share the understanding that the Yang energy is the source of life and that the Yin energy takes a secondary position. In addition, they all take the Chinese medicine classics and the Shang Hanlun as a model for understanding health and treating disease. When I followed their footsteps into the Chinese classics, my success with infertility increased tremendously.

SIGNIFICANCE OF SHANG HAN (COLD INJURIES)

The **Shang Hanlun** (Treatise about Cold Injuries) is one of Chinese medicine's main classical works. It describes life energy, how energy does and doesn't work, and what we should do to make it work. *Cold Injuries* refer to injuries of the Yang energy or an injury to the life force. In this work, author Zhang Zhongjing describes hot and cold symptoms, and shallow and deep conditions. He describes injuries to one's life force at the most initial stages and at the most terminal stages. His work encompasses the entire pathological development of one's energy.

The classical meaning of life-force is warmth, while the absence of warmth is the absence of life-force, thus it is called "cold injury." When the sun comes out, it is warm and when the sun is absent, it is cold. The presence of the sun gives life, while the absence of the sun eliminates life. In the same way, the presence of Yang energy gives life and the absence of Yang energy depletes life. The absence or disturbance of Yang is referred to as a "Cold Injury."

In Classical Chinese Medicine, all diseases, whether hot or cold, belong to cold injuries. This is because with all illness, the life-force is impaired – the Yang energy is impaired. If the Yang is deficient, a person will feel cold and if the Yang is too localized in one spot, the person may feel hot.

The Yang is the moving force behind the life mechanism. Thus, for thousands of years, the classical Chinese medicine view was to preserve the life-force Yang.

KEEPING THE YANG

Our Yang energy keeps us alive, it helps us reproduce, it helps us sleep, it helps us love, and it helps us do all the things that we accomplish in our lifetime. When we exhaust our Yang, we may feel cold, we may experience hot flashes, or we can become infertile. Stress, long hours at work, and emotional pressures can all weaken the Yang or cause it to stagnate. Greasy, cold and depleted processed food will do so too. However, the most significant cause of Yang deterioration is the ingestion of chemical substances.

Dr. Lu Chonghan is an accomplished and famous doctor in China. Patients from around the world seek his treatment for very rare and difficult cases. In his book **Fu Yang Jiang Ji** (Lectures on Supporting the Yang), he analyzes his usage of hot herbs to support the Yang energy. He prescribes these hot herbs for 95% of his patients, with a heavy emphasis on **Fu Zi** (aconitum), ginger and cinnamon. In 1992, he prescribed 20,076 herbal prescriptions, out of which 20,016 contained ginger in quantities ranging from 30 grams to 200 grams per formula. Cinnamon was an ingredient in 19,852 formulas, and 19,423 contained Fu Zi in quantities ranging from 60-250 grams per formula.

These three herbs are used predominantly in the Shang Hanlun to strengthen the Yang energy of the patient. In my practice, supporting the Yang in this way has restored fertility over and over again.

The method of supporting the Yang with herbs is a complicated art. The composition of the formulas is critical because incorrect composition will not only hinder fertility, it can also cause unnecessary side effects. In fact, I always discourage patients from self-prescribing herbs or medications of any sort, for it is imperative to have had a thorough classical herbal education in order to do so.

Cold herbs are harmful to the Yang, and although they are sometimes extremely necessary, they must be used sparingly and only when needed, which is in approximately 10% of patients. Nevertheless, in modern herbal medicine practices, 90% of the patients are given cold herbs, resulting in low success rates. This is why patients and practitioners alike have little faith when it comes to infertility and herbs. In contrast, IVF seems much more successful. In my practice, however, herbal treatments are at least as successful as IVF.

Infertility patients must look for an herbalist who specializes in classical Chinese medicine. To know how to find this information, ask the practitioner about the Shang Hanlun theories; also, be aware of the percentage of hot herbs in the herbal formulas you are receiving. To become fertile, you need your Yang to become stronger. If you are cooling off your Yang, or exhausting it, you are drifting away from your chances of becoming pregnant.

For the infertility patient, it is important to know what is at stake if one loses the Yang and how to prevent this from happening. The first step is to understand the six spheres we discussed previously. The second is to shy away from cold foods, cold herbs, cold medications and cold air. The third is to control the stress, emotions and pressures that deplete the Yang. The fourth is to refrain from hyper-stimulating the Yang, either physically or emotionally.

Too much physical stimulation, such as too much exercise, will move the Yang in the Tai

Yin, and too much emotion will move it in the Shao Yin. The Tai Yin organ is the spleen which nourishes the muscles. The Tai Yin is also damp earth. Excessive Yang will dry the earth, and dry earth is a dead earth. So excessive exercise will dry our earth – our bodies – and weaken our Tai Yin system. This is why many women athletes stop menstruating and become infertile.

The Shao Yin is where the kidney's water interacts with the heart's fire. The heart is where the spirit resides. When we think, contemplate, and study, we move the original Yang in the kidneys, helping the spirit revive itself. However, when we think excessively or become emotionally extended, the kidney's original Yang (water Yang) is exhausted and the spirit is lacking. This causes the water to dry, (see Yang Ming section about dry water) and the heart spirit floats.

When the sexual energy is stimulated, it goes directly to the Shao Yin heart-kidney relationship. Excessive sexual mental stimulation will dry the water. Today, we can see sexually stimulating images everywhere, resulting in a numbing down of sexual desire. In contrast, in the 1950s and 60s in China, where any reference to female sexuality was not allowed, young male villagers coming to the big city for the first time would find their pants wet from seminal emission just from riding a crowded bus. Most traditional societies and religions refrain from sex or sexual mental exploitations because free sexuality means low fertility and reduced sexual potency.

THE YANG IN THE CLASSICS

In the following section, I will quote several important Chinese medicine classics, then offer an interpretation of how they relate to infertility.

THE TREATISE OF ANCIENT TIMES AND THE HEAVENLY TRUTH: *The ancient sages knew the right path to longevity. They followed the rules of Yin and Yang and they harmonized themselves with the help of numbers. They well regulated their diet and sleeping habits and they never exhausted themselves. Because of this, their bodies and spirits thrived and they fulfilled their life expectancy. They lived to be more then 100 and then they passed away. Today's people are not the same. Harmful drinks are their nectar and exhausting themselves is the routine. They indulge in their desires, exhausting their essence and scattering their true Yang. Today's people don't know how to keep their energy full; they don't know how to regulate their spirit. They want to make their heart happy instead of true happiness. Even the sleep is not regulated and that is why they reach the age of 50 and their body has greatly declined.*

This quote is from the very first chapter of The **Yellow Emperor.** The main message is that we should all strive for healthier lives because it will enable us to fulfill our destiny, and allow women to become pregnant at the oldest possible age. Furthermore, this chapter introduces the concept of living in harmony according to the Yin and Yang. It tells us how to regulate our diet, as well as how to guard against exhausting our essence and scattering our true Yang.

THE GREAT TREATISE OF THE FOUR SEASONS AND REGULATING THE QI AND SPIRIT: *The three months of spring is when the old is expelled and new is born. The heaven and earth are born and the myriad things flourish. You should go to sleep late and wake up early. This is the right time to start exercising. It is also the right time to start thinking and planning as the energy spreads out and does not stagnate. In this season, there is only birth and no death, and there is only prosperity with no decline. This is the right path to nurture on the birthing energy of the spring. If you go against it, you will harm your liver. Your summer's energy will turn cold and the glory of summer will be scanty.*

The three months of summer are referred to as 'full glory.' The heaven and earth are in full exchange and the myriad things are in full glory. You should go to sleep late and wake up early. Do not feel bitter that the days are long and make sure that your mind is free of anger. Allow your spirit to flourish and your energy to expand as if the things that you love are all outside of your body. This is the right path to nurture on the summer's expanding energy. If you go against it, you will harm your heart.

The three months of fall are referred to as 'to even out.' The heaven's winds are blowing and the earth colors are changing. You should go to sleep early and wake up early following the rooster. Calm your mind and be peaceful as to join the fall's quieting down energy. Gather inward your energy and spirit as to match the fall's descending energy. Not thinking outward will cause the lung's energy to be clear. If you go against this path, you will harm your lungs. Your winter's energy will suffer drainage and the storage of winter will be scanty.

The three months of winter are called the storage. The water is ice and the earth is dry. One must follow the sunlight and go to sleep early and wake up late. All thoughts and desires should be directed inwards. Nothing should be radiating outward. Although it is important to dispel the external cold and keep warm, perspiration must be avoided. The Yang energy must be allowed to sink in deep. Going against this path will result in harm to the kidneys. The spring energy will suffer cold and infertility and the birth energy of spring will be scanty.

The main principle for maintaining health, according to **The Yellow Emperor,** is conforming to nature. Our behavior and actions should change every season according to the state of Yang energy around us. When the Yang energy expands in summer, we should allow our energy to expand, and when the energy moves into storage in winter, we should follow as well. This includes many aspects of our lives: the way we sleep, eat, exercise, think and express ourselves. For example, in the summer we should be outgoing and social, while in winter more inward looking and reserved. In the summer, we should sleep shorter hours, in winter we should sleep longer.

Our primary strategy to gain fertility is not with herbs or acupuncture, and certainly not drugs and surgeries. We should adjust our sleep, food, stress, emotions, and everything else according to the changes of Yang in the four seasons.

THE TREATISE ON LIFE'S ENERGY CONFORMING TO HEAVEN: *The most crucial aspect of Yin and Yang is that the Yang must become dense and consolidate. If Yin and Yang don't harmonize, it is like the spring without the fall, or the winter without the summer. When the two harmonize, it is called 'the way of the sage'. If the Yang 'opening' is too strong and it can't condense into storage, then the Yin energy will perish. When Yin is peaceful and Yang can withdraw back into storage, then the spirit is thriving. When Yin and Yang separate, our energy will extinguish.*

This section explains the importance of Yang within our energy. Yang gives us the ability to function, and even more importantly, it has the ability and need to withdraw back into storage. If the Yang can't withdraw, then the Yin energy will perish. The Yin energy is the energy within the matter – within every cell – of our body. When the Yin energy has perished, our life will become shorter. Over stimulation will cause the Yang to expand and not withdraw back. This can be over stimulation of the mind, or physical stimulation from coffee, smoking, or drugs. This is the reason many infertility patients suffer night sweats after taking fertility drugs. The Yang is expanded and is unable to retreat into storage, prompting the Yin to begin to perish.

THE GREAT TREATISE OF YIN AND YANG REFLECTIONS: *With strong heat, the energy will decline, while with mild warmth the energy will grow stronger. Strong heat is feeding on the energy, while the energy is feeding on mild warmth. Strong heat will scatter the energy, while mild warmth will give birth to energy.*

This segment explains the principle of balance, a key point in Chinese medicine. Warmth is beneficial, while strong heat can be destructive. This concept of keeping in balance is true for all aspects of life – diet, exercise, sleep – even for reproductive endocrinology.

In order to know where the correct balance lies, we must look to nature and the wisdom of our forefathers. Most scientific "new" ideas are here today and gone tomorrow. What is advised with confidence one year is reversed the next. I will continue to believe in the ancient wisdom of longevity and health when it comes to diet, exercise, sleep and treatment.

THE GREAT TREATISE OF YIN AND YANG REFLECTIONS: *A healer with great skill will treat a problem when it first arises at the superficial level of the skin. If he is too late, he will treat the disease at the flesh level. If he has missed it even more, he will treat it at the tendons and meridians depth. If the disease has formed already and the healer is late, he will treat it at the six Yang organs. If he has no choice and the disease has established itself in the depths, he can only treat it at the five Yin organs. When the disease gets to the deep level of the five Yin organs, it is a situation called 'half alive and half dead.' There can be only partial recovery.*

The wisdom of Chinese medicine is far reaching. **The Yellow Emperor** explains that the true remedy of all disease is prevention. But if not prevented, it is best to treat a disease early and correctly while it is at the skin or superficial level.

Every disease has a path of deterioration and a path of recovery. Regarding diet, sleep, stress and treatment of any kind, the correct measure will lead to recovery and the wrong measure creates disharmony and deterioration. Treating a disease, which has penetrated into the five Yin organs, however, is a difficult task and can ensure only partial recovery.

When a patient receives Western drugs, symptoms are removed from the exterior level, but are pushed inward into the five Yin organs. It is often difficult for the patient to discontinue the medication because of drug dependencies; the inner organs cannot function properly by themselves anymore.

THE GRAND TREATISE OF ESSENTIALS OF THE ULTIMATE TRUTH: *The Yellow Emperor asked: 'I know that the five weather phenomena interact with each other and there are excesses and deficiencies and that the six spheres take their place to rule the heaven and earth. What is the significance of all this?' Qi Bo bowed and answered: 'This is the big principle of heaven and earth and it reflects into the human spirit.' The Emperor said: 'I heard that in heaven this principle unites with the mysterious and on earth it joins with the unexplained. Why is that so?' Qibo answered: 'This is how the right path is born. This is also where ignorant doctors become suspicious.*

The five weather transformations of nature and the six spheres are a reflection of the human body. When we conform to this big principle, we can say that we follow the right path. The problem is that much of this principle is concealed in the mysterious ways of nature, and we as humans are uncomfortable with this mystery. We want to know why things happen. Our instinct is to understand nature so we can conquer it and not be conquered by it. Physicians who don't quite understand the "right path" nature is creating become suspicious of it, and ultimately come up with their own path which does not conform to nature.

THE TREATISE OF TRANSFORMING ESSENCE AND ENERGY: *The Emperor asked: 'I heard that in ancient times the sages could heal and transform essence and energy by using a blessing. In today's world, we use herbs to heal the inside of the body and acupuncture to heal the outside. Sometimes, the patient recovers and sometimes not. Why is this so?' Qibo answered: 'The sages lived among the animals. Their actions were tuned to avoid cold and their shelter protected them from extreme heat. Their emotions never harmed them internally and the external world never exhausted their physical body. Because of their harmonious lifestyle, a disease could not penetrate deep. In today's world, the story is different. Emotions harm our insides and the external world inflicts great damage upon our body. We do not follow the four seasons and we don't care to protect ourselves from cold and extreme heat. Diseases of all sorts attack us and penetrate deep from the skin to the bone marrow. Every little disease becomes a big one and every big disease results in death. This is why a little blessing cannot heal anymore and we need the use of herbs and acupuncture.*

"The ancient sages lived among the animals" means that the sages lived in harmony with nature as the animals do. They were in tune with the four seasons and understood the state of Yang energy in each season, and how it affects daily life. When we live in accord with nature, emotions come and go very easily; they cannot harm us. We do not hold grudges nor hold onto fear for extended periods of time. It is similar to a storm: the emotions of the sky are discharged gracefully and sun comes out immediately thereafter.

It is difficult to let go of the fear of infertility. When this fear is instilled by western physicians, it tends to stay with the woman and harms her chances even further by harming the kidneys' ability to hold the essence. If you live according to nature, this fear comes and it goes quickly.

In addition, the sages made sure that the external world would not harm their physical bodies. The external world is composed of two parts: our lifestyle and the external factors around us. We shouldn't subject ourselves to extreme temperatures, nor should we eat cold foods. Many of my patients report sitting entire days in a freezing office during their work week. Other patients take supplements because it is difficult to find the healthiest of foods.

We should, however, set priorities. The first and foremost is to keep our health, even if it means another job in a warmer office, or spending more time locating the correct food. We should not suffer through anything when it comes to our health, because everything else is secondary. We must attempt to sleep longer hours, eat warmer foods, and exercise less in the winter to insure that our kidney's energy will stay in surplus.

Additional influences are diseases that attack us and penetrate deep into the "bone marrow." This is not a literal description, but rather an expression describing depth on the energy level scale. If our body is strong, illnesses cannot go into a deep energetic level, but if our body is weak, then an illness can go deep. Another reason a disease can go deep is using the wrong treatment. When we become ill and take a drug to alleviate the symptom, this will push the disease deeper into a "bone marrow" depth. This is because a symptom is not a disease. When the true root of a disease, rather than a symptom, is remedied, then the disease will be cured.

For example, if one doesn't sleep enough in winter, the lower back may become sore because the kidney's energy is exhausted. If pain medication is taken to resolve the lower back ache, the pain might be temporarily relieved, but the kidneys are still exhausted and the sleep patterns are still off. The pain alarm that signals that the kidneys are deficient of energy is no longer felt. Later on, a severe disease surfaces and nobody knows why. This is why **The Yellow Emperor** says: *Every small disease becomes a big one.* In Chinese medicine treatment, the practitioner must strengthen the kidneys and advise the patient to sleep more during this season. This is a true remedy. The root is treated and the cause for the root problem is being addressed.

Western medicine has tried to adapt a preventative approach. The tracking of cholesterol and triglyceride levels have given birth to new drugs aimed at "preventing" heart disease. However, these discoveries are all man made and not derived from nature. My experience shows that following nature's rhythm results in unsurpassable health, and more importantly, it comes for free as an entitlement. We are part of nature and nature is part of us. Drugs for preventative reasons are unnecessary if one knows how to follow the path.

THE TREATISE ON PRECIOUS LIFE AND THE ENTIRE FORM: *First you must control the spirit, second you must know how to nourish the body, third you must know the real truth about 'toxic' herbs, fourth you must know the ins and outs of acupuncture, and fifth you must know how to understand and diagnose the inner organ patterns, the blood and energy. When you know all of the above, the right path is not mysterious anymore. It is open in front of you, but you may be alone on this path.*

The first element needed to pursue the correct path toward health, longevity and fertility is to control the spirit, meaning to conform to nature and the six spheres. The second principle is to nourish the body. The third, fourth and fifth principles of keeping healthy and following the right path are to know the truth about herbs, acupuncture and the art of diagnosis. The three combined represent the art of Chinese medicine. It explains that once your vibration matches the vibration of nature and you understand how nature works, you can use all natural resources such as herbs, grains, fruits, meats and vegetables to nurture your body. If you have failed the natural path to health and become ill, you should know how to assess and treat your illness using herbs and acupuncture remedies.

THE TREATISE ON STORING THE ENERGY AND LIVING ACCORDING TO THE SEASONS: *Toxic herbs can defeat a disease, the five grains will nurture, the five fruits will help, the five meats will benefit and the five vegetables will supplement. The energy and flavor of each will unite and enter the body. This will strengthen your essence and benefit your energy.*

Ingesting only natural foods and herbs is called nourishing the body. We must differentiate, however, between what is produced by nature and many other products that are labeled "natural."

TREATISE ABOUT ESSENTIALS OF MERIDIAN DIAGNOSIS: *The Yellow Emperor asked: 'What are the essentials of diagnosis?' Qi Bo answered: 'In the first and second months of the year (lunar calendar) the heaven's energy starts opening and the earth energy starts spreading. At this time, the man's energy is in his liver. In the third and fourth months, the heaven's energy is fully opened and the earth's expansion is full. The man's energy is in his spleen. In the fifth and sixth months, the heaven's energy is surging and the earth is high. The man's energy is in his head. In the seventh and eighth months, the Yin energy begins its decline. The man's energy is in his lungs. In the ninth and tenth months, the Yin energy resembles ice and the earth starts closing down. The man's energy is in his heart. In the eleventh and twelfth months, the ice is back and the earth energy is closed. The man's energy is in his kidneys.'*

When we realize that the energy surge is different in each organ during various times of the year, it is our first step toward learning how to become close to nature. It is our first step in understanding why, for example, we have allergies in spring and not in the summer.

THE TREATISE OF STORAGE IN THE SIX SECTIONS: *At the end of the year, the cycle repeats itself. The seasons take shape and their energies distribute accordingly like a circle without end. Because of this regularity, if the doctor does not know the additions of every year, the surge and decline of the energy in each season or the deficiency and excesses of each lunar segment, he is not qualified to practice Chinese medicine.*

Chinese medicine, without understanding the yearly changes, is like a car without an engine. It looks good from the outside but it cannot go anywhere. For example, when I see a patient, I must consider that particular moment in time. If a patient presents allergies in "Mid-Autumn" my assessment will be different than if it is in "Cold Dew." Mid-Autumn is the strongest metal element of the fall, where Cold Dew begins to bear more of the Kidney's water energy. The metal controls the wood and the water gives birth to the wood. Simultaneously in one year, the Yang Ming Dry Metal influences the second half of the year, bearing influence on the situation along with the guest energy during this two-month period, for example Shao Yang Minister Fire. The analysis goes on with different levels; because it is complicated, many uneducated practitioners choose not to consider it at all. Instead, they simply treat the symptoms of a disease.

TREATISE ABOUT PAINS: *The Yellow Emperor said: 'I heard that the one who knows the heaven rules must have good knowledge of people. The one who knows the ancient times must have good knowledge of the present, and the one who knows people must know himself well. In this way, the right path cannot be lost and the truth comes out. This is called true understanding.'*

To truly understand the right path for health, one must understand the heaven's energies, the wisdom accumulated in the past, and most of all, one must cultivate character and know oneself. It is important that we choose a way of self cultivation, such as meditation, Tai Chi, Qi Gong or Yoga.

DISCUSSION OF PULSE ESSENTIALS: *The Emperor asked: 'What is the method of diagnosis?' 'Qibo answered: Diagnosis is done early in the morning, before the Yin Qi moved and before the Yang Qi scattered, before any food or drink entered the mouth and the energy in the meridians surged. The meridians at this time are still in order and the Qi and blood are not yet chaotic. At this time you can diagnose the excess of the pulse.*

This quote explains the importance of checking the pulse early in the morning. However, the important hidden information is the understanding of Yin and Yang. In the morning, the Yin does not move yet and the Yang does not scatter. The ancient Chinese word for "move" is **Dong**, which has two elements: one means "weight" or "heavy" while the other means "force." The force and the weight brought together means momentum. The meaning of "move" is to move something of heavy weight with force. This is the action of the Yin. What does it mean to scatter? The Chinese character for scatter is **San**, and is composed of three parts. The first is hemp fiber or a stack of wood, the second flesh and third a component showing a beating action. All the components brought together mean that beating on a stack of wood or hemp fiber or flesh will cause it to break apart. **San** is the action that leads to breaking apart. The Yang action is then to break apart. What is the Yang breaking from? It is breaking from the flesh to go outward. What is the Yin doing? It is giving the momentum to the Yang to go out. When the Yang is silent or in storage, it cannot go out or break out. The Yin has the force to push this weight out. When the Yang is closing down, the Yin is also resting. They are actually not different from each other, but two sides of the same coin. The Yin is moving the momentum and the Yang is breaking out. That is why **The Yellow Emperor** says: *The knowledgeable sees the sameness and the fool sees the difference. The knowledgeable always has plenty and the fool is always in deficiency.*

DONG

SAN

STIMULATING DRUGS AND THE YANG DON'T ALWAYS MIX

Although Western fertility drugs are considered safe, I believe it is important to remember that certain drugs, which were initially found to be safe, were later found harmful. Such a drug was DES (Diethylstilboestrol), a synthetic estrogen that was prescribed by both obstetricians and general practitioners to millions of pregnant women in many countries from 1938 through the 1980s. Thought to prevent miscarriage and ensure a healthy pregnancy, over 200 brand names of this drug were sold; it never worked well and was eventually found to pose health risks, such as cancer and infertility, to the women who took the drug and the children they carried.

Patients who have had IVF treatments often come to me with a serious Yang deficiency caused by the over-stimulating drugs, and/or the cold herbs they've been taking. Stimulating drugs of any sort, including fertility drugs, stimulate the Yang to come out of the water. Their symptoms range from cold hands and feet, to feeling cold all over, to general exhaustion and repeated hot flashes. In addition to herbal supplements, I recommend seeking help from a qualified practitioner instead of purchasing herbal supplements from a health food store.

Infertility is becoming more prevalent as Yang deficiencies increase in the population. Zheng Qinan in his book **True Transmission of Chinese Medicine Theory (Yi Li Zhen Chuan)** explains that: *The true Yang resides below and penetrates the Yin. If the true fire is weak, it cannot control the lower orifices, blood and essence. When the true fire is weak, the Yin rises upwards, which can cause shortness of breath and a floating pulse. However, if the face is not red, the body is not hot and there is no sweat, then the true Yang is not rising with the Yin (which is a good prognosis). However, if there is red face, the body feels hot and there is sweating, then the true Yang is floating and truly wants to separate from the Yin (this is a bad prognosis).*

I have witnessed the deterioration of the true Yang in the kidneys of patients taking fertility drugs. Symptoms include hot flashes and night sweats. These hurt the body by hurting the Yang energy, which is responsible for conception and pregnancy; it also lessens fertility potential.

Even though my position on fertility drugs is generally negative, I am not opposed to their use. I have spent hundreds of hours in a Western fertility clinic as part of my doctoral program, and witnessed the miracles that fertility drugs can achieve. I have seen patients with deformed uteruses, abnormal ovaries and other anatomical situations, who would never have been able to give birth if it wasn't for modern technology and drugs. I know that Western doctors, especially many reproductive endocrinologists, are passionate, kind hearted, and want to help their patients get pregnant.

The problem is not with the doctors or even with the drugs. The problem is with Western medicine as a whole because it does not allow any other treatment modality to penetrate into the health care system. Due to public pressure, the system is finally changing now.

Acupuncture has begun to be accepted in some medical circles. Its efficacy is well documented, yet as recently as five years ago, most reproductive endocrinologists would not have referred their patients to an acupuncturist.

There is still a long way to go. Most patients who want to get pregnant don't have Chinese medicine as an option. Most Western doctors do not refer their patients to herbalists, and patients who try Chinese medicine usually discover it themselves.

This must change. It makes sense to inflict less damage on the patient. IVF procedures are useless in patients with Yang deficiencies. Because they only work in patients with a strong Yang, the deficiency must be remedied before IVF procedures are attempted. Except in extreme cases, infertility patients should be treated first via Chinese medicine, and if that doesn't work, move onto fertility drugs and IVF.

One reproductive endocrinologist who is a collaborator of mine tries to improve the health of his patients for the first six months, and if the patient has not conceived at that point, he begins the "shotgun approach" of fertility drugs. Unfortunately, such doctors are definitely the exception rather than the rule. I believe that 20 or 30 years from now, Chinese herbal medicine will be assimilated into the Western medicine dogma, the very same way acupuncture is today. However, for today's generation of patients, there is no time to wait.

THE FIVE REFLECTIONS – BANKING ON INTUITIVE KNOWLEDGE

Think about the two-phase method we use to differentiate information. In the first phase of understanding, we assess the data coming to us from the outside. In the second phase, we integrate what we've received with our intuition and inborn knowledge.

For example, it is claimed that food grown with pesticides is safe to eat, and studies are often cited to support this claim. While many people believe these studies, other people rely on their intuition which tells them that pesticides are never safe. In this case, external data, as convincing as it may be, must go through final approval in the heart before it is believed.

This intuitive knowledge, or as Chinese medicine calls it, "the heart thoughts" are naturally inside of us, and they differ from one individual to another. The "reflections" concept in Chinese medicine is tremendously different than modern science, and therefore can be difficult to understand for those of us who have been indoctrinated in modern science since childhood. In order to understand it, we must rely on intuition.

The Yellow Emperor: *The knowledgeable observes 'sameness', while the simple-minded observes 'difference'. The knowledgeable has always plenty and the simple-minded is always in a deficient state.*

We must use intuitive knowledge to make the leap into understanding Chinese medicine.

Chen Xiuyuan explains the above quote as follows: *The knowledgeable knows the heavenly truth that Yin and Yang spring out of the same place. When the Yang is kept healthy, the Yin is strong. When the spirit and essence are preserved within, the Yin flourishes and the Qi is strong on the outside. Since the knowledgeable knows the root of Yin and Yang, his energy is always plenty. The simple-minded thinks that Yin and Yang are different. When he has a problem outside, he treats the Yang, and when he has a problem inside, he treats the Yin. He doesn't know that strengthening the Yang will strengthen the Yin and that strengthening the Yin will strengthen the Yang. His energy forever will be deficient.*

What is this knowledge that **The Yellow Emperor** is talking about? In a poetic way, it describes knowledge in the **Origins of the Spirit** section: *The heaven in me is 'virtue,' the earth in me is Qi. The virtue flows downwards and the Qi pounces upwards and that gives rise to birth. When birth comes, we call this essence. When the two essences struggle with each other, we call this spirit. When the spirit comes and goes, we call this soul (**Hun**) and when the essence enters and exits, we call this physical soul (**Po**). Because of this, when we trust our attention in objects, we call this heart. When the heart remembers it, we call this idea. The idea stores and becomes 'will power'. Because the 'will power' accumulates and transforms, we call it a thought. When the thought is profound, we call this a 'deep thought'. If we use this 'deep thought' to assess the object to which we initially trusted our attention, then we call this knowledge.*

The basis of knowledge is heaven and earth. The natural connection that we have to nature and to heaven and earth is what gives birth to our instinctual knowledge in the heart. The heaven's ongoing virtue and the earth's energy unite in our heart as spirit. Data is absorbed by our heart and spirit, and is transformed into thoughts and "deep thoughts," finally becoming knowledge. If data comes to us and we skip the "deep thoughts" phase and simply accept it as knowledge, then The Yellow Emperor says we are engaging in the "simple-minded way".

True knowledge, as Chen Xiuyuan calls it, is "knowing the ways of heaven and earth to be able to nurture your body and health." With this knowledge, **The Yellow Emperor** says, "you will always have plenty".

CHEN XIUYUAN – SUPERFICIAL COMMENTS ON THE YELLOW EMPEROR: *The heaven's five directions, five energies and five colors enter into the five Yin organs to nourish the essence of these organs. This is because the heaven's Qi penetrates through the man and the man's Qi penetrates through the heavens, thus the five Yin organs store these five essences.*

The Yellow Emperor says that *the five Yin organs govern the storage of essence.* Western science and medicine believe that the human body is operating independently from nature; the different organs work independently from each other, and from other components of the body such as blood, tissues, muscles, bones, and tendons. In Chinese medicine, the opposite is the case. The body is completely dependent on heaven and earth, the organs are inseparable from each other, and the body components such as blood, tissues, muscles and bones are not stand-alone materials. As **The Yellow Emperor** reminds us, *there is nothing in our body, which is independent from nature.*

The Yellow Emperor: *Heaven is round and earth is flat, the man reflects it by having a round head and flat feet. Heaven has sun and moon and the man has two eyes. Heaven has wind and rain and the man has joy and anger. Heaven has thunder and lightning and the man has voice and sound. Heaven has four seasons and the man has four extremities (arms and legs). Heaven has winter and summer and the man feels hot and cold. Heaven has Yin and Yang and the man has husband and wife. Heaven has day and night and the man has sleep and activity. Earth, at times, has four seasons that don't give birth to grass and trees and the man has infertility. This is the reflection of man with heaven and earth.*

The knowledge of Chinese medicine is a knowledge of reflection. The principles leading the Yin and Yang energies into life, and out of it, are the same for the universe, heaven and earth, the annual seasons, humans, animals and plants. The energy cycle of Yin and Yang describes what is happening with our world and what is happening with us. The changes of the Yang energy from warm in spring, to hot in summer, to cool in autumn, and to cold in winter is the natural cycle happening everywhere. The Yang expanding, flourishing, declining, and storing is a universal law for man and nature.

The Yellow Emperor points out that the reason that we have two hands and two feet, two eyes, round head and so forth, is not random. Our body is shaped the way it is because we reflect nature. Our body follows the rules of Yin and Yang, as does our universe. For example, why are tendons flexible? Modern science tells us they are flexible so that the joints can be flexible. However, what factor decided that joints and tendons need to be flexible? Modern science does not really bother with the "why," instead simply assuming that the body is smart. But if we turn to a "deep thought" and look into our heart, we know that the tendons and joints are flexible because intuitively our body grows naturally in the same way heaven and earth evolves. Our body reflects the actions of the Yin and Yang energy around and within us. There is a reason for everything and the reason is "reflection."

THE GREAT TREATISE OF YIN AND YANG REFLECTIONS: *Heaven is deficient in north and west and the man's right ear and right eye are not as clear as the left ear and eye. Earth is not full at south east so the man's left hand and left foot are not as strong as the right hand and right foot. The east is Yang. The Yang's essence is to ascend upwards. If it is at the upper part of the body, then it is bright and not deficient on that side. This is where the heaven and earth, Yin and Yang cannot be complete.*

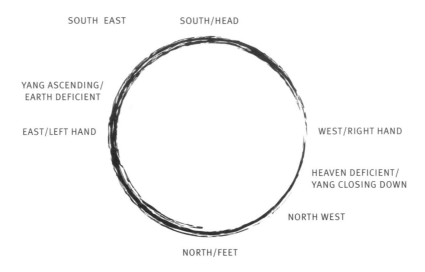

SOUTH EAST   SOUTH/HEAD

YANG ASCENDING/
EARTH DEFICIENT

EAST/LEFT HAND   WEST/RIGHT HAND

HEAVEN DEFICIENT/
YANG CLOSING DOWN

NORTH WEST

NORTH/FEET

If we look at the same energy circle we have previously explored, we can understand **The Yellow Emperor** statements. Our head is at the south or heaven, and our feet are in the north or earth; the right side of our body is in the west and the left side of our body is in the east. Because the Yang energy is stronger on the left, as its essence is to go upward, the left eye and left ear are stronger than the right. The right eye and ear are on the side where the Yang energy descends, so they are lacking energy in comparison to the left. The eyes, ears, and nose deal with Yang clear energy. There is no physical substance coming in and out of them, only energy, be it sunlight, sound waves, or air.

The hands and feet are different. They deal with substance and materials. They need Yin energy – the energy of the earth – to help them. The Yin and earth are deficient at the south east, where the Yang is most active. The Yin and earth are the strongest where the Yang is closing down (North West), thus the right hand and foot are stronger.

The five Yin organs, heart, spleen, lungs, kidneys, and liver, store the essences of the five directions. The five essences are the essences of heaven and earth. They are characterized by the five directions: east, south, west, north, and center.

DISCUSSION ON GOLDEN CHAMBER'S TRUE WORDS: *East has green color and it enters the liver, it opens to the eyes and stores its essence in the liver. Its ailment is trembling (**Jing He**), its flavor sour, its kind grass and trees, its animal chicken and its grain wheat. This is the spring, which is coming first. Its sound is Jue, its number is 8. The illness, you should know, is at the tendons. Its smell is rank.*

South has the color red, it enters the heart and opens into the ears, its essence is stored in the heart. Because of this, its disease is in the five Yin organs. Its flavor is bitter and its kind fire. Its animal is sheep and its grain broomcorn millet. You should know that its diseases are in the blood vessels. Its sound is Zheng and its number 7. Its smell is burnt.

Center has the color yellow, it enters the spleen, opens to the mouth and its essence is stored in the spleen. Because of this, diseases are in the root of the tongue. Its animal is ox and its grain millet. You should know that its disease is in the flesh. Its sound is Gong and its number 5. Its smell is fragrant.

West has the color white, it enters the lungs and opens into the nose. Its essence is stored in the lungs. Its disease is in the shoulders, its flavor pungent and its kind metal, its animal horse and its grain rice. You should know that its disease is in the skin and body hair. Its sound is Shang and its number 9. Its smell is rancid.

North has black color. It enters the kidneys and opens into the two Yin (anus and genitalia). Its essence is stored in the kidneys. Its disease is at Xi (the connection between the small muscles and bones). Its flavor is salty and its kind water, its animal pig and its grain beans. You should know that its disease is in the bones. Its sound is Yu and its number 6. Its smell is rotten.

The five directions have distinct colors. The colors are the manifestation of the heaven's energies. The red color feels hot, the green feels warm like spring, yellow is like the end of summer transforming hot to cool, white is cool and similar to the fall, and black is cold like winter. These colors or energies are natural expressions of Yin and Yang.

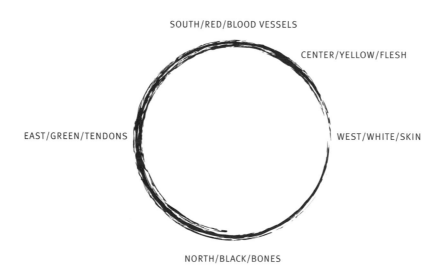

SOUTH/RED/BLOOD VESSELS

CENTER/YELLOW/FLESH

EAST/GREEN/TENDONS

WEST/WHITE/SKIN

NORTH/BLACK/BONES

The colors/energies are present in our body from our conception, when our father and mother mix their colors together and give it to us.

The quality of the colors, as **The Yellow Emperor** says, has many manifestations. For example, the energy of black enters our body and is stored in the kidneys. This energy opens up to the anus and genitalia. This means that regulating the bowel movement and urination is partially due to the kidneys' energy, as is sex and reproduction. The color black belongs to the north and it belongs to water. North, water, and black possess the same energy. Black in the Chinese language is **Xuan**, which not only translates to "black," but to "mysterious" as well.

XUAN

Looking at the classical meaning of Xuan in the earliest Chinese dictionary tells us that the color is conceived of black with a hint of red. Red is fire or Yang energy and black is water or Yin energy. The black energy of the kidneys embodies the seed of Yang – the seed of a new life. This is what we referred to as the energy of Shao Yin in the three Yin / three Yang system.

The Yellow Emperor goes further to explain that colors shape everything physical around us. The animals, the grains, the flavors and even our own body tissues, are all an expression of these colors. The quality of the black color, for example, is the core reason why our bones have formed the way they did, and the white color or white energy explains our skin. When we understand that, we can understand the holistic view of Chinese medicine. If, let's say, a patient has a disease of the tendons, we will treat the liver. The liver stores the essence of the green energy in the body, which is the same energy responsible for the formation of tendons. When the liver energy grows strong, the tendons can heal.

The same is true with most infertility issues. The reproductive system is weak because the black (with hint of red) is not sufficient. We strengthen the kidneys so the black energy of the body will become strong. When the black energy is strong, the sperm is good and the egg quality is at its best. If a physician refers to "poor egg quality" it signals that the black energy is not strong enough.

The energy of the five colors and five directions is the energy of heaven and earth. The heaven's energy comes down to interact with the earth and provides the earth with energy.

QI JIAO

This is called **Qi Jiao**, the space between heaven and earth where humans, animals, plants and trees live. The five colors or energies must follow a correct path for harmony to exist. The same is true with the five energies inside our body. They must follow a correct path or disease will result.

So for example, black energy is the strongest after midnight in the very early hours of the new day. If a couple has intercourse at this time, but the black energy is deficient, pregnancy will be impossible. It does not help if the black energy is strong in the middle of the day, when it shouldn't be. If the black energy is strong in the middle of the day, one feels tired, which will hinder conception.

Chinese medicine is not fixed like western medicine. A western diagnosis of "poor egg quality" means poor egg quality whether it is day or night, winter or spring. Chinese medicine recognizes that energy fluctuates in different times in different ways, represented by the different colors. My experience and results show that poor egg quality is not necessarily poor at all. When colors are deficient or when they are not in harmony, namely at the wrong place at the wrong time, the woman cannot get pregnant, and the quality of the egg does not matter. When the energies restore harmony, the woman will get pregnant even with "poor egg quality."

The Yellow Emperor explains that in the Qi Jiao, during the energy interaction between heaven and earth, six actions are occurring simultaneously: virtue, transformation, affair, effect, extreme change, and a possible disaster. These actions are happening between heaven and earth, but they also reflect in our body.

THE GREAT TREATISE OF CHANGES IN QI JIAO: *The east gives birth to wind and the wind gives birth to wood. Its virtue is to apply harmony. Its transformation is to birth and thrive. Its affair is to spread open. Its effect is wind. Its extreme change is anger. Its disaster is to fall down (like foliage).*

The south gives birth to fire. Its virtue is to appear obvious. Its transformation is luxuriant. Its affair is to be bright and dazzling. Its effect is heat. Its extreme change is obstructed glimmer. Its disaster is to burn down.

The center gives birth to damp and damp gives birth to earth. Its virtue is to steam. Its transformation is richness. Its affair is to become quiet. Its effect is dampness. Its extreme change is sudden rain. Its disaster is a long rain (where the earth is saturated and muddy).

The West gives birth to dryness and dryness gives birth to metal. Its virtue is to appear clean. Its transformation is to gather. Its affair is severe and fall. Its effect is dryness. Its extreme change is harsh fall. Its disaster is to green loss (its springing instead of falling).

The North gives birth to cold and cold gives birth to water. Its virtue is to appear cool. Its transformation is stillness. Its affair is to freeze. Its effect is cold. Its extreme change is freezing cold. Its disaster is ice, snow and frost.

One must inspect the movements of the five directions. They all have virtue, transformation, affair, effect, extreme change and disasters (De, Hua, Zheng, Ling, Bian, Zai). Everything on earth has it and the man reflects it too.

The Yellow Emperor tells us that to understand harmony and become fertile, we must understand how these five energies work. The energies of nature and of our body, reflected from nature, have normal functions and expressions. These energies also undergo extreme changes and disasters, making it impossible for the body to function correctly. Infertility is one issue arising due to such a change of energy. As many as 80-90% of my patients complain of feeling cold and having cold hands and feet. This is due to extreme change or even a disaster in the kidneys. The kidneys, water, and the black color are in trouble. If I succeed in alleviating this problem of extreme change, the patient conceives. If the black color becomes harmonious the patient will become pregnant. If the black color does not harmonize, neither the patient's youth nor her state of "perfect health" will enable her to become pregnant naturally through medical technology.

This principle seems simple, however in reality it is not. Even though most patients feel cold, it is not always the fault of the black color. There are other colors as well. The heaven's energies and the patient's body energies must be in balance. The art of Chinese medicine is first to recognize what is out of balance, then how to restore it. Because the essences of heaven and earth energies are stored inside our organs, the practitioner must know what is going on in nature daily. If he does not, he will not understand "reflections," and the treatment results will be poor.

The Yellow Emperor: *The emperor asked: 'There must be rules for the use of acupuncture.' Qibo answered: 'One must follow the heaven's rules and the principles of earth, unite the two until they shine bright. As for the method of acupuncture, one must first map out the stars and the moon, and know the seasons and the eight current energies. Only then can one utilize acupuncture. If the heaven is warm, the blood is flowing and the Qi is floating. If the heaven is cold, the blood is coagulating and the Qi sinks. When the moon has just begun to grow, the blood and Qi are thin and narrow in essence, and when the moon is full, the blood and Qi are full and the flesh is firm. When the moon is on the decline, the flesh decreases its firmness and the meridians are empty.*

In the past few years, there have been studies showing both the benefits of acupuncture for IVF, as well as those showing that acupuncture actually decreased IVF success. There is no answer, because to study acupuncture scientifically is wrong.

In the context of "reflections," **The Yellow Emperor** explains that the characteristics of the individual under treatment, as well as the season, moon phase, and time of day, will all effect the location of acupuncture points, the length of the needles, and how these needles will be twisted.

The Yellow Emperor – Miraculous Pivots states: *If you want to use acupuncture, you must first inspect the meridians to see if they are full or empty. You palpate the channel and follow its path; you press and knead it to find out its condition. Then you must look for the reflections. Only then can you choose which meridian to use and where to put the needles.*

This explains that each acupuncture patient must be checked carefully. Each meridian has to be observed and analyzed. Thereafter, the practitioner must study the current reflections of heaven in the body. These reflections change constantly. When the heaven changes, the reflections also change. Only then can the practitioner choose the meridians, needles, acupuncture points, and correct technique.

THE GREAT TREATISE OF FIVE TRANSFORMATIONS: *The heaven and earth, while alternating stillness and movement, advance in five steps to repeat the cycle over and over. What is the use of this birth and death cycle? The heaven reflects and the earth forms physical material. This happens on the horizontal and vertical lines in the empty space. It is the magnificent five elements (the empty space is Qi Jiao and the horizontal and vertical lines are Jing Wei – see appropriate sections). The earth forms physical matter. The empty space allows reflections of heaven's essence. The creation of the earth's form through the reflection of the heaven's essence is like the root and branches and leaves of a tree. Even though it is far and you can't see it, you can tell that it is there."*

Because we can't see the heaven's energies, we judge them by their color and we judge them by their "feel." Cold, black, red, and hot are, for example, tangible ways for us to sense these energies. We can't really grasp Yin and Yang, but can understand and experience water and fire, heat and cold. These are the reflections that we can see and feel – thus we know about Yin and Yang. We see the branches and leaves so we can tell that there are roots under the tree, even if we can't see the roots. When we look to the heaven, we can't see or feel Yin and Yang, but we can see and feel their reflections. There is a lot that we can learn about our health and how to become healthy and fertile by tuning in to these "reflections." For practitioners, learning this information is a must.

THE GREAT TREATISE OF YIN AND YANG REFLECTIONS: *Strong fire causes the Qi to decline, while mild warmth strengthens the Qi. Strong fire consumes the Qi, while Qi feeds on mild warmth. Strong fire scatters Qi, while mild warmth gives birth to Qi.*

When we study Western medicine pathology, we learn that numerous diseases are triggered by bacteria or viruses. This includes meningitis, prostatitis, herpes and other illnesses.

However, bacteria and viruses are often present in the body even though no illness has occurred. The viruses and bacteria attack or colonize only in selected people.

The above quote from **The Yellow Emperor** explains how the pathogens choose their victims. The principle that mild warmth nourishes the Qi is as true for culturing embryos for IVF as it is for culturing bacteria to make yogurt. If the temperature is very cold or very hot, nothing will happen. The temperature must be appropriately warm for the culture to grow.

The same is true inside the body with regard to reproduction. Warmth is the green energy of the spring and is the energy of the liver in the Jue Yin (see chapter 2). This green energy cannot translate into external temperature. This is an internal temperature that must be reached in the right place at the right time. Any woman who has charted her body's basal temperature knows that temperatures fluctuate during the menstrual cycle and ovulation. However, the temperature is only one aspect of green warmth. The other aspect of warmth (green) is its gentle spreading out, which occurs if the green essence of heaven is stored appropriately in the liver. This helps us understand why so many infertile women feel cold, and why bacteria and viruses attack some people and not others. It is the result of imbalances of reflected energy. It is not warm enough or it is too hot, it is not cool enough or it is too cold. This causes pathogens to move to one place or another, to attack one person and not another. This happens because the reflection and absorption of reflections is not harmonious.

The Yellow Emperor advises practitioners to treat the cause and not the symptoms. The root of the problem is disharmony in reflections, resulting from disharmony in the heavens or from an internal disharmony, such as emotions, that obstruct the body from absorbing reflections correctly. The practitioner's job is to know the heavens and the internal causes. He should look for the cause and cure it. Often patients tell me "you are a miracle worker." In reality, assisting my patients to become healthy has very little to do with miracles. It rather has to do with knowledge. Even though this knowledge is not easy to come by (it's not always in text books), it is worthwhile to invest the extra effort to attain it.

The Great Treatise of Yin and Yang Reflections: *Yang serves as Qi and Yin serves as flavor. Flavor returns to form, form returns to Qi, Qi returns to essence and essence returns to transformation. Essence feeds Qi, form feeds flavor, transformation gives birth to essence and Qi gives birth to form. Flavor harms form, Qi harms essence, essence transforms to become Qi and the Qi can be harmed by flavor.*

When we talk about reflections, we can't really do without the above quote from **The Yellow Emperor.** Nevertheless, it is one of many confusing quotes which leave the reader with a headache from excessive thinking. It becomes easy to comprehend, however, if the underlying logic is clear.

In total, this quote has 12 thoughts grouped together in three groups of four. The first group is the "returning" group, the second is the "giving birth" group and the third is the "harming" group.

GROUP 1: "RETURNING"

A) FLAVOR RETURNS TO FORM: Flavor is extreme Yin and it returns to the earth, meaning it belongs to the earth. The earth shapes physical forms. Flavor is used here as an example, explaining that physical form, such as a mountain, a piece of wood, a diamond or any other material, still contains some Yin essence within. This Yin essence is called flavor.

B) FORM RETURNS TO QI: The earth's myriad forms are the result of Qi, or energy, penetrating into the earth. The physical matter of the earth is lifeless without Qi.

C) QI RETURNS TO ESSENCE: Qi is the energy in the empty space between heaven and earth. Earlier we described it as Qi Jiao (Qi crossing from heaven to earth). Essence in The Yellow Emperor is the essence of the heaven's movements, including the heavenly essence of the north, which is stored in the kidneys, and the heavenly essence of the east, which is stored in the liver. **The Yellow Emperor** explains here that the Qi between heaven and earth exists because heaven has 'essence' of constant movement. Constant movement of heavens means that the stars, the moon, the sun, and the seasons are moving without stopping.

D) ESSENCE RETURNS TO TRANSFORMATION: The above essence of heaven belongs to transformation. Transformation here refers to spirit transformation. We discuss this aspect in greater detail in chapter 8 'Shen Ji, Qi Li' (spirit mechanism and Qi axis). The idea behind spirit transformation is that there is a higher energy above the heavens that causes it to move all the time. In a similar way, we have described flavor as the Yin essence inside the form. Transformation of spirit is Yang energy outside of heaven. The heaven's constant change is due to this spirit transformation in the universe.

The first group of sentences explains the hierarchy between Yin and Yang and between heaven and earth. We have five components in the process of reflections from heaven into earth and from heaven into man. If we list them from top to bottom, from heaven to earth, or if we compare it to our world (the planet we live on) with its ball shape, from the outer stratosphere to its inner-most core, the five levels are:

SPIRIT TRANSFORMATION

↑

HEAVEN'S ESSENCE OF MOVEMENT

···················· ↑ ··················

QI BETWEEN HEAVEN AND EARTH

···················· ↑ ··················

EARTHLY FORM

↑

YIN ESSENCE OF FLAVOR

The two lines in the chart represent the heaven that we see above us and the earth we see below us. The human being is living in this area between heaven and earth (between the two lines). In the first group, **The Yellow Emperor** explains that in the process of life we do have these five levels taking place, and he does show us where we humans live our life in comparison to these five components.

GROUP 2 "GIVING BIRTH"

A) TRANSFORMATION GIVES BIRTH TO ESSENCE: The spirit of transformation outside of heaven is the force giving birth to the heaven's "essence." The heaven's essence is the constant movement of the stars, moon, seasons and directions.

B) ESSENCE FEEDS QI: Heaven's essence comes down to the empty space. This is called "the essence feeds the Qi." In Chinese, this coming down motion is **Xia Lin** and the empty space is called **Qi Jiao**. When the essence comes from heaven into Qi Jiao we feel the weather and seasonal changes. We feel the warmth of spring, the heat of summer, the coolness of fall, and the freeze of winter.

C) QI GIVES BIRTH TO FORM: Qi from the empty space comes down into the earth, causing the earth to give birth to myriad things. All material things around us that we can see and feel come from earth and contain Qi including human beings, plants, trees, rocks, and buildings.

WEI

D) FORM FEEDS FLAVOR: While we can see the heaven and we can feel the earth, we cannot see the spirit transformation above the heaven (Yang) and we cannot feel the flavor (Yin stillness) inside the earth. The Chinese character for flavor, **Wei**, is composed of two parts – the first section is a mouth, and the second means "not there yet." For Chinese, flavor means almost there, but not yet there. The same is with the Yin inside the earth. When we feel the earth we get a taste of Yin, but not pure Yin. The form feeds flavor means that Yin can exist inside because there is earth around it. Yin energy cannot exist without the earth's form.

GROUP 3 – "HARMING"

In group 3 we learn about possible and impossible interactions between these five levels. Some can harm each other. In this group, we must read hidden meanings "between the lines."

A) FLAVOR HARMS FORM - Flavor, or Yin stillness, is closely related to form. However if we look in group 2/c we learn that Qi gives birth to form. Qi is a moving energy or life force. When this moving energy sinks into the earth, the earth can shape forms. At the same time, flavor is Yin stillness, which is the opposite of movement. If this formless "stillness" is too strong, then forms suffer. The moving energy (Qi) coming down into the earth is halted. The excessive Yin action can harm the form by neutralizing the Qi movement and preventing the earth from shaping forms. This is the reason for old age; the Yin grows stronger and the Qi becomes weak, the body begins to suffer and deteriorate. Ultimately, when we die, the Qi is completely gone and the Yin has occupied the entire body into stillness.

B) QI HARMS ESSENCE - The essence comes from heaven down into the empty space (Qi Jiao) and gives birth to Qi. The Yellow Emperor says that the heaven's energy penetrates the man and that the man's energy penetrates the heaven too. The heaven's five essences of green, red, yellow, white and black enter into the five Yin organs – liver, heart, spleen, lungs and kidneys respectively. At the same time that the man resides in Qi Jiao, the empty space between heaven and earth, the Qi of Qi Jiao, is the four seasons' energy around us. This Qi, if abnormal, can harm the heaven's essence in the organs. For example, if the spring is cool instead of warm, the Qi can harm the liver's essence (heaven's green essence). In addition, if the Qi in the empty space around us is abnormal, let's say because of a big forest fire or modern day pollution, the essence coming down from heaven cannot be absorbed properly in our body.

C) ESSENCE TRANSFORMS TO BECOME QI - The heaven's essence transforms downward to become Qi here on earth. It is not the Qi on earth that transforms into heaven. This means that the heaven is always in a giving mode. The Qi in Qi Jiao (where we people live) is always in a receiving mode. This means that our Qi cannot really harm the eternal heaven up there. The essence of heaven, which is harmed by Qi in the previous sentence, is the reflected essence on earth, or the reflected essence inside our body, that can be harmed by abnormal Qi. If one understands this concept, one can no longer be afraid of infertility. Heaven constantly gives and renews Qi. It is important to stay in tune with nature, and to stay away from pollution, chemicals, drugs, and processed food that obstruct the absorption of healthy reflections of heaven. Nature's true products will not obstruct.

D) QI CAN BE HARMED BY FLAVOR – Qi is the energy of our life. Qi likes movement, as Qi itself is the result of eternal movements of heaven (essence). Flavor or Yin is energy stillness. It wants to take the movement out of the form. It wants to make the form still and motionless. We must have Yin, otherwise the Yang opening motion will not return into storage. Without Yin there can be no form. We will have no physical body to live in. The Yin, deep inside the earth and unable to be felt or seen is the real reason that the spirit transformation and the heaven movements want to reflect down here on earth where we live. So even though the Yin is responsible for death, it is also responsible for eternal life on our planet. In a small cycle of one man's life or one year's seasons, or one day and one night cycle, the Yin is the reason for the decline. However, in the big cycle of eternal human lineage; generation after generation, year after year, day after day without ever ending, the Yin is the attracting force of life.

The Yellow Emperor explains that the wise man knows that both Yin and Yang are the same. They are both responsible for life from different angles. One is calling for the energy to come and the other is giving the energy that it has to give. That the Qi can be harmed by flavor means that the small cycle has to end for the big cycle to continue. The Yin has to bring the Yang down into storage or into death so it can attract new Yang to emerge in the next cycle. Death is not the end. Death is the end of the small cycle. If we do not die, we will not be able to bear children. Because we die at the end of the small cycle, we can bear children in this cycle if we make the right choices during our lifetime.

The science of reflections is the marvelous heart and soul of Chinese medicine.

THE GREAT TREATISE OF YIN AND YANG REFLECTIONS: *When the (physical) form is deficient, use Qi to warm it up, and when the (heaven's) essence is deficient, use flavor to strengthen it.* Chinese herbs, food, and drinks, have two aspects – energy and flavor. The five energies are warm, hot, even, cool, and cold. The five flavors are sour, bitter, sweet, pungent, and salty. With infertility, as with other disharmonies, if the physical body has a problem, such as fibroids, cysts, blocked tubes, endometriosis, poor eggs, or a tilted uterus, we must determine which energy can remedy the situation (warm, hot, even, cool, or cold). Only then can we choose the most effective herbs. Because energy or Qi enters the form and gives it life, energy heals the physical body and flavor (Yin) heals the energy. This new life in the form can change its physical shape, which is why patients sometimes regard the healing as a "miracle." Flavor (Yin) is the power attracting the heaven's essence to come down here into reflections in our organs. Essence gives birth to Qi. Qi is energy. When the energy is missing, the only tool we have is to give the appropriate flavors at the appropriate time in the right quantity. Strong fire consumes the Qi and mild warmth strengthens the Qi. Strong fire means that flavor brings down the heaven's essence of the south, which is fire and hot energy, but it can also bring the essence of the east, which is mild warmth.

THE FEMALE ENERGY – BY THE LIGHT OF THE MOON

TREATISE OF THE EIGHT MAIN SECTIONS AND A CLEAR SPIRIT: *When the moon begins to grow, the blood and energy begin forming essence and the protective energy starts moving. When the moon is full, the blood and energy are full and the body's flesh is solid. When the moon is empty, the flesh decreases its firmness, the meridians are relatively empty, the protective energy is missing and the physical body is stripped of energy.*

One must recognize these heavenly changes and then regulate the blood and energy accordingly. When the heaven is cold, avoid cold acupuncture, and when the heaven is warm, avoid moxabustion (burning of herbs). When the moon is growing, avoid reducing methods and when the moon is full, avoid tonifying methods. When the moon is empty, do not treat (tonify or reduce, use only even methods) and this is called following the changes of heaven in harmonizing the patient.

Why is the female menstrual cycle one moon long? This is a question related to Yin and Yang. If we take our world and mix into it an energetical polarity, we get life. Life is a constant mixture of two polarities, like the plus and minus of electricity. There is a man and a woman and when the two are brought together, life results. But what makes a man Yang and what makes a woman Yin? Is it because the man received a Y chromosome and the woman didn't? Is that just a coincidence?

Chinese medicine does not believe in "coincidences." There is a reason for everything, even if we don't understand why. **The Yellow Emperor** calls it "the mysterious way of heaven." But when one analyzes this mystery, one can see many things, including an obvious polarity. The day turns into night and the night turns into day. The summer turns into winter and the winter turns into summer. The male has genitalia which are meant to give, and the female has genitalia that are meant to receive.

Lao Zi wrote in chapter "Four Infinities" of the Chinese classic **Dao De Jing:**

> *Before the World exists*
> *Much is mysterious:*
> *Quiet, depthless,*
> *Solitary, unchanging,*
> *Everywhere and ever moving,*
> *The mother of the World.*
> *I do not know its name, so I call it Dao;*
> *I do not know its limit, so I call it infinite.*

Lao Zi uses the description "mother of the world" to describe the energy responsible for creating this world – a feminine energy first captured by the moon. Just like a woman receiving the male's essence, or sperm, the moon is the recipient of the sunlight Yang energy. The growth of this Yang fullness, coming concurrently with the changes of the moon, is the time when the "mysterious" happens and a new life is created. The times of the moon are, as we previously discussed, the times of the three Yin; Tai Yin, Shao Yin, and Jue Yin. A new Yin energy is born as the Yang energy goes into rest. These are the times where we end the life of one day, going to sleep for the night. The moon – the mother of the world – then births us into the dawn of a new life.

The female receives her energy from the moon – the reflection of the sun's Yang energy, which we call Yin energy. So in **Treatise of the Eight Main Sections and a Clear Spirit**, Qi Bo writes:

When the moon starts growing, the blood and energy start forming essence and the protective energy starts moving. When the moon is full, the blood and energy are full and the body's flesh is solid. When the moon is empty, the flesh decreases its firmness, the meridians are relatively empty, the protective energy is missing and the physical body is stripped of energy. One must recognize the above heavenly changes and regulate the blood and energy accordingly.

The woman's blood and energy conform to the moon and increase in volume when the moon is full, allowing the Yang essence to enter. Her energy decreases when the moon is empty, Yin taking over. This is the same principle that causes the water in the sea to rise and sink with low and high tides. The increase in blood and energy when the moon is full allows the Yang essence to enter.

If during the menstrual cycle the Yang essence is introduced into the female and a new Yang is born, the Yin energy will continue to flourish and attach to the new baby, which is a pregnancy. However, if the Yang is not introduced, or if it is introduced but no new Yang is born, the Yin will increase and energy will decline. All the extra Yin energy amassed during the first and second halves of the cycle is discharged out of the body. This is the menses: the extra Yin energy for which the woman's body no longer has any use. The Yang has declined and the Yin energy goes with it into hiding. During a pregnancy where the Yang continues to grow, the woman's Yin and blood can double or even triple, insuring the baby's ability to attract Yang.

The woman's menstrual cycle follows the moon movements in the increase and decrease of Yin energy. It increases to receive the Yang and decreases when there is no new Yang created. It is the best teaching example that our body vibrates in accord with nature.

Why don't all women menstruate when the moon is empty? Our bodies are impacted by a variety of factors in addition to the moon, and it is even more so because we have distanced ourselves from nature. Because of external and internal influences, some women start their cycle before the moon starts its birth and others start their cycle thereafter. A few of my patients tell me that they menstruate like clockwork every time the moon is full or empty, but most women do not conform to this pattern to an exact degree. However, it is clear that the menstrual cycle, at 28 days, is one moon long. When the body is in disharmony with the moon, the period can come every 14 days or every two months, or even not at all. According to **The Yellow Emperor**, the menstrual cycle stops after seven cycles of seven years, or after 49 years. At this point, natural fertility stops and the woman's Yin does not increase and decline with the lunar cycles.

It is important to understand here that the menstrual cycle is not the result of the uterus "wanting" to shed its lining. It is rather because the body is conforming to nature and to the lunar movements. This closeness with nature is important to understand, because if conventional medicine theory is followed instead, birth control pills and/ or fertility drugs will induce menstruation at odd times. This will distort the Yin cycles of the body, taking the patient further away from giving birth to a new Yang. This is not what Lao Zi calls "the mother of the world."

Of course, Western medicine does not recognize the relationship between the female menses and the lunar cycles. Why? As **The Great Treatise of Essentials of the Ultimate Truth** states: *The Yellow Emperor asked: 'I know that the five weather phenomena interact with each other and there are excesses and deficiencies (lunar surge and decline) and that the six spheres take their place to rule the heaven and earth. What is the significance of all this?' Qi Bo bowed and answered: 'This is the big principle of heaven and earth and it reflects into the human spirit.' The emperor said: 'I heard that in heaven this principle unites with the mysterious and on earth it joins with the unexplained. Why is that so?' Qi Bo answered: 'This is how the right path is born. This is also the reason why uneducated doctors become suspicious.'*

MALE AND FEMALE UNITE

The man's energy comes from the sun, while the woman's energy comes from the moon. The menstrual cycle is a Yin action, and its implication is to receive the Yang. The Yin action occurs in the lower part of the body, also called the lower heater. This includes the uterus, kidneys and liver. The man's desire to reproduce is the Yang action. It happens in the upper part of the body, also called the upper heater. This includes the heart, head, and lungs.

THE GREAT TREATISE OF YIN AND YANG REFLECTIONS: *Yin and Yang are the paths of heaven and earth, it is the reason for everything on earth, it is the mother and father of transformation, it is the root of birth and decline, it is the palace of the clear spirit.*

The relationship and harmony of Yin and Yang happens on many different levels. Some levels are physical while some are spiritual. Some levels are easy to understand while some are difficult.

NOTE TO THE READER: This discussion of spiritual and physical levels may be difficult to understand. It may require more than one reading. If you come across a section that is vague and/or obscure, please leave it behind and read further. Later on, you can go back to it.

NINE MONTHS PREGNANCY – THE SECRET OF LIFE AND DEATH

Pregnancy is the story of life and death, two events which are very much dependent on each other. In Chinese medicine, this dependency is referred to as the secret of life and death.

In today's mechanical world, we believe that a sperm enters an egg, then chromosomes unite and the cells begin to divide. A fetus develops out of this mutation – arms and legs, brain, heart, and other organs – and we have a baby.

I believe that pregnancy, which is life and death, carries a different story. It is a story of a dying man. A man who lived to 80, lived his life to its fullest, and spawned many children and grandchildren. This man had many stories throughout his life. How he loved and hated, worked for many years to support his family, and how his eyes filled with tears of joy as he saw his children becoming successful and having their own children. On his death bed, this handsome man of life battled a grave disease of death. As life was running out, his wishes and desires began to change. He saw no use for clothes, food, and entertainment. His only desires were to enjoy the warm morning sun and sip water.

Treatise on Acupuncture Prohibitions: *The liver is born on the left and the lungs are stored on the right. The heart distributes to the exterior, while the kidneys rule the interior.* This statement makes no sense from a modern anatomical point of view. The liver is not on the left and the lungs are not on the right, the heart is not outside and the kidneys are not necessarily more inside than other organs.

We must discuss the art of numbers of Chinese medicine to understand. **The Yellow Emperor** says: *Heaven One created water and the earth Six completed it. Earth two created fire and the heaven Seven completed it. Heaven Three created wood and the earth Eight completed it. Earth Four created metal and the heaven Nine completed it. Heaven Five created earth and the earth Ten completed it.* A chart of these numbers, called **He Tu** ("The River Chart") represents the foundation of Chinese medicine and dates back at least 2500 years. It contains hollow dots, representing odd numbers (1, 3, 5, 7, 9) also known as heaven's numbers, as well as solid dots representing even numbers (2, 4, 6, 8, 10), also known as the earth's numbers.

HE TU

As we already know, the circle explains much of Chinese medicine's understanding of life and death, of pregnancy and birth. The east is where the sun rises and the west is where the sun descends. The east is where the spring begins and the west is where the fall enters into storage. The east is where the morning begins and the west is where the evening descends.

As previously explained, the east and west ascending and descending are the levers of the exiting of the Yang energy and entering of the Yang's storage. Rising and descending are the two handles that cause the Yang to go out of storage or "exit" and back into storage or "enter." These two planes, east-west and north-south, are called Jing and Wei. The north-south plane, or Jing, connects heaven and earth and is where water and fire unite to create life. The east-west plane, or Wei, is where the two levers of ascending and descending give us the motions of life.

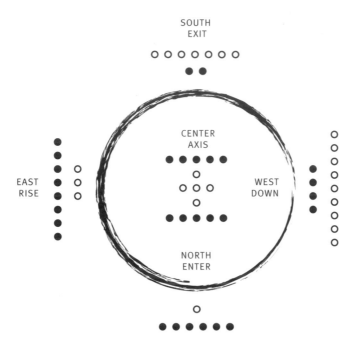

This plane causes the Yang to exit and enter, to expand and contract with every breath we take, on every daily cycle, on every month, and on every year. Every cycle of life's energy is pulled and pushed by the east-west levers.

The Yellow Emperor says that the Qi has four directions: rising, descending, exiting and entering. The River Chart below depicts the attachment of the five Yin organs to the five directions.

The liver, which belongs to the east, is on the left. The lungs, which belong to the west, are on the right. The heart, which belongs to the south, is on the "exiting" and the kidneys, which belong to the north, are on the "entering." The liver and lungs are on the east-west axis, while the heart and kidneys are on the north-south axis. **The Yellow Emperor** says that the heaven One, which is the heart, descends into the north to create water. He also says that the earth Two, which are the two kidneys, ascend to the south to create the fire. This is the reason that we have two kidneys. At the same time, secondary but not less important, are the heaven Three that create wood in the east (or left) and the earth Four that create metal in the west (or right). This is the east-west axis that ensures life is cycling after the initial creation. The heaven Three

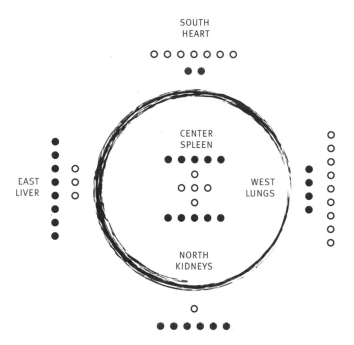

is an odd number and is why there is one liver, while the earth Four is an even number and why we have two lungs. Finally, we have the number Five, which creates the earth and the spleen. This is the center axis for the Jing and the Wei, as it is likewise the center point for the east-west and north-south axis. As in a revolving wheel, the center of the wheel is the focal point. It has to fix the axis so that the wheel can rotate smoothly without jumping in disarray. The spleen, which is the only organ in the center of the body, has a harmonizing function of all four directions. It is the focal point for the axis.

While the east-west axis is the action during life itself, the north-south axis is the creation and end of life. The heart and the kidneys, or what we previously described as the Shao Yin, is the axis for the creation and end of life – it is the axis for the "entering" and "exiting" of life. When **The Yellow Emperor** described the heart as distributing to the exterior and the kidneys ruling the interior, it corresponds to this description of the "entering" and "exiting" axis.

Now, let's return to the story of the man who lived his life to its fullest. On his deathbed, he desired only water and to spend time in the warming sun. He felt no desire for food, clothes or entertainment. Water and sun make-up the north-south axis, the origin of life which unites with death on the same axis. We enter and exit life from the same axis which connects heaven and earth, water and fire, and Yin and Yang. The heaven One gives birth to water and the earth Two gives birth to fire, The heart warms up the kidneys and the kidneys cool off the heart. One cannot do without the other.

This basic north-south axis requirement for life is the same for fertility and pregnancy. Pregnancy needs the north-south axis. It needs the one and the two, the male and the female. The One and Two start from the male and female hearts as represented by their emotions – love, passion and desire, and ends with the male and female kidneys represented by their genitalia and reproductive organs. These are a must for a healthy pregnancy and healthy future generations.

The ten months of pregnancy take place in the center of the female body. This is where Yin and Yang are in their most advanced state of harmony, at the spleen pivot point of the two axes. The north-south and east-west cross through the center, and it is because of the center that the north-south axis can transform into the east-west. The primordial life creation (pregnancy) can turn into life itself (baby).

There is a very specific reason why nature designed a man and a woman, a One and a Two, and brought them together. It was to enable the creation of this north-south axis, which during a pregnancy, passes through nine stages, or months, of pregnancy that corresponds to the entire transformation of the "River Chart." Again, the transformations of the "River Chart" are Heaven One gives birth to water and Earth Six completes it. Earth Two gives birth to fire and Heaven Seven completes it. Heaven Three gives birth to wood and Earth Eight completes it. When the entire cycle is complete at the number ten, the fetus can exit the mother with its own east-west axis. It will go back to the north-south axis before death. When conception occurs, the mother and father are horizontal in the east-west axis, but immediately thereafter they stand up and go back to the north-south axis, which is heaven and earth. The fetus is initially horizontal and as the months go by turns into the vertical axis south-north with the head pointing down, but emerging, turns upside down so the head can be pointing upward to heaven.

The baby will still spend the first few months of his life in a horizontal position, crawling until he matures to the point where he can maintain his own north-south axis, when he can sit, stand up and walk. He will then return to the east-west axis every night when going to sleep. This changing of axis from east-west to north-south is instrumental when it comes to insuring the prosperity of future generations.

I have questioned a midwife for statistics regarding women who begin labor at night. She estimated that 80 percent of pregnant women going into labor between 11 PM and 3 AM, the time of the Shao Yin. It is the time of the day where the north-south axis is dominant. I asked an oncologist about similar statistics for terminally ill cancer patients, and was told that approximately 70 percent expire at the same Shao Yin time. It is statistically significant that 70 percent of the people die in 17 percent of the day.

During nine months of pregnancy and the tenth month of delivery, a fetus will develop its physical and energetical body as it proceeds through the numbers: the creation of water, fire, wood, metal and earth. During the different stages, different body parts and organs are created and different aspects of the energy and spirit form. Chen Xiuyuan writes in his work **Superficial Comments on the Yellow Emperor**: *This is because the heaven's Qi penetrates through the body and because the body's Qi penetrates through the heavens.* The reason that the fetus develops is not because it is a "coincidence." It is because it is influenced by heaven's Qi or by the life-force around us. This is what gives us life. This is what causes our development inside the womb and outside of it.

For all of this to work properly we need a healthy One and Two. We need a healthy man and woman for a perfect north-south axis. The baby will enter the world with an east-west axis and live his life to the fullest until going back to the north-south during the exit.

When **The Yellow Emperor** says that the heart distributes to the exterior and the kidneys control the interior, this refers to the 'entry' and 'exit' of life. The kidneys are used for reproduction and they are the tool for "entry," while the heart is used to connect the spirit to heaven and it is the tool used for "exit." **The Yellow Emperor** says that the five Yin organs transmit their essence to the heart and that the heart connects to the five heaven energies via the eyes. On his deathbed, the old man closes his eyes and this connection between the Yin organs and the heaven's energies subsides. The connection to heaven becomes looser and looser.

When one tries to alter the north-south or east-west with artificial medications and procedures, it is going against nature's intention and is bound to fail. I believe in the old adage: "If you mess with nature, it will mess with you." If you are not in good health and your kidneys are weak at the time of conception, the north-south will not meet, and infertility will result. On the other hand, if you are healthy according to Chinese medicine, your kidneys are strong and your north-south can meet, you are fertile and can become pregnant, whether or not Western medicine has diagnosed you as infertile.

When the parents are healthy in the "north-south fashion" they should trust that the pregnancy they achieved is real. Most intervention in the shape of pills and foreign substances impacting the mother will offset this balance.

QUESTION "THE PILL"

A woman's health and fertility should not be decided by a male dominated health insurance industry, nor be decided by a pharmaceutical industry heavily influenced by western medicine associations. The decision about a woman's fertility should be given to the woman who is seeking the treatment.

Let's take the female menstrual cycle for example. In my practice, I have seen thousands of patients who have taken the birth control pill for different reasons. Of the patients who had irregular periods before taking the pill, and became regular while on the pill, none of them retained the regularity once discontinuing the pill. Of the patients who had regular periods before taking the pill, and regular periods while on the pill, quite a number became irregular when discontinuing the pill.

In Chinese medicine, we seek harmony with nature and with the lunar cycles when we attempt to regulate the menses. I have witnessed many patients who regulated their periods while taking herbs and Chinese medicine. Not only did their period become regular, it also stayed regular for years after stopping the herbal consumption. In addition, treating infertility with herbs aims at restoring harmony. The goal is to ovulate one egg per lunar cycle, not 30 eggs, which is the goal of modern drugs.

Estrogen and progesterone that occur naturally in the body to regulate the menses is the body's response to the lunar cycles in nature. This cycle will be changed after conception and during pregnancy. The progesterone will not decline but rather increase to maintain the pregnancy. Even though these hormones are physical chemicals, they are not the cause for the menstrual cycle, but are rather a response to the Yin energy changing and the growth and decline.

When a patient who is irregular begins menstruating like clockwork on taking the pill, it is clear that the blood deficiency is still there and even aggravates with time. The drugs may be prompting the menstruation bleeding to happen regularly, but the blood is not strong. This will desynchronize the woman farther from a lunar cycle harmony. In other words, not only is she losing blood every month, the blood is deficient. From the Chinese medicine science perspective, this is not possible according to nature. It is unnatural and in fact is considered "miraculous".

THE MALE ENERGY – NOT AS QUICK AS IT LOOKS

The man participates in the process of creation for approximately two minutes. After that, the woman does it by herself. However, if we can briefly peek into a different dimension – a dimension of spirituality – then the scenario is completely different.

In Chinese medicine, as in many religions, the spirit is an integral part of the body. In Judaism, for example, the body and spirit are analogized as a candle and its flame. The candle is a cup or a vessel holding olive oil, and when it is lit, the flame feeds on the olive oil. The flame cannot exist without the vessel, and although the vessel can exist without the flame, it is just a useless cup. So is the case with our body and spirituality. The body is like the vessel and the spirituality is like the flame. The primary element in our existence here on earth is our spirituality, but we cannot be spiritual without our body and our health.

The two most obvious phenomena we can see in nature are the sun and the moon. In Judaism and in Chinese medicine, the sun is the male, constantly radiating hot energy, and the moon is the female, receiving the sun's warmth.

While we are warmed and sustained by the outer most layer of the sun, the inside essence of the sun must be transmitted to us in order to create life. To do this, nature created the moon to reflect the sun's inner energy back to us without reflecting its intense heat. This reflection of the essence is the moon's job, but the essence itself is the sun's essence.

The reason that we have a sun and a moon, a male and a female, a Yin and a Yang, is to enable the Yang essence to find a place in the Yin. The sun's essence can be reflected into the moon and then onto earth. The male's essence can be deposited in the female and reflected into the baby. According to the Jewish Kabala, the life's energy begins from above the male, travels into his brain, down his spine, into his kidneys and out through his penis into the female, depositing this sun's essence into the moon to create new life. The new life has started from the sun's essence, or in other words, has been spawned from the male's spirituality.

Again, if we only think in physical terms, then the sperm is just a piece of material produced in the male's testes. The only difference between sperm and a rock is that the sperm has a genetic code on it and genetic code makes life.

In my view, the modern scientific idea that human genes alone contain the code of life is so superficial and redundant that it is difficult to understand how widely it is accepted. Simply consider that a sperm, which is microscopic, creates an embryo, fetus, baby, toddler, adult, and an old man – a 100-year cycle of emotions, physical and spiritual worlds. A sperm must be more than just a microscopic piece of matter. It is similar, in fact, to a nuclear reactor in terms of the power imbedded within.

The sperm is the Yang energy that gives life. It is spiritually powerful. It is transferring the power that resides in the male's health and in his spiritual clearance into the child to come. If the husband's spirit is down, depleted or disturbed, conception cannot happen. This is why so many IVFs fail – because it is difficult to unite the husband's spirit with his sperm in a laboratory. There is no romance or intimacy or love involved. Love, in fact, is spirituality. It is the vehicle which takes the husband's spirituality into the sperm. A woman becoming pregnant without a loving husband is like the moon existing without the sun.

As **The Great Treatise of Yin and Yang Reflections** states: *Yin and Yang are the paths of heaven and earth, it is the reason for everything on earth, it is the mother and father of transformation, it is the root of birth and decline, it is the palace of the clear spirit.*

The palace of the clear spirit and the root of birth are closely related. Clear spirituality provides the optimum conditions for birth. Of course, both parents must be of clear spirit, but the father must develop his spirituality specifically for the purpose of conception, and nurture it from the day he is born until the day he conceives. By contrast, the mother's spirituality is of great importance from the time of conception until the moment she gives birth. After birth, the spirits of both parents unite in an effort to grow the spirituality of their child so that he or she can bear children when the time is right.

The female can take the male essence and make a new life out of it. She takes the light of the male and transforms it into a new kind of light she reflects forward, transforming the previous generation into a new one.

Chinese medicine theory is so developed that most people simply can't understand it today and modern science lags far behind it. Nevertheless, some bright western scientists are looking beyond the normal quota. For example, Dr Johanna Budwig, a seven-time Nobel Prize nominee, writes in her book **Flax Oil as Aid against Cancer**: *The living mass of mankind derives its being, as does all life in nature, from the sun! This has been forgotten until now in biology and medical science.* She also writes: *Solar energy electrons are both wave and matter! Nobel winner De Broglie writes that light is the fastest, purest, lightest and most beautiful form of matter we know, as well as the fastest and purest form of energy we are aware of. As the fast emissary from star to star, sunlight electrons are always, whatever their condition, both wave and matter. The electron is a form of matter always surrounded by magnetism. It can be measured as either matter or wave. This borderline situation between energy and matter overturns all classical physics, and is extraordinarily interesting as well as of vital importance in respect of physiological, medical and biological problems.*

What is "energy and matter" if not the concept of heaven and earth, and Yin and Yang? The next step in modern science development will be the improvement of Western medicine into a different realm, from a physical world into an "energy and life force" world. This will then become closer to the Chinese medicine realm.

MALE VITALITY – ALL YOU NEED IS LOVE

The "thought" that is the seed of conception descends from the male brain, down his spine, to his kidneys and out his penis as a white drop ready to enter into his female partner. The penis is like a dead organ. Ninety nine percent of the time it is shrunken and useless. For a brief moment every day, or every week or every month, the penis becomes alive due to the "thought." The testicles are simply the home of the physical sperm, the sperm's energy emanating from the "thought" and from the spirit.

Many men are devastated by the infertility treatments administered to their wives. Physically, the sperm seems to be fine. All the drugs, laparoscopies and procedures are aimed at the prospective mother. The husband, longing to impregnate his wife, has an inborn need to imbue the next life in the woman just like the sun gives its essence to the moon. He also has the innate impulse to protect his wife from harm at a time when infertility treatments are placing her in harm's way due to side effects, surgery, pain and financial stress. This situation creates havoc in the male's spirit. It is nearly impossible for him to transfer his spirituality into the sperm, and hence, it is nearly impossible for the wife to become pregnant.

In a couple's relationship and desire for a baby, the male's spirituality is key. The vitality of his spirit is just as or more important than the vitality of his physical body. In the past, women were considered inferior to men. Although this has thankfully changed today, the new dynamic that men and women are equal has spawned a new assumption that no matter what happens, the male will never feel inferior, emasculated, and spiritually broken. This is a big mistake. Many men have a broken spirit because of this new dynamic. You can't see it from the outside, but the problem is there.

The solution is love, for that alone is what will make the dynamic work. Love means that the wife feels she will do whatever her husband wants, and in turn the husband feels that he will do whatever his wife wants. No husband wants to see his wife get hurt and no wife wants to see her husband emasculated. The male vitality is kept intact by the woman making the man happy through vibrating the message to him that she loves him and he is enough. This in turn, allows him to protect and provide for the wife, the true joy of the husband.

The wife does not rely entirely on her spirituality to nourish the fetus. She rather relies on her Yin energy, as well as her blood. When the wife's Yin spirit and blood suffer, the couple can still become pregnant, but it is highly likely that there will be a miscarriage.

In my practice, both partners receive herbal treatment, although the wife does receive more of the treatment as she does with Western procedures. The difference is that with my treatment, the husband knows that his wife is growing healthier, and hence, he has the ability to protect his wife, and his vitality is not compromised.

THE ESSENCE OF SPIRITUALITY

The sun, as far as we know, is a great ball of fire. Yet it is different than the fire in your kitchen, which must be cautiously fed in order to keep itself going. The sun, on the other hand, is eternal. Its flame runs on a different source: the internal essence of the sun.

The sun reflects in us as human beings and especially in men. It keeps us running with its eternal essence. In Judaism, Christianity, Buddhism, Daoism, and all other religions, this essence is virtue – the will power to do good deeds, charity, and other beneficial actions for others. It is what makes us want to love our child or help a friend.

This virtue is the spirituality source of life. Although women have virtue too, virtue is the male's strongest quality. This is the same source that feeds down to the male brain and "thought," down the spine, the kidneys, and out the penis into the female partner.

The moon receives the essence of the sun, becomes pregnant with it, and then reflects it to women on earth. This energy is about bravery, which means that courage and strength are the female's strongest qualities. Because the moon predominantly impacts the woman, the woman's strongest quality is courage and strength. When a woman becomes pregnant and delivers a baby, her courage is beyond anything a man can imagine.

When a man deposits his virtue through his white drop (semen and sperm), the woman possesses the courage to harbor it, and becomes pregnant with it. The courage continues by the internal source of the moon. Every month the moon disappears, but then has the courage to come back for another cycle. The woman will find the courage in her to become pregnant and deliver a baby, to raise the child through difficult times and hardship. Without the courage of the woman, there would be no life.

The virtue quality that men possess is also about "letting go." He lets go of his sperm – and the necessary accompanying spirit – when he releases it into the woman. The courage of a woman is embodied in "holding on," even clinging to things. This spirit is needed for holding on to the sperm and onto pregnancy. This energy is also needed for building a home for the family.

Virtue and courage are needed by both men and women throughout their lives, but when a man has too much courage, or when a woman has too much virtue, problems may result. It is the same as relying on the moon to warm us, or the sun to reflect on us. The sun, although warming and lighting the way during the day, cannot dispel the darkness at night as the moon can. The sun is simply absent altogether at night. It does not have the brave quality that the moon exhibits.

Yaron also mentions a case involving Dan, who suffered from erectile dysfunction, which only occurred around his wife's ovulation. Dan's doctor recommended Viagra. Nevertheless, Dan and his wife did not conceive for three years, even with two IVF cycles. Yaron says that Dan then received herbal treatment and within three months the erectile function recovered and within two more months the couple conceived. His problem, according to Yaron was a deteriorated heart fire aggravated by 'trying to conceive' pressure. Yaron says that he improved to the point that his wife no longer needed to chart temperature or use ovulation kits. Dan says that it was so easy without all the pressure.

UNDERSTANDING INFERTILITY
THE RIGHT WAY

THE LIFE INSIDE YOUR WOMB

"Goodness-of-fit" is a child psychology term first used by Thomas and Chess in 1977. It explains that the social environment of a child will impact the child's future development. A mother has certain expectations from her child even from before it is born. She doesn't want her child to be sick or misbehave. She does want her child to be healthy, strong, and intelligent. When a child behaves the way his mother wishes, it is referred to as a "Goodness-of-fit."

It is the same case in the reverse role. A child has certain expectations of his mother. He wants her to be nourishing, warm, and understanding of his frustrations. He does not want his mother to abandon him, ignore him, or shout at him. When a mother behaves in a way that fulfills the child's wishes, it is "Goodness-of-fit."

Thomas and Chess explain that "Goodness-of-fit" allows the child to develop in a positive way – to grow into a fulfilled adult. Without it, the child will no doubt have emotional issues as an adult.

This "Goodness-of-fit" is just as important in the womb as it is outside. In Western medicine, the most important priority to insure that fit is making certain the baby is receiving the proper vitamins. But the baby needs much more than that. The baby needs a lifeline. Where there is no life to carry, the child cannot be born.

THE SIX SPHERES OF ENERGY

To understand lifeline we must first be very clear about the significance of Yin and Yang. The six spheres include three Yin and three Yang, both sides comprised of opening, closing, and pivot. To understand the difference between the three Yang and the three Yin, it is helpful to put things into the concept of "time." As we have seen in previous chapters, each of the six spheres has a different time during a Yin and Yang full 24-hour, 29.5 day, or 12-month cycle.

For simplification purposes, I will only use a 24-hour day cycle and A, B, C instead of the Chinese names of the time periods (A-Zi, B-Chou, C-Yin, D-Mao, E-Chen, F-Si, G-Wu, H-Wei, I-Shen, J-You, K-Xu, L-Hai). First, let's review the locations of the time periods during the day.

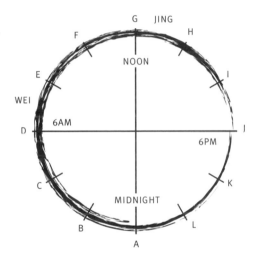

Each time period extends two hours in length, giving us a total of 12 time periods within one 24-hour period. Segment "A" is from 11 PM to 1 AM, "B" is from 1 AM to 3 AM, "C" is from 3 AM to 5 AM and so forth.

The Tai Yang phase starts from "A" and finishes at "G." "A," around midnight, is the time where the new Yang energy is the coldest, having just been born. "G," around noon, is when the Yang energy is opened up the widest at the warmest time of the day. Yang Ming starts at "G" (noon), the Yang slowly closing down until it reaches its most closed state at "A," or midnight.

This "opening" and "closing" process requires a pivot, the Shao Yang minister fire. The more the Yang energy opens, the higher goes the temperature – whether that corresponds to the time of day, or the seasons of the year. To open, the Tai Yang needs the help of the minister fire.

While Tai Yang needs to be close to the minister fire, the Yang Ming needs to distance itself from the fire in order to close. Consequently, Zhonging explains in the **Shang Hanlun** that the Shao Yang minister fire time is in the east from "C" until "E", while the Yang Ming time is exactly opposite, from "I" until "K" in the west. The Shao Yang minister fire helps warm up the Tai Yang because it is overlapping the same time period, and also helps cool off the Yang Ming because it is far away from the Yang Ming or opposite to it. This is the "pivot" function of the three Yang spheres.

If the three Yang spheres – opening, closing and pivot – occupy the entire 24 hours of the day, where do the three Yin spheres fit in? According to Zhang Zhongjing's description in the Shang Hanlun, the Tai Yin sphere begins at "L" and continues to "B." Shao Yin is from "A" until "C," while Jue Yin is from "B" to "D."

The three Yin occupy a much shorter time period than the Yang, from 9 PM until 7 AM. The Yin and Yang, then, are not equal in quantity.

The Yellow Emperor classics explain in great detail the three Yin and three Yang. Each one of the six spheres has a root energy and a manifestation, which was explained in chapter 2. These are the Tai Yang cold water, Shao Yang minister fire, Yang Ming dry metal, Tai Yin damp earth, Shao Yin emperor fire and Jue Yin wind wood.

Within the three Yin, Tai Yin is "opening," Jue Yin is "closing," and Shao Yin is the "pivot." From a superficial point of view it seems that "opening," "closing." and "pivot" is quite easy to understand. The Yin opens up, the Yin closes down, and there is a pivot that helps harmonize their opening and closing. In reality, this is not so. It is not like a simple machine.

Observe the four seasons. In three of the four – spring, summer and fall – we are able to watch the state of the Yang energy with our naked eye (leaves budding, flourishing and falling). However, in winter we cannot see the Yang energy in storage (trees are naked). We can, however, sense it with our heart.

This same phase is the storage phase that Zhongjing attributes to the Yin spheres – the time of darkness. So why do we have Yin altogether? We need to look back to the Chinese medicine classics to understand. **The Yellow Emperor** describes the annual four seasons in five phases, including the birth and growth phases representing the spring and summer, and the wood and fire elements respectively. Then there is a transformation phase, "Hua", which represents the late summer and the earth element. Following "transformation" are the decline and storage phases representing the fall and winter, and metal and water elements respectively.

HUA

BIAN HUA

The Chinese word **Hua** (transformation) historically has a pair word, **Bian** (Change). Together they are widely used as Bian Hua (changes and transformations).

However, if we study these two words closely, we learn about the difference between them. In the classics, it is said that when a substance is born, it is called Hua (transformation) and when the substance dies, it is called Bian (change). Together Bian Hua translates to birth and death of a substance. Birth and death are the ultimate changes that anything or anyone can go through. As we have seen, The Yellow Emperor inserts Hua (transformation/birth) between the birth/growth and the decline/storage phases. At the same time, he does not insert the word Bian (change/ death) between the storage phase of winter and the birth phase of spring. This hidden idea is very important for us in order to understand the meaning of Yin.

The Yang commences opening at midnight and stops opening at noon, when there is transformation (Hua), allowing the Yang to return into storage to become stronger. If the Yang energy goes into storage and does not re-emerge, this is death (Bian). **The Yellow Emperor** then omits the word Bian from the sequence. He does not insert "death" between the winter's storage and the spring's birth. Here, where the word "Bian" was supposed to be, we are allowed to enter the realm of the three Yin, from where the Yang re-springs the next morning. The reason we are able to wake up every morning is the three Yin, which are the root of life.

Our next step is to understand what actually happens in the three Yin that propels our life forward, and why the Shao Yin emperor fire serves as an axis.

For this purpose, we turn to several quotes from the classic **Miraculous Pivots – Chapter of Ying and Wei.** This classic often refers to Shao Yin and Yang Ming as the core of Yin and Yang and in this chapter it also mentions the function of the Tai Yin and Tai Yang. It says: *"The man receives his energy (Qi) from the food, the food enters the stomach and then the energy is transported to the lungs, then the five Yin and six Yang organs all receive energy."*

From this ancient text we can see the function of the three Yang and some of the function of the three Yin. When water and food enter our stomach, they are transformed into our Yang energy. This Yang energy takes many shapes and forms. It can be the energy of the inner organs, it can become the protective energy that defends us from harmful influences or it can also be the nutritive energy that nourishes our body. **The Yellow Emperor** describes this energy as reaching the "four seas," meaning every aspect of our life.

The ancient text explains: *When Yang energy reaches the Yang phase it starts moving and when it reaches the Yin phase it stops.*

Knowing that our energy circulates 50 times in our body during one day and one night, the ancients explained that the Yang stops *"50 cycles and the energy returns to Da Hui (big meeting place)."* Da Hui means at midnight or at the time of A – 11 PM-1:00 AM. The text then explains that *at midnight, where Da Hui happens, all the people are asleep.* Midnight is the time where all the Yang energy returns. This is the time when the three Yin take action.

As we have learned, Tai Yin is earth dampness, Shao Yin is emperor fire and Jue Yin is wind wood. The Miraculous Pivot states: *The human being reflects heaven and earth and responds to the sun and the moon.* Reflecting heaven and earth means that the human being contains a heaven element and another earth element. Heaven contains the six spheres, while earth contains the five elements. Heaven is three Yin and three Yang energy, while earth is bones, tendons, muscles, skin, and hair. Our Yin and Yang energies come from heaven, while our body comes from earth. The interplay of Yin and Yang is such that Yang opens up during the day and closes down in the evening. Yin is the bridge allowing the Yang to reopen. This happens in three stages. First Tai Yin earth has to create dampness. Dry earth is a dead earth, and dryness as we've seen in chapter 2 is the absence of Yang in the water. Tai Yin earth occupies the time when the daily Yang is closed, starting at 9 PM. The daily Yang is called Xing.

In order for the earth to create damp, it needs Yang. This Yang comes from the Shao Yin emperor fire as the second step. Its fire is called Ming or true fire. Xing and Ming are two types of Yang energy. The first belongs to the three Yang, while the latter belongs to the three Yin. Xing is the Yang energy we receive from food and drink and which we use for our daily activities. Ming is the pre-natal Yang energy we receive from our parents. The Ming energy is transmitted to the baby during conception and it is stored in the Shao Yin. The third step

XING   MING

allows the Jue Yin to put a pause in the true fire, keeping it from being wasted. The Ming or true Yang energy of the Shao Yin is what we call "lifeline." It comes swiftly at midnight to revive the sleeping Xing and allows life to continue.

When we talk about the Yin and Yang energies in our body, they are not heaven and earth but rather water and fire. The Yin of our body is coming from the three Yin of heaven (Kan- water) and the Yang of our body is coming from the three Yang of heaven (Li – fire). What we get from the earth is our body. When a person dies, even though the Yang energy separates from the Yin energy and are both extinct, the body of the person is still lying on the ground lifeless. The dead body does not have any Yang energy or any Yin energy. It belongs to the earth. It has no Xing or Ming. The energy of the body – three Yin and three Yang – belongs to heaven.

INFERTILITY AND SHAO YIN – ESSENCES EXCHANGED

Our life relies on "true fire," which belongs to the same category as the Yang energy, yet it is not the same as Yang energy. "True fire" is the Shao Yin emperor fire. In the Shao Yin there are two organs; heart and kidneys. The heart represents fire and it is the emperor organ in the Chinese medicine anatomy, while the kidneys represent water and are responsible for reproduction and the sex organs. Heart and kidneys compose the post-heaven water-fire relationship needed for life.

The book of changes **Yi Jing** states: *"The male and female exchange essences and then the myriad things are born."* What is the meaning of this quote? Fire is the man's heart desire for the woman and the woman's heart desire for the man. Water is the reliance on the sex organs for sexual activity and reproduction. The exchange of water and fire is necessary for the exchange of male and female essences. When the water or fire is deficient, the exchange cannot be complete. If the exchange of essences is not complete then the likelihood of a pregnancy is decreased. This is what we call infertility.

In modern medicine, all research is focused on Xing, the material, and nothing is focused on Ming, the lifeline energy. This is why patients and doctors alike are occupied with physical findings such as hormones, fibroids, cysts, and fallopian tubes, as if something "physical" must be obstructing the conception's "physical" process.

In reality this is not the case. The main cause of infertility is an obstacle with the "lifeline." The essences of the fire and water from the father and/or mother have a problem. This is why many of my male patients have "perfect" sperm, but cannot conceive with their wives until their Shao Yin is brought into balance. This is also the case with many of my female patients who suffer "unexplained" or "explained" infertility and yet, when their Shao Yin true fire is fixed, they can get pregnant.

In **Miraculous Pivots, The Yellow Emperor** explains that when food and water enter the stomach, the body separates the energy into clear and turbid. The clear energy enters the inner Yin spheres of the body, while the turbid energy enters the external Yang spheres. The famous commentator Zhang Zhicong wrote: *The pre-heaven state of heaven-earth has just reached the post-heaven state of water-fire.* This is in essence how our body uses nature around us to sustain life, transforming the Xing into Ming.

We can see that the clear and most purified energy derived from our food, water, and the air we breathe, enters into the Yin spheres to help with the emperor fire's activity of "saving life." The father and mother have Shao Yin water-fire activity. The embryo needs it as well. If the father and mother are lacking the essences of water and fire, then the embryo cannot form. Treating infertility is the treatment of water and fire. It is the treatment of Shao Yin. After seeing many patients, I can testify that at least seven or eight out of every ten have a Shao Yin problem, with symptoms such as cold hands and feet, hot flashes followed by a cold feeling, slightly red face with a thirst for warm liquids, thin and small pulse, and exhaustion as a result of insomnia. I normally use herbal formulas to strengthen the Shao Yin water and fire, and many of my patients are blessed with beautiful babies.

THE CONSTANT LINK

Shao Yin disease, then, is the main cause of infertility. This statement seems simple but in reality has many variables. Many religions explain that when we die, our bodies return to earth, and our spirits return to heaven. However, from one generation to the other, there is a continuous link. It is not only heaven and earth that we need, but rather the direct lifeline from our parents. If this lifeline is broken, life stops.

As we explained above, there is Ming – pre-heaven – and there is Xing, which is post-heaven. Diseases can arise in either of these states. In our daily life (Xing) we can do the wrong things that will make us sick; in our embryonic life (Ming) our parents can do the wrong things that will make us sick or shorten our life. The cervical cancer cases from DES, for example, represent a pre-heaven disease, in that they were a direct result of actions taken by the mother. Even though most of us want to do the right things when we are pregnant so our baby will be healthy, we may have a serious problem fulfilling that wish because we are relying solely on the knowledge of modern science. Medical doctors are occupied with the prevention of immediate birth defects, however, defects beyond birth are no less important. How will the baby grow up to be an adult? How will he or she reproduce and create another generation? These questions are completely outside the scope of Western medicine. In contrast, Chinese medicine has researched the long-term effects of treatment, passing the knowledge down from one generation to the next.

MEDICINE IS IN THE DOCTOR'S HEART

"Yi Zhe Xin Ye" is an ancient Chinese idiom that means: medicine is heart. Chen Xiuyuan in his book **Prescriptions Poems from Chang Sha**, wrote: *The good or bad fortune of the patient is entrusted to the doctor. Thus the doctor's responsibility is great. However, the power is not entrusted in the hand of medicine, but rather in the hand of the person practicing the medicine.*

The natural desire to assist another person in need was designated by Confucius as "virtue." The desire to help the sick was designated by the sage as **Yi De** meaning "medicine's virtue," which, all who learn to practice medicine must have. A sick person is defined as anyone who has lost his or her balance, either within himself or with his surroundings. Whether it is the Yin or the Yang, the doctor's responsibility is to know the origin of the problem, which medicinal remedy to use for treatment, and how to bring this patient back to harmony. The reason behind studying medicine and becoming a doctor, according to the sages, is only one: to help sick people become healthier. If the doctor follows this path of virtue he becomes one with the Dao. He is a true doctor.

The doctor's virtue pushes him on an endless quest for knowledge. He wants to know how to insure the safety and health of his patients. When a doctor adopts a path that causes his patient's health to deteriorate, even if he is not aware of it, the offense under heaven is unparalleled. With heavy weight on their shoulders, the sages put their lives at stake in the quest for truth in medicine. When and if the physician made a mistake at the imperial court, he would lose his head the next day.

Today, many doctors in Western and Chinese medicine save lives on a daily basis and their work is unmatched. On the other hand, many others ruin lives. The difference lies in their possession or absence of virtue.

For example, a patient who recently underwent IVF began the drug protocol perfectly healthy and with no complaints. Within a few days of ingesting the drugs, her tongue coating began to deteriorate, and a week later, the rear half of the tongue coating was completely missing. She suddenly began feeling weak and tired, and the skin over the front of her leg became sensitive as if there were needles underneath it.

I treated the patient with acupuncture, but this could not save her kidney's essence, nor could it help her original Yang. I felt as if an invisible hand entered my heart and squeezed it. The pain stayed with me until the evening. When she asked her doctor about these "side effects" he plainly dismissed them as "normal".

The situation is not as grave with modern Chinese medicine, however it has similarities. Patients with deficient original Yang are often diagnosed as Yin deficient and receive greasy, thick, cold herbs harming their lifeline further.

The job of the patient is to educate herself and tune herself into her condition. If she believes her condition is worsening with treatment, she must transition to another option.

IVF AND THE ROOT OF LIFE

As we now understand the importance of a lifeline, I want to share with you my personal Chinese medicine experience with IVF and fertility drugs. During an IVF treatment, heavy doses of various synthetic drugs and synthetic hormones are utilized. Patients typically suffer side effects, such as feeling hot flashes followed by immediately feeling cold, a bloated lower abdomen, irregular periods, headaches, lower back pain, red tongue, slow pulse, as well as the deterioration of the tongue coating to patchy or completely missing.

From a classical Chinese medicine point of view, these symptoms are all under the same category of deteriorating Shao Yin and diminishing "true fire." **The Yellow Emperor says:** *When the Yang is born, the Yin flourishes, and when the Yang retreats, the Yin stores.* The first part of this quote refers to the Shao Yin emperor fire (Ming). When the Shao Yin true fire is born, then the kidney's water is flourishing, and the Shao Yin is thriving. The second part of this quote refers to the three Yang's Yang energy (Xing). When this Yang energy retreats inward, then the Tai Yin begins preparing the storage or the Yin function of saving life.

We can see from the following diagram that the Yang energy description of "born" and "retreat" sits on the horizontal Xing line and the Yin description of "store" and "flourish" sits on the vertical Ming line. In chapter 2, we described this as Jing and Wei. The relationship of the water and fire, or Yin and Yang, within the Shao Yin and the relationship of the three Yang and the three Yin, are completely intertwined. The one cannot do without the other. The Xing and the Ming are inseparable.

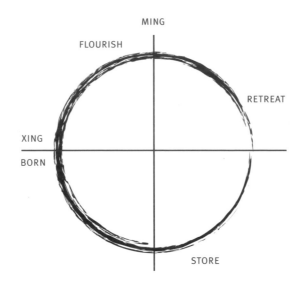

The Yellow Emperor says: *The core principle of Yin and Yang is that the Yang condenses and then the Yin becomes resolute.* This means that when the Yang can condense inward, the Yin can begin performing its three steps of preserving life as we discussed previously: prepare the earth, add true fire to create damp/mist, and quickly finish the process of the first two. When a patient uses fertility drugs and hormone therapy, according to Chinese medicine thinking, either the three Yang are harmed (feeling cold or tired) or the three Yin are damaged (hot flashes, bloated abdomen, clouded spirit). The Yang energy is unable to condense and the Yin energy cannot be resolute.

Under normal circumstances, a woman is able to discharge one egg per menstrual cycle. How then, while using fertility drugs and hormones, is she able to discharge 20 or 30 eggs? According to Chinese medicine principles, this excessive extraction of "true fire" is able to sever the root of life, and any such severing can last for several generations. For example, studies many years after WWII have shown that the stress resulting from widespread famine in Holland during the War caused impairment in genes for at least two successive generations.

With aggressive fertility treatment, when the father's or mother's heart fire and kidney water are damaged by drugs and synthetic hormones, what will the consequences be for their children and grandchildren? It is unclear at this point, and I cannot pretend to predict the future. However, Chinese medicine explains that we must do our best to preserve the lifeline we hand down to our children. This lifeline is all within the Shao Yin water and fire essences we exchange with our husband or wife. In Chinese medicine, we say that the most important element when treating a disease is to correctly differentiate the syndrome before treating it. We differentiate and treat for one reason: to preserve the root of life.

Let us think about it from a logical point of view. In your opinion, if you are ill and you become pregnant, could that impact your child's future? We can't give a definite answer. It might not impact your child. But let us reverse the question and ask: if you are very healthy, on a honeymoon or vacation, and feel great while you conceive, could that be beneficial for your baby? It will not hurt and probably will be beneficial. When we undergo excessive drug therapy, or for that matter any kind of therapy, and suffer "side effects," does that mean we are healthy or not healthy? In conventional medicine, where the disease is the target and not the person, we are taught that "side effects" are known to the drug manufacturer and thus, should learn how to "live with it". But from the Chinese medicine point of view, there is nothing "side" about "side effects". For example, if a woman undergoing IVF begins to experience hot flashes, one mechanism in the body is out of order and disharmony and illness symptoms result. Although it is difficult to prove that this will harm the baby, because it would be necessary to follow the study for several generations, we can use logic to assume that it may.

Another point that must be considered when we discuss IVF is the low success rate. Why is there only 5% success for patients older then 42? Modern medicine claims poor egg quality. In reality, the situation is quite different. As we age, the original Yang declines until it is consumed completely when we die. A 40 year-old patient has less original Yang then a 20 year-old. When using fertility drugs, where the original Yang is undergoing heavy extraction in order to produce more eggs, the 40 year-old patient is exhausted beyond her "true fire" reserves. Three days later, when the woman undergoes an embryo transfer, it cannot be supported by true fire because there is none left. This is why 19 out of 20 patients fail. However when using donor eggs, the success rate rises again because the donor egg is much younger, or so assumes modern medicine. My experience shows differently. In a donor egg cycle, the patient is not stimulated, and thus her true fire is not exhausted. It is the donor woman who is losing her true fire during stimulation. So the 40- year old patient receives an embryo while she still has some true fire left. I am certain that 100 years from now, Western doctors will look back at the procedures and drugs used today and view them as archaic. I will not be surprised if Chinese medicine herbs and theory will occupy a bigger role.

5

FERTILITY OBSTACLES

By presenting several patient stories and threading them together, I want to share with you my view, sitting on the practitioner side of the table, of what I believe are the major obstacles to achieving fertility.

DRUG CRAZY

Patient 1 is a 27 year-old female. She discontinued birth control pills approximately a year ago after ten years of use. Since stopping, menstruation has stopped. A reproductive endocrinologist induced a period with fertility drugs and estrogen/progesterone. While using fertility drugs, the patient produced in excess of 20 follicles and was disqualified for IUI (artificial insemination). The RE recommended IVF. His diagnosis for her condition: "The patient is very athletic and thinly built and this is the reason for her absent periods." While questioning the patient about her weight, she explains that she gained 10 lbs in the past year and according to my calculation her weight is normal. The patient is in complete agreement with the RE and she has started an IVF cycle. She is eager to get pregnant with the help of the drugs. In her words "I don't want to waste anymore time.'"

Patient 2 is a 45 year-old female who has undergone seven IUI procedures and six IVF procedures during a two-year period. All the procedures failed. After using the Hunyuan herbal treatment for two months, she conceived naturally. After conception, the patient expressed worry about consuming herbs during her pregnancy, and discontinued use. She returned to her doctor and began receiving progesterone shots. A miscarriage followed.

Patient 3 is a 38 year-old female who underwent three IUIs with clomid and later with injectable drugs. She reported feeling sick to her stomach with severe night sweats and anxiety attacks. After one month of herbal treatment with the Hunyuan Method, the symptoms subsided. The patient went back to the doctor who asserted that the dosage had been too weak in the previous cycle, and decided to begin another medicated IUI with twice the dosage. The cycle failed and all the side effects returned stronger then ever.

Patient 4 is a 46 year-old female who suffered secondary infertility. She received Hunyuan herbal treatment and acupuncture for six months. Although she did not conceive, her symptoms of achy joints and arthritis-like pain disappeared during the course of herbal protocols. Returning to IUI with medications, the pain returned within the first ten days. The patient expressed concern yet commented: "I know the drugs are harmful, but I can always come back so you can fix me up. My plan is to do a few cycles and hopefully I can come out of it fast enough before I am burned out."

CONVENTIONAL DIAGNOSIS BREEDS PSYCHOLOGICAL FAILURE

Patient 1 is a 33 year-old female. She conceived naturally but suffered a miscarriage. A Dilation & Curettage (D&C) was done to speed up the cleaning of the uterus lining. The patient could not conceive for a year after the D&C. The Western diagnosis was that she had poor egg quality.

Patient 2 is a 43 year-old female with secondary infertility. The Western diagnosis was that she was too old to get pregnant.

Patient 3 is a 39 year-old female. She failed three IVFs. The Western diagnosis was that she had elevated FSH levels.

Patient 4 is a 40 year-old female. She suffered recurrent miscarriages. The Western diagnosis was that she had genetic abnormalities.

Patient 5 is a 37 year-old female who cannot get pregnant. The Western diagnosis was unexplained infertility.

Is there a negative impact on a woman when she is told by an authoritative doctor that her eggs are too old? Or that she is unexplainably infertile? I have seen many patients, who, when told that their eggs are too old, have broken into tears and fallen into depression for days and even months. On the other hand, I have never seen a patient become depressed when hearing that she had a kidney Yang deficiency.

Why is Western diagnosis so devastating? Because it has a tone of finality. The mind goes into a state of shock. The more it is believed as truth, the more devastating. The new emotional blockage is infertility inducing. In Chinese medicine, this is referred to as "diminishing the emperor fire." The belief in one's ability to produce a baby has just diminished. I have seen patients become pregnant simply by restoring their self belief. When FSH levels of 15 are considered a sign of infertility, I have had patients with FSH levels of 20, 30 and even 80 who conceived naturally.

The emperor fire is in the heart and the will power is in the kidneys. When they are both functioning correctly, the Shao Yin sphere is intact and fertility will happen.

MAKING BABIES – IT TAKES TWO

When it comes to conception and making babies, it is a job for two: the husband and wife. In Chinese medicine we call this Yin and Yang. The two are inseparable. When the Yin is impaired, the Yang is in trouble, and when the Yang is obstructed, the Yin is malnourished. There is no such a thing as the problem of the Yin or a problem of the Yang. It is always the problem of Yin and Yang.

In modern Western medicine, when the diagnosis strikes the Yin or the Yang, it creates a separation of the Yin-Yang bond. It becomes the problem of the wife or the husband.

In Chinese medicine, the emperor fire plays a major role in allowing conception to transpire. If the husband's emperor fire is lacking, conception will not happen even if his sperm is viable. I have had experiences where I have boosted the morale of the husband over the course of an hour conversation, and then seen the couple conceive within the month. The wife became much more content during that month, which was enough for her to become pregnant.

What happens when the wife is diagnosed with poor egg quality and the husband is celebrated with excellent sperm count? This is a terrible blow to the Yin and Yang bond. Even in modern Chinese medicine, practitioners will pronounce the Yin as deficient but the Yang as fine, and vice versa. The Yang cannot be fine if the Yin is deficient, for it means that there is no healthy bond between the two. They are separated.

THE INTERNET – JUST THE BEGINNING OF KNOWLEDGE

We know that the quest for knowledge is an important one and that the Internet is certainly a significant tool. However, because Chinese medicine is an art that has crystallized over thousands of years, we must be careful how we take the Internet into account.

On-line research gives us pieces of information in greater and greater volume but with diminishing quality. While it gives us facts, it does not necessarily provide real knowledge or understanding. In the past, one would have borrowed books from a library, or taken a course on a particular subject. This might have taken days, months, or even years to accomplish. In a world of easy and rapid information disbursement, it becomes difficult for us to know who we should follow and what we should learn.

One cannot get to the essence of Chinese medicine from pieces of information even if it is accurate, let alone if it is wrong. We are far better off relying on the wisdom of the past tested in the laboratory of history.

We must understand science to grasp the heart of the problem. Science is emotionless. Its principle is to find the cold facts and its goal to replicate the results. If I analyze data scientifically, the results must be reliable. This means that if I analyze similar data later, the results must be the same, otherwise the first results were wrong. This instrument of science is, of course, very useful in many areas, including modern medicine, aviation, or technology.

Yet when we talk about art, the concept is different. When we look at a painting, or listen to music or watch a movie, something happens in the object we see that moves our heart. Art has no cold scientific boundaries. Rather, it has to do with the skill of the artist and the eye of the beholder.

In the art of Chinese medicine, the eyes of the practitioner and the health of the patient are both unique. The skill of the practitioner plays a crucial role. This can be a disadvantage, as some practitioners are less skilled than others. But the skills of the practitioner can also exceed normal levels and his touch brings a cure. Achieving results are not as simple as duplicating a procedure, which is the case with modern medicine.

This unique position of Chinese medicine brings big promise and responsibility simultaneously. The practitioner must be on a quest to improve his or her skills for an entire lifetime. The more skill and experience brought to bear, the more effective the cures will be.

The patient gathering pieces of information on the Internet is putting herself in a maze that it is difficult to maneuver. She must take two steps away from the monitor. It is fine to gather information, but she must know that this is not knowledge. It is just the beginning of knowledge.

Sarah and James could not conceive for four years. Their doctor explained that James's sperm count was low and that the sperm motility was below normal. Four IUI and two IVF cycles proved fruitless and their frustration grew. The couple heard from a co-worker about Yaron and the Hunyuan Method and decided they had nothing to lose. Yaron's conclusion was that Sarah had a Shao Yin kidney Yang deficiency. After five months of Sarah taking herbs and undergoing acupuncture treatments, the couple conceived naturally. James was startled and excited after so many years of believing that it was solely his problem.

6

HERBS, ACUPUNCTURE, AND DIET – DEEPENING UNDERSTANDING

THE TREATISE ON PRECIOUS LIFE AND THE ENTIRE FORM

First you must control the spirit, second you must know how to nourish the body, third you must know the real truth about 'toxic' herbs, fourth you must know the ins and outs of acupuncture and fifth you must know how to understand and diagnose the patterns of the inner organs, the blood and energy. When you know all of the above, the right path is not mysterious anymore. It is open in front of you, however you may be alone on this path.

These are the methods known for the past 3000 years that bring us closer to health and fertility. We must control the spirit and nourish the body, know herbs and acupuncture and understand how to diagnose the problem according to Chinese medicine.

THE MIRACLE HERB

The "miracle herb" in Chinese medicine is an herb that performs wonders in your body. If you are very ill, it can make you healthy, if you are sad, it can make you happy. This miracle herb can even give you longevity.

The name of this miracle herb is "Chinese herbs," and there are hundreds of them, each one offering its own specific miracle. Herbs are Chinese medicine's main tool to restore health and fertility, and combined with acupuncture, they have been the single most practiced and tested healing method for the past 3000 years.

The challenge is that each single herb must be used exactly at the right time, in the right quantity, and in the right combination with other herbs. It must be prepared correctly, cooked exactly the appropriate length of time, and administered in the correct way. When a patient visits me for the first time and says that she has heard that *Dang Gui is good for infertility*, I can only politely disagree. The herb is neither good nor bad. If one knows how to use it, it can make miracles. If one doesn't know how to use it effectively, then it is all a matter of chance. As I've stated before, Chinese medicine is not about luck, but rather about knowledge: how to, when to, why to? That is the reason I urge patients to avoid buying herbs for a "quick fix" solution. The patient must be thoroughly versed in the herb, and aware of the long-term effects; that do not mean the results of a study done over a period of six months or two years.

I recently visited an herbalist friend in California whose back yard garden is full of medicinal herbs. Every morning he picks a different set of herbs to brew his morning tea. When I looked at him harvesting his herbs, I asked myself: is he going to have a long healthy life? The answer was absolutely. Sometimes you look at something and you just know in your heart that it is right. Harvesting his home-grown herbs fresh every morning is in accord with nature. A double blind study is not necessary to prove it true.

The Treatise of Storing the Energy and Living According to the Seasons: *Toxic herbs can defeat a disease, the five grains will nurture, the five fruits will help, the five meats will benefit and the five vegetables will supplement. The energy and flavor of each will unite and enter the body. This will strengthen your essence and benefit your energy.*

Herbal formulas are not made-up of a bunch of herbs put together, but rather of ingredients carefully chosen to go into the mix. The famous scholar Su Shi (1037-1101) wrote in his work **Noble Prescriptions of the Shen Family**: *Treating a disease has five difficulties: differentiating the disease, choosing a correct treatment plan, knowing the individual herbs, knowing how to put the herbal formula together, and knowing how to distinguish between the herbs in the formula.*

The practitioner must have adequate knowledge in a variety of areas in order to put an effective formula together. As Su Shi writes in the introduction of this same book: *When the sages prepared herbs, they had rules for cooking and rules for drinking the herbal teas. Some herbs need to be cooked for a long time, while other herbs cannot be cooked for long. Some herbs require strong flame, while others require low heat for their cooking. These are the main rules of cooking. For drinking, some herbs need to be consumed warm while others cold, some need to be sipped slow while others fast. Some herbs need to be consumed with emotions such as anger or happiness and these emotions help the action of the herbs, while other herbs are contraindicated to emotions. For these contraindicated herbs, the emotions are enemies. These are the rules for drinking the herbs. In addition, some spring water is good and some is bad, so if the patient receives herbs and they don't always work, don't blame the herbs for that. This is because there is difficulty in determining the right way to prepare and drink the herbs.*

While establishing the basis for herbal treatments, **The Yellow Emperor** defines the strategy needed for healing: *When the disease is hot, then cool it off, and when the disease is cold, then warm it up.* This is the most basic approach for using herbs in classical Chinese medicine. However, **The Yellow Emperor** does not stop there. In **The Great Treatise of the Five Common Affairs**, he says: *To treat hot disease you use cold herbs and you need to drink it warm. To treat cold disease you use hot herbs and you need to drink it cool. To treat warm disease you use cool herbs and you need to drink it cold. To treat cool disease you use warm herbs and you need to drink it hot.* For the herbs to be effective, the method of delivery must be correct.

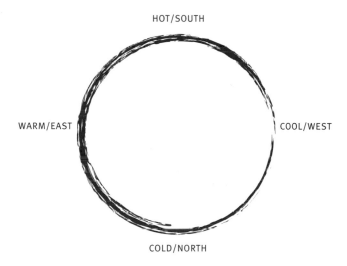

If the disease is hot, its energy is in the south, and cold herbs from the north are necessary to instill balance. However, in order for the north cold energy to travel to the south hot disease, east warm energy is needed, making it important that the tea be consumed when warm. If the disease is cool, its energy is in the west. The herbs must be warm from the east to bring balance. The tea must be hot, possessing the energy of the south. The south hot energy is a bridge between the east warm herbs and the west cool disease. The energy, as in the four seasons, is moving clockwise from the east to south to west to north. If the disease is cold, its energy is in the north. The herbs needed are hot from the south and the tea temperature needs to be cool from the west. If the disease is warm, its energy is in the east. The herbs should be cool from the west and the tea needs to be cold. The cold energy of the north will take the energy of the west and bring it to the warm disease in the east.

The book **Stories of Famous Physicians of the Past** includes a story about the famed physician Li Shicai: *One patient suffered cold injury. He felt very agitated and his face was red. His mind was in chaos and at times he wanted to drink cold water. The patient was waving his hands and kicking his feet so that the doctor could not feel his pulse. It took five or six people to subdue the patient for the doctor to take his pulse. The pulse was surging big and without rhythm. When he pressed down on the pulse it felt like a thin thread. Doctor Li said: 'Floating and big, while deep and small it is a Yin disease that looks like a Yang disease. I will give the patient 'strengthening the center decoction' (hot herbs) and he will live.' His student said: 'Ten out of ten doctors would have used cold herbs, but you instead used hot herbs. What is the logic behind it?' Dr. Li answered: 'With warm herbs the patient will live, while with cool herbs he will die. Following this, the doctor decocted the formula 'strengthening the center decoction', which included four ounces Ginseng and one ounce of Fu Zi. The finished tea was inserted into well water to cool off, and the patient drank it cool. Within one hour the erratic behavior stopped and one cup of tea later, the patient's spirit became clear. With the help of five pounds of herbs, the patient completely recovered.*

In this story, we witness the great skill of the physician. The symptoms the patient displayed – red face, waving his hands, etc. – were all hot symptoms, but within the pulse the doctor found the real cause of the disease, a cold disease. Furthermore, in addition to using hot herbs to counter the cold disease, the patient was ordered to cool off the tea before drinking. Doctor Li understood that to bring the hot herbs into the cold disease, the tea must be cool; to bring the south into the north we need the west.

USING HERBS WRONGLY THE WESTERN MEDICINE WAY

Normally I treat patients suffering from night sweats and hot flashes with hot herbs in a formula such as Tong Mai Si Ni Tang (penetrating the vessels Si Ni decoction). The prevailing reason for night sweats and hot flashes is a deficiency in the Yang energy due to the Yang's inability to root in the kidneys. It is not, as some people believe, a Kidney Yin deficiency.

When do women suffer hot flashes most frequently? It is as they approach menopause in their 40's and 50's, when the Yang energy is declining for both men and women. If the decline is abnormally rapid, the Yang may have a problem anchoring into the Yin and it begins floating to the surface of the body, triggering a hot flash or heavy sweat in the middle of the night. Using very hot herbs to strengthen the Yang solves the problem.

Fertility drugs, which also disturb the Yang rooting process in an abrupt manner, can have the same effect, forcing the Yang to the surface, and prompting hot flashes, or flickering of the Yang.

Because the hot flashes can be symptomatic of another condition, Chinese medicine always recognizes that each patient must be treated individually. In fact, hot flashes and sweats can be caused by the opposite of Yang deficiency – by excessive heat accumulating in the Yang Ming sphere, driving the Yang energy and body fluids outwards toward the exterior. Very cold formulas like Bai Hu Jia Ren Shen Tang (white tiger decoction with ginseng), are used to treat this condition. I had a patient who was an MD; she was using hormone replacement therapy for several years to control her hot flashes. She sought my assistance in helping her discontinue the hormone treatments, but when she stopped, the hot flashes came on at a relentless pace. She could barely function as a physician. Normally, I would consider a case like hers a Yang deficiency, but after considering all the symptoms she displayed, it became clear that even though she was 46 years old, it was a case of too much heat building in the Yang Ming. I gave her Bai Hu Jia Ren Shen Tang and two weeks later the symptoms were completely gone. The patient did not use hormone replacement therapy again.

The strength of Chinese medicine is the individual assessment of each patient. In today's world of Western medicine, all women who suffer from hot flashes are treated with the same hormones, and even in modern Chinese medicine, the situation is the same. Hot flashes and night sweats are considered to be the same Yin deficiency for all patients and are treated with the same herbs. **The Yellow Emperor** says that observing a symptom and automatically attaching to it a formula is the lowest form of medicine. In most cases, this treatment will prove itself wrong. Each patient has to be individually examined and the symptoms analyzed.

The same is, of course, true when it comes to solving infertility. Each person is unique and different. That is why we have our own different genetic codes, fingerprints, emotions, and desires. We need to see the difference in us to realize that there is no one drug that is good for everyone, and no one herb that is good for any one symptom.

TOXIC EXTREMES

Lu Chonghan in his book **Lectures on Supporting the Yang** writes: *Toxic herbs in classical Chinese medicine mean potent herbs.* You are in health when your energies are balanced and are sick when your energies are off balance. The farther away you are from the balance point to the left or to the right, the more potent an herb is needed. If you are just a bit off balance, then just a mild herb is needed.

The Yellow Emperor repeatedly mentions the necessity of acquiring the knowledge of toxic herbs. This knowledge is the knowledge of how to use potent herbs in the process of healing. Oddly enough, there are times when I hear medical doctors comment that herbs may be toxic and dangerous. Toxic means potent and dangerous means that there is no knowledge on how to use them. This will be true if a Western doctor, none of whom receive any herbal education in medical school, were to prescribe herbs to their patients.

Potent herbs can do great miracles if recommended by a skilled herbalist who has studied the subject for many years. Lu Chonghan, in studying one so called "toxic" herb in his herbal prescriptions, found out that out of 27,000 herbal formulas he prescribed in one year, he had used the herb Fu Zi (aconitum) in well over 90% of his formulas and there was not one negative reaction to the herb. The key for that was the knowledge of how to compose the formulas.

In fact, Western drugs can be far more toxic than eastern. With fertility treatments, for example, if a patient were to inject herself with higher dosages than prescribed the patient could die within a few days. In Chinese medicine, "toxic" herbs occupy a different level of harm. If the patient ingests a Chinese "toxic" herb at the wrong time in the wrong quantity, he or she will suffer undesired side effects, but those will subside as soon as the herbal intake is stopped.

To put this in perspective, let's take Ephedra for example. This herb was abused outside the scope of Chinese medicine without any appropriate knowledge. Some greedy companies have used the herb as a weight loss substance, using its diaphoretic properties. In Chinese medicine, a patient may use this herb only for a very short period of time and only for a very specific illness, not weight loss. It is contraindicated in many cases. Nonetheless, these greedy companies manufactured dietary weight loss supplements with Ephedra and sold it to millions of people for many months. A few of these people who used the herb in excess of 1000 times the dosage allowed in Chinese medicine, died as a result. This is a toxic herb in Chinese medicine. If millions of people were to abuse a Western drug in excess of 1000 times the recommended dose, more than just a few people would die.

When I speak about Chinese toxic herbs, it is important to distinguish them from many kinds of toxic herbs strong enough to kill an elephant with a tiny dosage. This kind of toxicity is not medicinal toxicity, it is deadly toxicity. This is the reason some people are afraid of herbs. Three thousand years of Chinese herbal experience does not deliver these kinds of herbs. Even Ephedra does not have this kind of deadly toxicity unless it is driven to an extreme abuse. Additionally, a practitioner must know his herbs and how to differentiate between a good and bad herb. For example, the herb Fu Zi (aconitum) is considered toxic and hot. It is the single most important herb strengthening the Shao Yin true Yang. Hence, Dr. Lu Chonghan uses it in more then 90% of his patients. However, this herb, as many others, has been subjected to abuse, mass produced in China in inappropriate climates at the wrong time of the year with harmful toxic chemicals. Traditionally a farmer would be able to process 50 kilos (100 lbs) of

Fu Zi per day, while a factory can produce (with chemicals) 1000 kilos per hour. The chemicals added, such as Dan Ba, render the herb very toxic, when in reality it is not. As a result, pure quality Fu Zi must be imported individually from Jiang You prefecture in Sichuan, China. There is none to be found in North America of traditional quality. A practitioner who is unaware of this and doesn't have his own acquisition source, cannot use the locally sold herb. With a pure, traditionally produced herb, one can use 20-200 grams in a formula, while with the modern toxic variety, only 3-6 grams. Side effects come from chemicals added to the herbs, and sadly practitioners believe they come from the herb itself.

Because of the conflicting and confusing information available to us, it is sometimes hard to make the right choices. My recommendation is to seek real knowledge. The patient must become his or her own healer. It is not satisfactory to say "studies have shown that this works."

In Chinese herbal pharmacology, the knowledge of herbs has shifted as the centuries have passed. The origin of Chinese herbal pharmacology is with the emperor Yan Di, also known as Shen Nong (sage of agriculture) and his book **Shen Nong Ben Cao Jing** (the classical pharmacopoeia of Shen Nong) dating back 2500 years ago.

Shen Nong, as legend goes, tasted 100 herbs per day and was said to have established Chinese pharmacology along with **The Yellow Emperor,** who established Chinese medical theory, and the Duke of Yi (Yi Yin) (1648 BC-1549 BC), a famous Prime Minister of the Shang dynasty who is said to have established the art of combining Chinese herbs into formulas. Between the three of them, it is said that the art of Chinese herbal medicine was complete. In reality, the ancient scholars were simply following the ideal of selflessness, giving all the credit to these three sages. When we say that Shen Nong, **The Yellow Emperor,** and Yi Yin are the three Chinese herbal medicine pillars, we actually refer to a thousand years of accumulated knowledge.

The herbs in the "Shen Nong Ben Cao Jing" were divided into three categories; upper, middle, and lower. "Upper" herbs were non-toxic, "middle" herbs were mildly toxic and "lower" herbs were very toxic. However, "toxic" in ancient China constituted the meaning of "vigor." If the vigor is applied in the wrong direction, its impact is devastating, while if it is applied in the correct direction, it is very beneficial. For example, when an Israeli woman who had been hospitalized in Tel Aviv for three months unable to get out of bed was referred to me as a last hope, I suggested a formula with 250 grams of Fu Zi (aconitum). Within one day, the patient rose from her bed, and within 3 days of taking 750 grams of Fu Zi was ready to be discharged from the hospital. How can you say that Fu Zi is toxic when it saves lives? Yet this "magic" could not have been accomplished without knowledge and without the traditionally produced pure herb.

To understand herb toxicity or non-toxicity, one must be knowledgeable in medicine, health, the year's energy, the stars and the moon. When one understands all of this, then herbs are not toxic. If you do not understand the entire picture of heaven, earth, and man, even mild common herbs will become "toxic."

ACUPUNCTURE – 365 POINTS WHERE ENERGY GATHERS

The doctor who was sitting in front of my desk said: *Correct me if I am wrong. As far as I know, acupuncture is the use of needles to stimulate a network of energy channels. When you stick needles in certain points, it triggers the energy to circulate in the energy channels and thus it helps the patient recover.* I had only one minute to explain myself before the next patient would step into the room. I had no choice but to reply that this was partially true. In fact, the doctor's understanding of acupuncture was much less than just "partial." It wasn't much more than at a 1% level.

The main classical work in Chinese medicine that pertains to acupuncture is the **Ling Shu,** also known as **The Yellow Emperor's Miraculous Pivots – Nine Needles and Twelve Origins,** where it is written: *The crossing of joints have 365 gatherings. The meaning of 'joints' is the traveling, exiting and entering of the spirit and Qi. It is not the skin, flesh, tendons and bones.*

This quote explains the meaning of the 365 acupuncture points we have in our body, the points where true energy and the spirit gather. The true energy comes from the food we eat, while the spirit comes from the interaction between heaven and earth within our body. This gives us the first glimpse into what acupuncture is all about. When we insert needles into one of these 365 points, we influence our own energy and influence the connection of our body with heaven and earth, or with our spirit.

While the body's true energy is inside our body, the 365 acupuncture points are the doors where the external heaven and earth energies – the three Yin and the three Yang – are waiting to enter. They are led inside by the spirit, or **Shen Ji**. When the inside energy is strong and healthy, it will harmonize with the external energy. But when the internal energy is weak or ill, then there will be disharmony between the energies and we will become ill.

When I place a needle in an acupuncture point, there are many aspects I consider. Using a modern day example, it is like going to the airport to catch a flight. I plan my transportation to the airport. If I decide to take my car, I must know where to park and how to proceed to the terminal from the parking lot. I should know what I will need at the security checkpoint, from which gate my flight is leaving, how many bags I am allowed and so forth.

In the practice of acupuncture, I need to be aware of the energies outside the body at the time of treatment. Is it a full moon or empty moon, is it spring or fall? What are the dominant and guest energies at present? I must know the situation inside the patient. Is the liver energy strong or weak? Is the fire too strong or the water too weak? Then I must decide which acupuncture points I should use, how deep the needles should be placed, how much the needles should be rotated, and in which direction they should point.

Miraculous Pivot states: *You can't head on the coming and you can't pursue the going.* This means that when the entering energy is too strong, the practitioner cannot tonify with acupuncture, and when the heaven's energy is departing, the practitioner can't sedate with acupuncture, because the inside energy is growing weaker. The state of one's health is always the result of an interaction between the inside energy and the outside world. This is fundamentally different than Western medicine. This is why there is a difference between western drugs and herbs, and between surgery and acupuncture. Western medicine deals with the body as an independent unit, while Chinese medicine does not separate the body from nature.

The behavior of energy is universal. The heaven's three Yin and three Yang outside our bodies contain the same components as does the energy inside our body. In modern Chinese medicine, it is falsely perceived that the six heavenly influences – wind, cold, damp, dryness, warmth, and summer heat – are the cause of symptoms in our body. (ie: Heat attacking the body provokes hot symptoms, cold attacking provokes cold symptoms, etc.)

It is actually the three Yin and three Yang inside our body that create the symptoms. This means that when cold enters, we can have cold symptoms, such as aversion to cold, or we can have hot symptoms, such as fever, or we can have dry symptoms like dry mouth and lips. This is because energy enters the body and then transforms within our own three Yin and Yang.

Why is there a therapeutic effect when inserting a needle into the body? This question is very illusive and its answer is very difficult to comprehend. In modern acupuncture, considerable scientific research has been done into the efficacy of acupuncture. However, the common approach is from the perspective that acupuncture works by stimulating the nervous system – efficacy must work on the physical level of nerves, flesh, skin and bones.

An infertility patient sits in my office and tells me the following: In addition to irregular periods, she has a problem with depression in the spring. In the summer, she tends to gain weight, while in the winter she loses weight. All of these symptoms are contrary to what most other people generally experience. Now, which acupuncture points should we use and in what way?

We must consider that the spring is when the Yang energy rises. It is the wood energy of the Jue Yin and the warmth energy of Shao Yang. Depression is the emotion of fall, of metal and the lungs. The metal's job is to control the wood. Overactive wood will demand much of the metal. Because the outside energy of the spring enters our body via spirit and 365 gatherings, the wood becomes strong and the metal weak. Given that the patient feels depressed in spring, the outside energy is clearly impacting the inner three Yin and Yang. The summer belongs to fire and fire controls metal. The weak metal is over controlled in the summer and is weakened even more. The lungs are Tai Yin and together with the spleen, they are responsible for food metabolism. In the summer, the patient gains weight because the Tai Yin is impaired. In the fall and winter, the energy descends and helps the metal downward movement, thus making the metal and Tai Yin stronger, and the metabolism improves.

From this analysis, we can learn what needs to be strengthened and what needs to be reduced. The lung's metal is weak and liver wood is too strong, over-controlling the spleen earth further, weakening the metabolism in the summer. However, in addition to strengthening the lungs and spleen and reducing the liver, we must consider the seasons. In the fall, we must strengthen the lungs metal and in the spring we must reduce the liver wood. In the summer, we must moderate the heart fire. We must consider the inside and outside of the problem.

UNDERSTANDING ACUPUNCTURE AND HOW IT RELATES TO DISEASE

Miraculous Pivots says: *Yin and Yang have different names, however they are of the same kind. Above and below gather to penetrate through the meridians and side channels in an endless cycle. When evil energy attacks the patient, it can enter into the Yin or enter into the Yang. Above and below, right and left, they all have different reasons for attacking. When deficient evil enters the body, it alters the physical shape, however when upright evil enters the body, one can only see slight changes in color. The changes cannot be seen in the physical body, as if it is sometimes there and sometimes not, as if there are sometimes physical changes and at other times not.*

This quote explains the relationship of our energy to heaven's energy and how disease comes about. Yin and Yang means the energy inside and outside the body. They are seemingly different, but inherently are not. The energies of heaven are above, and the inside energies are below. Our energy and heaven's energy combine together to create the energy in the channels. This is why the spring can influence us in one way, while the summer will influence us in a different way. The summer will cause one patient to gain weight and the winter will cause the same patient to lose weight. Above and below, or inside and outside, energies will gather to penetrate through the meridians and side channels.

The Miraculous Pivot continues on with a discussion of deficient evil and upright evil. This again concerns the relationship between the inside and the outside. If our three Yin and Yang are healthy and upright, while the heaven's three Yin and Yang are ill, it is referred to as upright evil. If heaven's energy is ill, there is too much fire, not enough cold, or too much dryness. This will influence us negatively. However, since our own energy is healthy and in order, our body will withstand this harmful energy. Only slight changes will be in evidence in the color of the face, lips, tongue, or skin.

If, on the other hand, our three Yin and Yang are ill and the heaven's three Yin and Yang are ill, it is called deficient evil. At this time, our body can't withstand the attack and we fall ill.

When the **Miraculous Pivot** states: *You can't head on the coming and you can't pursue the going*, it tells us what acupuncture is all about. The practitioner must know if the patient displays an upright evil or a deficient evil. He must know if it's important to tonify or sedate; and he must consider the energy outside in order to come up with the correct assessment. A modern approach to acupuncture is that each point has a specific action--one point is good for the tendons while another is effective for the uterus. This is not acupuncture the way the sages intended. So when I hear a statement such as "This acupuncture point helps increase the blood flow to the uterus," I can only raise an eyebrow in dismay.

I believe that Chinese medicine must be integrated with Western medicine, because both have strong points. But I don't believe that Chinese medicine should be compromised in order to do so. In my practice, I collaborate with Western doctors on a regular basis. They work with me because they see results. The same goes for me. When I see results, I am likely to agree to work with the doctor involved. However, results for me do not mean that patients are conceiving, but rather that they are conceiving as naturally as possible. Dr. Karol Chacho, a reproductive endocrinologist with whom I often work, tells his patients that if they have a pimple on their little finger, cutting off the finger to eliminate the pimple may do the job, but that it's not necessarily the best way to treat the issue. Dr. Chacho is actually able to use Western

SHU

medicine's non-invasive procedures to assist many of his patients become pregnant. In my opinion, this is a successful physician.

Some of the 365 acupuncture points are more potent than others, at least from the angle of harmonizing heaven and earth with man. These are the **Shu** (transport) points;

Shu also meaning to bring a tribute from one place to the other. The character Shu is composed of two components. One is a cart with wheels and the other is a boat, meant to signify that a tribute can be brought via land or sea. **Miraculous Pivot – Nine Needles and Twelve Origins** states: *The Yellow Emperor asked: I heard that the five Yin organs and the six Yang organs have a place where they exit? Qi Bo answered: 'The five Yin organs have five Shu each, and the six Yang organs have six Shu each. Five times five* *is 25 and six times six is 36. Where the Shu exits, it is called Jing, where it trickles away it is called Ying, where it pours, it is called Shu, where it is marching, it is called Jing and where it enters, it is called He. The energy interaction of heaven and earth in the 20 channels and side channels are all in these five Shu points.*

The main acupuncture points that harmonize the entering of heaven energy and the exiting of body energy, then, are below the elbows and knees.

Miraculous Pivot: *Yin rules the Yin organs and Yang rules the Yang organs. The Yang is received at the four extremities and the Yin is received at the five Yin organs.* The Emperor explains that the heaven energy (Yang) enters at the four extremities, while the earth energy, or the inside energy, of our body is in the five Yin organs. The five Shu points at the arms and legs below the elbows and knees are where all the interaction happens. The He points, at the elbows and knees, are where the heaven energy enters. The Jing points, where the body's energy exits, are at the finger and toe tips.

In ancient China, numbers had great significance. One and two are the numbers of water and fire, and represent the pre-heaven state before life, while three and four are the numbers of wood and metal, and represent the post-heaven state where life begins. Three is the number of the east and spring, which is the beginning of life, where heaven and earth energies emerge. Four represents the west, where the energy declines.

In traditional acupuncture, each acupuncture point has a Chinese name. In the West we have erased all the names because it was too difficult to remember for non-Chinese speakers, names such as Da Dun, Xing Jian, and Tai Chong now referred to as "liver 1, liver 2, liver 3." Each of the five Yin organs – lungs, heart, liver, spleen, and kidneys – has a meridian, and each of these meridians have five different types of Shu points: Jing, Ying, Shu, Jing and He. The third point on each meridian is the main Shu point, which carries the name of the entire group of points.

Exiting and trickling from the fingers and toes upwards and entering and marching from the elbows and knees downwards, the heaven energy and the body energy pour and merge together at the Shu point. This is why the five Shu points are named Shu and not Jing or He or Ying. Among the five Shu points along the meridian, the Shu point is the third point or the middle point. It is the third point from the elbow down or the third point from the finger tip up. It is the center of the action. Heaven and earth are mixing together to enter the body at the Shu point and thus it is called Shu; to bring the tribute inside the body.

DA　　TAI

The character Da and Tai are very similar and often interchangeable in classical Chinese. They both translate to big, huge, or extreme, and in ancient script they represent a human being.

The character Da on the left is composed of two components. The horizontal line represents heaven and the two other lines represent man. The heaven crossing over the man means that the heaven and man are merging together. In the character Tai, there is also a small extension at the bottom of the foot signifying roots going into the ground.

When we look at the names of the five Yin organs Shu points (third point on each Yin meridian) and their corresponding organs, we can understand the difference.

TAI YUAN – lungs

DA LING – heart

TAI CHONG – liver

TAI BAI – spleen

TAI XI – kidneys

We can see that each Shu point on each Yin meridian has the meaning "big," however the heart has "Da" and the other four organs have "Tai." We know that out of the five elements – wood, fire, earth, metal and water – only the fire is formless and flares upwards. All the other elements have physical forms and substance, and therefore, will gravitate downward toward the earth. The sages went to show us that within the five Shu points of the organs, the heart is purely connected to heaven with "Da," while the other four Shu points are connected to heaven too, but already gravitate to the earth with "Tai."

Now why would the Shu points of the Yin organs be "big?" This is, as we explained before, the place where the heaven's energy merges with the body's energy, hence it is a big place.

When we talk about the five Shu points, we must also know that the sages attributed the five elements to these points. For the Yin meridians, the distribution is as follows:

JING – wood

YING – fire

SHU – earth

JING – metal

HE – water

The Shu points are earth element. The sages realized that the heaven energy mixes with man's energy on the Yin meridians on the earth points. This distribution is not random. It is rather a description of natural phenomena. Our human energy comes from the Yin organs, and when it surfaces to the meridian, it exits at the Jing, trickles at the Ying, and becomes the biggest at the Shu-earth point on that same meridian. From the other side, the heaven's energy enters at the He point, increases, or marches, at the Jing (this Jing is a different character then the first Jing even though it is pronounced the same) and becomes the biggest at the Shu earth points where it merges with human energy.

155

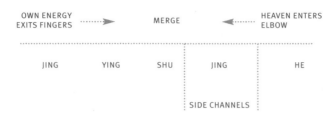

In the meridian system, **Luo,** or side channels, is where the meridians connect with each other. It is also where the energy splits off, entering our body from the meridians. When we look at the Yin meridians we discussed above, we can see that the side channel always starts either between the Shu-Jing points or between the Jing-He points.

The location where the energies mix is full or abundant, allowing the energy to enter into the body's deeper layers.

When standing upright with arms dropped, the elbows, where heaven's energy enters, are high, and the fingers, where human energy exits, are low. Similarly, the knees are high and the toes are low. High reaches to heaven and low reaches to the earth.

When the mixed energy enters the body, it is distributed within the body's three Yin and Yang, mixing with food energy and breathing air energy to become blood and nutrients to sustain our health. **Miraculous Pivots – Pathogenic Qi Zang Fu Organs, Disease and Physical form** says: *All types of small pulse show that the Yin and Yang, physical form and Qi are deficient. You can't use acupuncture to treat it, but rather you have to use sweet herbs to strengthen it.* States **Miraculous Pivot – Beginning and End**: *If the Qi is not enough, the different pulses on the neck and wrist are all small. This is because the Yin and the Yang are both deficient. If you tonify the Yang with acupuncture, the Yin dries up, and if you drain the Yin, the Yang will separate. At this time you can use sweet herbs.*

"Sweet herbs" does not necessarily mean herbs that are sweet. Sweet is the flavor of earth, the place where the myriad things are born. Sweet herbs mean herbal formulas in general and herbs from the earth instead of acupuncture. When the Yin and Yang are deficient and when the Qi and blood are not enough, herbs must be used because they store the heaven's five essences and bring them into the five Yin organs. Acupuncture, on the other hand, harmonizes the heaven energy with the body energy, treating deficient and upright evil. Clearly both acupuncture and herbs are very useful in assisting infertility.

When needling a patient, the practitioner's intentions must be fully present or else the treatment is useless. States **Miraculous Pivots – Beginning and End**: *The intentions of your spirit lead will into the needle. For male on the inside and for female on the outside. Strengthening to prevent exiting and protecting to prevent entering. This is called reaching the Qi (De Qi). For* treatment to be effective, the practitioner must reach the Qi, which in Chinese is **De Qi,** by using his heart intentions and spirit to guide his will into the needle. For a male patient, the practitioner intentions must go inward, because male is Yang and his energy naturally wants to travel outwards. For a female patient, the practitioner intentions must travel outside, because female is Yin and her energy naturally

DE QI

wants to travel inward. The practitioner intentions aim to strengthen the upright energy of the patient, preventing it from exiting, and enabling it to prevent the evil energy from entering.

The correct movement of energy, entering or exiting, can be controlled. When I administer acupuncture, the patient can feel gurgling in the stomach, electricity running along the channel, heaviness, tingling, and pressure. Also, the area around the needle becomes red. This is all part of the concept of De Qi. However, if the patient is very deficient in Yin and Yang, she will not feel any sensation and acupuncture is not beneficial. She rather needs herbal formulas to strengthen the Yin and Yang first, and then recommence acupuncture. Herbal formulas should be composed of raw herbs and not capsules or other patent pills that are depleted of heaven's energy.

For the Qi to arrive and for the acupuncture to be effective, the acupuncture needle must be inserted in the correct location. **Miraculous Pivots – Pathogenic Qi Zang Fu Organs, Disease and Physical Form** says: *The Yellow Emperor asked; what is the correct method of acupuncture? Qi Bo answered: The needle must be placed in the Qi hole. It must not be placed in the muscles and joints. Needling the Qi hole will cause the needle to float in its harbor. Needling the muscles and joints will cause the skin to ache and the disease will aggravate.*

As we explained before, the 365 acupuncture points are the junctions where the heaven's energy mixes with the body's energy. For the energy of the body to emerge, or for the energy of heaven to enter, one must needle these 365 points exactly. The points, or what the emperor calls "holes," can be felt by palpating with the finger, and are between the muscles and joints, or between different muscles and tendons, so that the energy can gather. When we needle these holes, the energy can go one way or another, scattering or gathering, exiting or entering. Some of these "holes" are very small and hard to detect, some are large and easy to feel, but the experienced acupuncturist can feel them all.

The He points at the elbows and knees are big and deep, distributed on a large area of the skin. They contain the vast Yang energy, which while entering, will become increasingly more condensed. The Jing points at the finger/toe tips are small and superficial, and they contain the condensed Yin energy which will gradually expand. They march toward each other, meeting at the middle Shu point. Yin and Yang are opposite in character and this is the natural way of heaven.

The needling depth is very important too. **Miraculous Pivot**: *When the Qi is in the meridian, the evil Qi is on top, the turbid Qi is in the middle and the clear mist Qi is at the bottom. When the needle is placed superficially, the evil comes out, when the needle enters midway, the turbid matter comes out, when the needle is too deep, the evil Qi to the contrary enters inwards and the disease aggravates.*

This quote is telling us that if the needling is too shallow, the body's energy will not exit. Turbid energy refers to the individual's own Yin energy, while evil Qi refers to heaven's Qi, as in deficient evil or upright evil. If one enters with the needle too deep, not only will the energy fail to emerge to mix with heaven's energy or to repel evil Qi, but it will cause the evil to enter.

When I hear about acupuncture courses of short duration such as medical acupuncture, which is a course for physicians ranging between 150 and 300 hours, I feel that a great disservice is being done to patients. I am also chagrined by the claims that medical acupuncture is superior to acupuncture administered by acupuncturists who have thousands of hours of training. On the other hand, I am also aware of medical doctors who receive real acupuncture training for three years, which makes them competent acupuncturists as well as medical doctors. This I believe is honorable and the patient should note the difference between the two.

ACUPUNCTURE: CHANNELING NATURE'S ENERGY INTO THE FERTILITY ZONE

Miraculous Pivot: *The twelve meridians are where a person is born. It is where a disease culminates. It is where a person is healed. It is where disease arises. The acupuncture novice will begin his learning with this and the accomplished acupuncturist will end his study with it. A low level practitioner finds it easy, while a master practitioner finds it very difficult. The first will frequent his mistake while the latter dwells in it as not to go wrong.*

The twelve meridians are where heaven's energy enters and the body's energy exits. It is where the two energies merge to form and shape your health and longevity. When you have energy, you are born. Without energy, you have no life. This is true for the mother and father as well as for the new baby. Furthermore, the intricacy of the Miraculous Pivot text reveals a much deeper idea the sages conveyed to us. The author conceals a special message in the first four sentences: A person is born, disease culminates, a person is healed, disease arises.

"Where a person is born" refers to our own energy. If our energy, three Yin and three Yang, is not healthy and harmonized, then a disease is already culminating. "Where a person is healed" refers to the external influence that enters and impacts our body. Disease will form and aggravate if we fail to control the exterior energy entering. The classics explain that the harmonizing of the internal energy or the control of the external energy all happens within the realm of the meridians. The meridians transform the three Yin and Yang. Therefore, an acupuncturist must always focus on learning as much as possible about these meridians.

The practice of acupuncture involves the spirit of the practitioner concentrating on the needle. The spirit, as we learned many times so far, is the vehicle for entering and exiting of energy between heaven and man. When the practitioner connects the heaven's energy and his energy to the needle, we call this **Qi arrival**. Many of my patients comment that when they received acupuncture elsewhere they felt nothing, but in my acupuncture sessions they feel many strange sensations. They literally feel the energy moving at all times. Yet my needles are not connected to any electrical outlets, only to my intentions. When I twist the needles I do not twist a piece of metal, but rather turn left and right, spring and fall, entering and exiting.

Miraculous Pivot: *The heaven is so high that you can't measure it and the earth is so wide that you can't weigh it. The person's life is born in between the heaven and earth. He is born within the six unifications. The heaven's height and earth's width, which is the root of his life, is not something that can be measured or weighed by man.*

I was once sitting in on a lecture by Dr. Jiao Shunfa, a famous Chinese neurosurgeon who invented scalp acupuncture in 1970 as a way to help stroke patients. His methods became so famous that the WHO (World Health Organization) and the United Nations recognized scalp acupuncture as a major invention from China and recommended its method for clinical applications. But the story of scalp acupuncture was not always so famous and wide spread. In 1984, a conference of neurosurgery department heads from all over China took place in Shanxi Province. A patient paralyzed in her right hand showed up at the outpatient clinic of the hospital where the conference took place. Dr Jiao invited the neurosurgery chiefs to check the patient and come up with a diagnosis. The majority of doctors concluded that the reason for the paralysis was cerebral thrombosis, or blood clotting in the brain. When Dr Jiao suggested to this group of senior doctors that scalp acupuncture would enable this patient to regain the ability to use her hand within five days, the crowd looked at him in disbelief. Dr. Jiao went further to predict that on the sixth day the patient would be able to roll dumplings with her hand. "If the patient does not recover her ability to use the hand as a normal person, I will stop practicing acupuncture," he said to the now dumb-struck audience. Five days later, the patient recovered full functionality in her right hand. On the sixth day, when Dr. Jiao arrived at the class, all the guest patients and doctors were gone. They had taken the patient to the cafeteria to check her ability with dumplings. When they came back to the conference hall they all praised him for his success. From that day on, scalp acupuncture spread far and wide in China and around the world.

The practice of acupuncture for infertility is exactly like that. You can only believe it if you have seen it with your own eyes. My eyes are there in my office every day to see how patients improve and recover and become pregnant.

The acupuncture points that I use are below the elbows and below the knees. They are between point Jing at the finger/toe tips and He at the elbows and knees. The forearms and the lower legs are the location for the heaven's energy to enter, the body's Yin energy to exit, and the Yin and Yang to mix. **The Miraculous Pivot** says that heaven is Yang and the earth is Yin, and therefore the body's upper half corresponds to heaven and the body's lower part corresponds to earth. Thus the upper limbs correspond to heaven and the lower limbs correspond to earth.

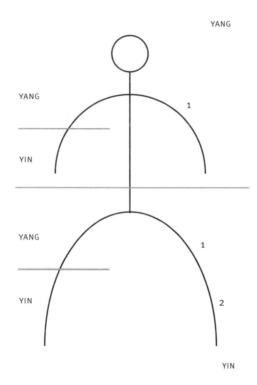

The lower legs are the Yin among the four limbs, while the forearms are the Yang. This is because the arms are close to heaven and correspond to Yang, and the legs are close to earth and correspond to Yin. Within the lower legs, the knees are the Yang within Yin and the toe tips are the Yin of Yin. As for the forearms, the fingers are Yin and the elbows are Yang. As explained earlier, the numbers occupy a special meaning. "Heaven 1 descends to create water, earth 2 ascends to embrace the fire, heaven 3 creates wood, and earth 4 creates metal." Numbers 1 and

2 represent the connection of heaven and earth and the connection to the pre-heaven state. Numbers 3 and 4 complement the first two in creating the post-heaven. In order to create harmony between our energy and heaven's energy, we need to use these four numbers. First, I must establish a connection between heaven and earth or between the outside energy and my body's energy. I use one needle at or around the elbow, which is the Yang of Yang. This brings the heaven's energy down into the body to create water. The water trigram has one solid Yang line in the center. One needle at the elbow represents this 1 Yang that creates the water. To bring the Yin energy of our body to exit and to mix with the Yang of heaven, I use two needles. I insert them close to the ankles, or at the Yin of Yin. I use the most Yin energy and two needles to create the effect of earth 2. This gives birth to fire. In the Li (fire) trigram we see that in order for it to take place, there are two solid Yang lines, one on top and one at the bottom. There is also one broken Yin line in the center. Two needles close to the ankle represent the broken line in the middle of the trigram. This is why the Classics say that Earth 2 gives birth to fire.

WATER TRIGRAM

FIRE TRIGRAM

When I use two needles at the Yin of Yin, the body's own Yin energy exits to the surface to meet the heaven's energy. Under normal circumstances, this is what I want to reach with acupuncture. Heaven 1 is close to the elbow at the Yang of Yang, and earth 2 is close to the ankles at the Yin of Yin. The acupuncture points that I normally use are Tai Xi (vast brook/ kidney 3) and San Yin Jiao (crossing of three Yin/spleen 6) if the patient is at her first 14 days of the menstrual cycle. If the patient is at the second half of the menstrual cycle, I substitute San Yin Jiao (spleen 6) with Fu Liu (repeated current/kidney 7). I avoid the use of San Yin Jiao (spleen 6) if there is a possibility that the patient is pregnant because it can induce a miscarriage.

The first two rules of Hunyuan acupuncture are heaven 1 and earth 2 mixing and creating fire and water. This is the pre heaven state before life turns into the post heaven state. Two needles at the ankles and one at the elbows already gives birth to three needles. It is enough to create a trigram, or a state of energy, which needs at least 3 lines as we have seen in the Li (fire) and Kan (water) trigrams. The father of Daoism, Lao Zi, wrote in his book **Dao De Jing**: *One gives birth to two, two give birth to three, and three give birth to the myriad things.* We need one of heaven and we need two of earth and together they are three. Water and fire together establish the pre-heaven connection. But we need the post- heaven state. We need the physical world we live in. We need the wood and the metal. We need the 3 and the 4.

To create this effect with acupuncture, I need a third needle on the leg in addition to the heaven 1 and earth 2. Heaven 1 and earth 2 comprise the vertical line of Jing, but I need the Wei horizontal line as well. This time I use the Yang of Yin or points close to the knee. As explained,

1 and 2 are descending and ascending to create water and fire (Sheng Jiang), while 3 and 4 are right and left and are also exiting and entering (Chu Ru). Three is the number giving birth to the east while 4 is the number giving birth to the west. In the east, the sun rises and we call this "sun exits from the earth." In the west the sun sets down. We call this "sun enters into the earth." This is what 3 and 4 exiting and entering means. The sun rises in the morning and the spring comes out after the winter. These two phenomena are the beginning of life. This is why the number 3 is the beginning of the post-heaven state; the state of life as we know it. The third needle of the leg gives new meaning to the harmony for which we strive. The 1 needle and the 2 needles mix the water and fire to create life's energy. However, we need the sunrise of spring needle. This third needle of the leg causes the mixed energy to spread in the body.

After we establish the use of three needles to bring the mixed Yin-Yang energy to spring into the body, we must plan our exit. We cannot have the sun rising without setting down, nor can we have the spring arriving without the fall to follow. This is a universal rule of our post heaven state. Without left and right, and without entering and exiting, we find ourselves in the pre-heaven state – before life.

For the "exit" to come about, we do need 4 needles, but the fourth needle in acupuncture was already established when we entered the third needle of the leg: it is the needle in the arm which makes four needles. When I enter into the realm of the third needle, entering into the post heaven state, there is already an "end" in sight. The pre-heaven state of heaven and earth is eternal. There is no end to it. But our life of post-heaven and right and left, east and west, entering and exiting is a state with an "end." When I insert the spring with the third needle, I have already established a post-heaven state with an "end" or "exit."

This means that with the third needle, I must be able to look far into the future. I am not inserting the needle to solve an immediate symptom, but creating the beginning of a long life cycle to come.

The 1 needle of the arm and 3 needles of the leg work in different ways on different areas, but I must have oversight of the entire action. The harmony of the 4 needles is crucial. This is dissimilar with Western medicine where a specialist will treat one problem and only one problem. With four needles, I need to solve the problems at hand and make sure that other problems will not arise in the future as a result of the acupuncture I perform. Sometimes I see acupuncturists inserting 10 or 20 needles in all parts of the body without any logic or rules. The classics say that inserting needles at random without knowledge or correct purpose can inflict great harm.

ACUPUNCTURE AND PREGNANCY

I have discussed the celestial bodies in different chapters about Yin and Yang and about harmony with nature. The ancients observed the five brightest stars: **Tu** (earth), **Mu** (wood), **Huo** (fire), **Jin** (metal) and **Shui** (water). For reference, consider the following: Mercury is the water star, Venus is the metal star, Mars is the fire star, Jupiter is the wood star, Saturn is the earth star.

If we consider the sun as the center of our galaxy, and that all the other stars revolve around the sun, we end up with chart below. Our planet makes a full orbit of the sun in one year. Each star has a different size orbit, the stars closer to the sun orbiting faster around the sun as they have less distance to travel. We measure the speed of the stars as they relate to our planet, as well as how they impact us.

During 60 years and 60 cycles of planet earth around the sun, the water star, which is closest to the sun, orbits 240 circles around the sun and the metal star orbits 96 circles. This is because these two stars are closer to the sun than our planet earth. During the 60 orbits of planet earth, the fire star orbits 30 circles, the wood star orbits five circles and the earth star, which is the farthest from the sun, orbits only two circles. The significance of 60 years, as the sages found, was that all these stars align with the sun into one line every 60 years.

```
EARTH · WOOD · FIRE · PLANET · METAL · WATER · SUN ·
STAR    STAR   STAR  EARTH    STAR    STAR
        X2.5    X6     X2      X1.6    X2.5
2        5      30     60       96      240      1
```

If we observe the difference between the orbit speeds of the stars, we get the above results. The wood star travels 2.5 times faster than the earth star. The fire star travels six times faster then the wood star. Our planet earth travels twice as fast as the fire star. The metal star travels 1.6 times faster then our planet earth. The water star travels 2.5 times faster then the metal star. This difference in speed between neighboring stars is our first set of numbers. When we multiply the difference in speed between the stars we get the following: 2.5 x 6 x 2 x 1.6 x 2.5 =120. The number 120 is

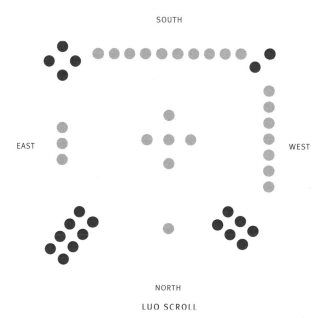

SOUTH

EAST

WEST

NORTH

LUO SCROLL

a complete number. It equals two 60 years cycle, or one Yin and one Yang cycle. In chapter 3, we discussed the river picture with the numbers 1-10 falling on all four directions and the center (the diagram with the black and white dots). Number 1 is in the north, number 2 in the south, 3 in the east, 4 in the west and 5 in the center. When we multiply 1 x 2 x 3x 4 x 5, we get 120. This is the number needed to establish the five directions.

In the image from the Luo scroll, the set of numbers emphasizes the circular motion of the universe, as compared to the four directions in the "river picture." We can see that in any direction – horizontal, vertical or oblique – when the numbers are added together, the result will be 15. The numbers in this chart can be added in eight different ways, and will always equal 15 for each strand, and 15 x 8 gives a total of 120 again.

Lao Zi, in his book **Dao De Jing** says: *Dao gives birth to 1, 1 gives birth to 2, 2 gives birth to 3 and 3 gives birth to the myriad things.* Myriad things mean everything under heaven; mountains, rivers, animals, plants, men, women and babies. "3" gives birth to all of these. So what are these 1, 2, 3?

EARTH STAR	WOOD STAR	FIRE STAR	PLANET EARTH	METAL STAR	WATER STAR	SUN
2	(3) 5	30	60	96	240	1

Dao is the core principle for life and is the invisible part we need our heart to envision. This invisible Dao principle gives birth to the sun. Out of the sun comes the Yang energy needed for all life forms to exist. Second to that, and in extreme opposite side to it, we have the earth star, making only two orbits within a 60-year period. Because this star is the farthest away from Yang and the sun, it has the least Yang energy. At the same time, it has the minimum Yang energy required for movement. The minimum movement of the earth star and the maximum Yang energy of the sun is the relationship needed to begin life. Thus Lao Zi said 1 gives birth to 2.

This relates directly to the human ability to become pregnant and begin a new life cycle. "1" gives birth to 2 means the male energy goes into the female body. 1 and 2 are on both extremes. But this by itself is not enough to create "everything under heaven." That is why Lao Zi said that 2 must give birth to 3 and then 3 can give birth to the myriad things. From the numbers point of view, 3 is the difference between the earth star and the wood star (see chapter 2).

As we mentioned, the Wood and fire stars are to the left of earth, and metal and water stars are to the right. This gives our planet and our life the balance we call Yin and Yang. It is not that the stars give us this balance, but rather that these stars follow the principle that we are to follow as well. The sages did not believe that the stars were influencing us, but rather the stars serve as the database, giving us the information we need to be able to use our heart to see the invisible principle of Yin and Yang. Even though our earth is in the middle between wood, fire, metal and water, we are even more in the middle between the sun and the earth star. There are three celestial bodies to our right and three to our left. These are what **The Yellow Emperor** called the three Yin and three Yang.

When we start talking about "3", there is a more complex relationship. It is no longer just Yin and Yang, but rather Yin and Yang + plus one other thing.

EARTH STAR (3)	WOOD STAR	FIRE STAR	PLANET EARTH	METAL STAR	WATER STAR	SUN
2	5	30	60	96	240	1

This new relationship is between the two extremes and the axis. The two extremes are the sun and the earth star, and the axis is our planet earth. We can clearly see that wood, fire, metal, and water distribute on both sides of the axis. The spring and summer are to our left and the fall and winter to our right. When we begin having this kind of a relationship, we call it "life." We have the most Yang source on the one hand and the most Yin source on the other, and in the middle we must have the axis for both of them. When these three come together we can say that the **myriad things** are born.

In the book of changes, **Yi Jing,** it is said that when the male and female essences exchange, the myriad things are born. The father is on the right and the mother on the left. The two come together to exchange their essence in order to create the center axis, a new wheel of Yin and Yang forming. This is called an embryo. This embryo axis starts revolving in an opposite direction, counter-clockwise, until becoming a baby, emerging out of the mother 10 months later.

This 1,2,3 – or father, mother and an axis – is the fundamental basis for conception. For this, we need the Yang energy to be in storage and to grow stronger. After pregnancy has been established, we must learn how to maintain and to nurture it so a healthy baby will be born.

In the Chinese language, the word **"Zhi,"** or cure, literally means "to control." When the above 1, 2, 3 travel in a wrong direction, the doctor's job is to put it back on track. In today's "pregnancy world," western doctors feel obligated to constantly intervene with blood tests and examinations. Many

治

ZHI

drugs and supplements are given to the pregnant woman. In Chinese medicine, the more a woman progresses with her pregnancy, the less treatment she needs.

However, a woman may need help conceiving because her conditions are not optimal. A pregnancy, aside from having a connection to the five elements and the numbers as we previously discussed, must be connected to the moon's principle, and if it isn't, there can be problems.

Miraculous Pivot – Discussion of Revealing the Year: *A man is a reflection of heaven and earth. He reacts to the sun and the moon. Therefore, when the moon is full, the ocean is full to the west, the person's energy and blood are accumulating, and his hair, skin, and flesh are all supple. At this time, evil can attack only on a superficial level. When the moon is empty, the ocean is full to the east, the person's energy and blood are depleted, his defenses are down and his body stands alone in the fight. His hair, skin, and flesh are deficient. At this time, evil can attack to a deeper level.*

We can see that the sages understood the relationship between the moon and our body. The opening statement says that the human body reacts to the sun and the moon movements. The sun, in reality, is not static. It moves in circles in relation to our planet.

SUMMER EXTREME

SPRING SPLIT — FALL SPLIT

WINTER EXTREME

In the Chinese lunar calendar, the year is divided into 24 segments. Each segment is approximately two weeks long. Even though it is a lunar calendar, it is divided according to the sun's movements. The sun travels every year from north to south, back and forth. When the sun arrives at the most southern point, it is referred to on the calendar as **Dong Zhi** or "winter extreme." When the sun returns toward the north and crosses the equator, it is called **Chun Fen,** or "spring split." When the sun continues its travel to the north until its most extreme point, it is referred to as **Xia Zhi,** or "summer extreme." When the sun then travels back southward and crosses the equator again, it is referred to as the **Qiu Fen,** or "fall split." The sun's circular motion establishes the four seasons. The entire planet reacts to the sun accordingly.

The same is true with the moon, but on a different platform. The moon orbits our planet earth every 29.5 days and circles around itself every 29.5 days, creating a special phenomenon, enabling us to view the same side of the moon all the time.

When the moon is full, it contains all the Yang energy. This is similar to the storage of Yang in our body. We can also use this principle to learn about the development of our pregnancy and baby.

The moon has eight phases, but for simplification purposes, we will divide it into four phases to match the four seasons. An empty or new moon is 1, the half moon growing is 3, the full moon is 5, and a half moon waning is 7. Thereafter, it is back to an empty moon 1. The new moon always rises at sunrise. The first half moon rises at noon. The full moon rises at sunset. The waning half moon rises at midnight. From this, we can see that the moon behaves differently depending on the amount of Yang energy within it. When the moon begins filling up with Yang energy, it rises at sunrise and when it is full with Yang energy (full moon) it rises at sunset.

This is very significant. Let's imagine that the moon is an energy tank where the "Yang energy reserves" are kept. When this tank is empty, it fills up on the sun's energy when the sun is in the sky. By the time the sun disappears, the tank is full and the tank is able to provide energy for light.

The Yellow Emperor says that we react to the sun and the moon. We wake up every morning for sunrise using new Yang energy, and we charge our energy every night when we go to sleep. The moon relates to our ability to recharge, or bring the Yang energy into storage. When the moon is full, it rises at sundown and stays with us throughout the night. This is why **The Yellow Emperor** says that when the moon is full, the energy and blood are full and evil can enter only at a superficial level, but when the moon is empty, the energy and blood are weak and evil can enter deep into the body.

A woman's menses preferably occurs when the moon is empty and the energy and blood are weakest. Her ovulation should occur when the moon is full and her energy and blood are at peak strength. The time for successful conception is when the moon is full. However, women often get their periods at different times of the lunar cycle.

In the classics, the sages stated that when the woman's period is irregular, the practitioner must regulate it in order for the woman to be healthy. Modern practitioners believe that the sages meant to regulate menstruation by making it occur every 28 days. The sages, however, meant that a regular menstruation is a period conforming to the moon cycle.

Synchronization with the lunar cycle is extremely important for pregnancy. The reason the body allows pregnancy is because our cycle is in sync with the moon and sun, with the ability to store Yang energy. When the body functions well, it knows that the baby can be healthy and it allows the woman to conceive. The system of male sperm and female ovum and the essence behind them is extremely potent. If the body is correctly storing Yang energy, the sperm and ovum have no problem finding each other. If Yang storage is impaired, then the code is broken and the essence is weak.

We must understand that if the body is not healthy, then it is not in a position to become pregnant or to keep a healthy pregnancy. When young children are sickly, it can partially be blamed on poor lifestyle and diet, but it is also because a pregnant mother couldn't harmonize with the lunar Yang storage phases.

The locations of moonrise and moonset at the horizon show the same variation during a month that the locations of sunrise and sunset do during a year. For those in the northern hemisphere, when the sun is in the south it is winter and the north when it is summer. The same happens with the moon every month. The lunar rising and setting change locations, which impacts our ability to store Yang energy. One Qigong exercise, which is very effective, is to stand outdoors in the evening when the full moon comes out and simply watch the moon and inhale slowly, harmonizing with it. You can only do this exercise when the moon is full.

The Yellow Emperor says that man (and woman) responds to the sun and the moon, and that the female reaction to the moon stops at the age of 49, meaning at menopause. The period can still come but the ability to conceive and create new life stops.

The ten heavenly stems, **Tian Gan,** are distributed around the circle. **Jia** is the first heavenly stem, while **Kui** is the last heavenly stem. Jia is the first step in the opening of the Yang energy, while Kui is the last step in the closing of the Yang energy. Every day, month and year, the cycle ends in Kui but breaks through into Jia to start a new cycle. When The Emperor says that at age 49, the woman's heaven Kui is finished, he means that there is no more lunar Kui. The new cycle, the cycle that conforms to the moon, does not start. This is the monthly cycle of ovulation

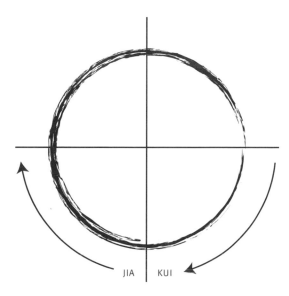

JIA | KUI

and menses. The moon and the storage of Yang are in the heaven Kui. The sun and the birth of Yang are in the heaven Jia. Because the heaven Kui is finished, the woman cannot get pregnant, but because the heaven Jia is not finished, she will still live a long life. The reproduction phase of her life ends.

Kui and Jia belong both to water and the north. Kui is Yin and Jia is Yang within the water as in the water (Kan) trigram. This is called the female essence. When this essence dries out, pregnancy is no longer possible. **The Yellow Emperor** explains that the female accumulates seven cycles of seven years, while the male accumulates eight cycles of eight years, until both their essences dry out.

Aside from helping our body become strong every month by knowing the moon, we can also learn about the development of the baby during pregnancy. The female becoming pregnant is the result of the female acting as the Yin counterpart of the moon. Its action of regenerating storage is the story of the "new life." The way that it recharges reflects the way a baby is developing. When the moon starts as a crescent new moon, it appears at the northwest, or rather the northwest part of the moon appears. This is the time when the baby is conceived. Thereafter, the moon gradually grows upwards toward the south and leftwards towards the east until the first growing half moon fills the right side of the moon (the west side). The moon continues to grow to become a full moon, which is the south, and this is mid pregnancy. The moon then starts to wane down to the east (to the left).

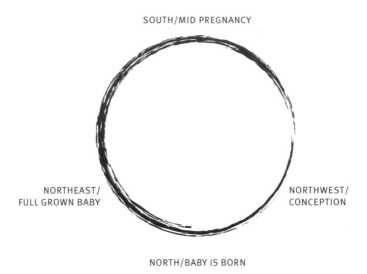

SOUTH/MID PREGNANCY

NORTHEAST/
FULL GROWN BABY

NORTHWEST/
CONCEPTION

NORTH/BABY IS BORN

The moon wanes until only the half moon remains at the east (left side). Then the moon wanes to a declining crescent moon that is visible at the northeast. At this time, the baby is fully grown and ready to emerge. The last phase of the moon is an empty moon. This is month 10 of a pregnancy when the baby is delivered.

Premature babies are often healthy, but are generally slightly less healthy then fully matured babies. This is because their five directions are established in the first five months of pregnancy.

When we understand the two phases of a pregnancy, we begin to have an insight into Chinese medicine miscarriage prevention and how to treat a pregnant woman. A pregnancy has two phases and not three trimesters as Western medicine pioneered. The first phase is the first five months of pregnancy, which includes the pre-conception phase. Infertility treatment falls under this category. I treat the mother and the father, not only so they can conceive, but rather so that their creation will survive the first five months.

The doctor's job is to ensure that conception will get to a full moon. He must have the vision that his treatment of infertility does the job for at least the first half of the pregnancy. It is also his job to make the second phase of the pregnancy proceed smoothly as well.

I had a patient who had suffered five miscarriages, three of which were during week 14, before coming to see me. In each case, she was treated with different Western medications unsuccessfully, but these medications could not correct her lunar cycle. With herbs and acupuncture during the first phase of pregnancy in order to restore harmony with the moon, she carried to term.

Before continuing with the two phases of pregnancy, I want to explain another point regarding fertility and successful conception, as this relates to phase one of pregnancy. The moon grows from the northwest to the south, however our Yang energy opens up in the reverse direction, from northeast to the south. When the moon grows, the Yang energy increases, because it increases the Yang energy storage. However, when the Yang energy opens up in the east or northeast, this starts the process of spending the Yang. At the same time, the spending of the Yang is a daily cycle, while the storage of the Yang as it relates to the moon are monthly cycles.

When the storage of the moon is full, the body's overall energy and blood are full. This is the time for conception, or as Western medicine might put it, "ovulation." This time is in the south. At the same time we must understand the other side of the chart. The north, or the time Zi, (11pm-1am) is the Shao Yin time. It is the time of the emperor fire, when the heart's fire warms up the true Yang of the kidney's water. This causes the Yang energy to exit.

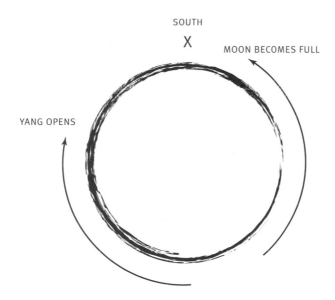

SOUTH

X

MOON BECOMES FULL

YANG OPENS

NORTH/NEW MOON/YANG RISE

The east is the time of Mao (7 AM – 9 AM). It is the time of the Shao Yang's minister fire. The minister fire pushes the rising of the Yang energy until it gets to the south where it is most open and used up. In general, the Yang opening up combined with the full moon is the time where libido or sex drive peaks. It is the time of conception as well. This is why many women

171

experience an increase in libido around the fertile time. "Sex drive" is connected to fertile time and reflects the health of the stored Yang. The seasons are spring and summer and correspond to the time when animals move into "heat" and are intent on reproducing.

After the male and female essences have exchanged and a new life is created, the whole process of the baby developing in the first five months is the process of the moon becoming full. The mother nurtures this process of establishing the child's five directions. In the second phase, when the directions are complete, the child begins to be demanding. In the baby's fetus world, the moon cycles are dominant, the rotation of the fetus moving counterclockwise from the northwest to the northeast.

Come month 10, the baby emerges into our world, his Yang revolution becoming the same as ours. It revolves clockwise from the northeast to the northwest. At this time, the baby's energy walks the same route as adults and the treatment must adapt accordingly.

In the first phase of pregnancy, the treatment goal is to help the baby as its five directions form. If anything is wrong with the harmony, we must help the child first. During the second phase, the moon declines. This means that the energy and blood of the mother decline. The job of the doctor in the pregnancy's second phase is to strengthen the mother and prepare her for delivery. Of course, strengthening the baby is no less important; however one should remember that the five directions have been established and simply need to be completed, represented by the numbers 6, 7, 8,9,10. In the first phase, the mother creates the baby's five directions, while in the second phase the baby pulls from the mother the resources needed for its completion. In this second phase, it is most common to see a pregnant woman diagnosed by Western doctors with gestational diabetes or anemia. In reality, this is a natural process and it merely means that the mother's resources are over taxed by the baby.

The first phase and second phase of pregnancy is the designation made by the sage to insure a healthy future generation. The first phase of pregnancy is called the pre-heaven phase, while the second is called the post-heaven phase. During the pre-heaven the mother is giving and during the post-heaven the mother is taxed by the baby.

The Yellow Emperor explains that the minister fire comes down to earth to create fire, shaping the 10,000 shapes and forms. The emperor fire, or "heaven's essence," doesn't come down to earth, instead it reaches the Yin organs and store as essence. When form (Xing) and essence (Jing) unite, we get "birth" (Sheng Hua). In this

形 精 生 化
XING   JING   SHENG HUA

context "form" refers to the female ovum and the male sperm, and what we call "essence" refers to the mother's and father's Shao Yin. The man reflects the heaven and earth, and so he has the heaven's Yang essence as well as the earth's Yin form.

There is the form and the essence. The form alone can't do the job, nor can the essence. **The Yellow Emperor** says that the kidneys rule the storage of essence. The kidneys in Chinese medicine are the Shao Yin emperor fire. The essence that **The Yellow Emperor** is talking about is the essence that can give birth to a new life. It is the essence of the five directions; north, south, east, west and center, the same five directions needed to establish the first phase of pregnancy and the first five numbers of the baby – 1,2,3,4,5. This whole dynamic explains what the emperor means when he says that minister fire comes down to the earth and emperor fire does not. The minister fire is the fire creating the "form," or sperm and egg. The emperor fire is the fire stored as essence which we call Shao Yin essence. This is why we say that the man reflects the heaven and earth and he has two fires.

Minister fire leads the Yang and emperor fire pilots the Yin. Our Yin energy is the heaven's energy stored in our body as essence. The Yang energy is our body's functions. Therefore, when we treat a pregnant woman, we want to help the mother and the baby. To help the mother, we help the Yang energy and the minister fire, and to help the baby, we help the Yin or the emperor fire. Helping the Yin and baby is never ever clearing heat or using thick herbs to obstruct the Yang, the way it is widely practiced today. Yin is emperor fire. It is heaven Yang stored within the body as essence. Using acupuncture or herbs to obstruct the heaven's Yang and the Shao Yin is what the sages called "putting the patient under the sword of medicine".

ACUPUNCTURE PRINCIPLES AND GUIDELINES

During the first phase of pregnancy, the primary treatment principle is to help the baby, acupuncture the preferred treatment modality. If the father and mother are not in optimal health at time of conception, then herbal formulas can be considered as well. What is most necessary, however, is neither acupuncture nor herbs, but rather Chinese medicine. Many think that herbs used in the Chinese herbal pharmacy equal Chinese medicine. This is not true. A cup of hot water could be Chinese medicine, while popular Chinese herbs like Dang Gui (Dang Quai) may not be. If the practitioner understands Yin and Yang well in the way that the sages did, he can use a cup of hot water to cure the patient. Speaking for myself, I have helped many of my pregnant patients recover with a cup of hot water.

Many patients in mid pregnancy experience heart burn. Over the counter remedies are often prescribed by the ob/gyn, but shouldn't be. When the baby grows in the uterus, the Ren and

WATER TRIGRAM

Chong meridians are obstructed and the stomach descending motion is hindered, heartburn, as well as nausea and belching can result. Hot water is water with extra Yang energy. This is the Yang energy in water as described earlier in the book, represented by the water trigram.

When extra true Yang energy from hot water enters the stomach, the stomach can recover its natural function of descending and the heartburn stops.

The same is true with acupuncture. When the practitioner understands the nature of the problem, the number of needles used doesn't matter. If the acupuncturist does not understand the nature of the problem, then even 20 needles will not do the job.

The most important aspect, and at the same time the most difficult, is to know when it is best to treat a patient, and when to avoid intervention. The basic and most fundamental principle of Chinese medicine is to restore balance. If the patient is already balanced, it is possible that treatment will put her out of balance. Some modern practitioners, when treating a patient, use Western methodologies to determine when to treat. They may decide to treat ovulation issues during the follicular phase and menstrual problems during the luteal phase. They may treat based on assessment of Yang energy according to basal body temperature. This kind of approach, however, is not Chinese medicine, but rather Western medicine with needles and herbs. With true Chinese medicine, the appropriate time for treatment is solely based on whether or not the patient is in harmony.

Along the same lines, the Western system often discovers pregnancy issues as a result of doing routine interventions or tests. Sometimes the mother and/or baby are already in trouble. In Chinese medicine, these issues are resolved before they happen, which is of course far preferable.

With regard to stopping and starting treatment when pregnant, if the patient feels uncomfortable symptoms, such as nausea, back pain, hemorrhoids, heart burn, or acid reflux, treatment can be very useful. Other symptoms, such as very mild nausea in the first phase, are normal and no treatment is needed

ACUPUNCTURE IVF AND EVIDENCE BASED SCIENCE

Acupuncture has made large strides in modern medicine. Today it is a popular treatment modality. Many health insurance companies now cover acupuncture treatments. Many medical doctors are referring their patients to acupuncture practitioners.

It is clear to me that the reason acupuncture has been found to be beneficial for IVF patients is that the acupuncture does make a woman healthier and more able to withstand the IVF procedure. However, these women who become healthier with acupuncture are just as likely to then go on and have a baby naturally as they are to start IVF procedures. Instead of supporting the IVF procedure, the acupuncture should be seen as a stand-alone answer. It is far less invasive, has far fewer side effects, and will not be as costly.

SUPERMARKETS OUT, LOCAL FARMS IN

The centralization of the food chain and the ruining of food with artificial ingredients, can have a negative effect on our health and fertility, and its effects on future generations is as yet unknown. We have to make the right choices when it comes to our food.

The Chinese sage Sun Simiao named his classical book **Emergency Prescription Worth a Thousand Gold,** meaning the life and health of a person is most precious. But for whom is it precious? It is only precious for the individual himself. With regard to modern food, an individual's health is not precious to the big companies producing the food. Therefore, it is up to the individual to ensure quality. Of course, if manufactured food were to be harmful upon digestion, authorities would shut down the companies involved. But if food products are harmful over a period of many years, the companies are not held accountable and are safe to make their profits.

Big food companies have tremendous resources when it comes to manipulating public opinion. This can be done through advertising, government lobbying, and the sponsorship of "studies" that prove desired results.

How do we know what we should eat and where to get it? I think we should all look into our heart and find our belief. We should look for what makes sense to us that creates our belief. When my oldest daughter was born, I became very worried. I had an overwhelming desire to find out the truth about food and be able to give it to my family. I went on a difficult quest where I met controversy. It was difficult to know right from wrong, but I always fell back onto my heart. I looked for the warm place in there, where I asked myself, what would my mother, grandmother, and great-grandmother have done? What would they decide?

The answer has always been the same – to rely on the generations. They didn't choose what to buy at the market, or what to cook at home, because of a study they read. In today's world, we have stopped listening to our mother's voice. We are listening to science now.

We must go back to the time where the reason for cooking food was to make it delicious and healthy. It was a time when the mother would put love into cooking for her children and go out of her way to acquire the best possible ingredients. These are diets that have been created over many centuries for only one purpose; creating and sustaining a healthy next generation.

RECOMMENDATIONS OF THE GENERATIONS

We provide ourselves with an abundance of food year round. We can buy summer fruits in winter and tropical fruits in Alaska. Even though this may seem fine to the naked eye, it is not. When fruits and vegetable grow in a certain climate or in a certain season, they can supplement a real and current bodily need. If we eat a watermelon, which is watery and cool, in summer it can actually slow down the Yang expansion, restoring harmony in our body.

At this time, eating a watermelon is beneficial to our health. However, what happens when we eat a watermelon imported from South America in the middle of winter? Our Yang energy is in a contraction state in accordance with the winter season. A watermelon will overly shrink the Yang into contraction, harming the true Yang of the kidneys.

The Yellow Emperor says if it's hot, cool it off, and if it's cold, warm it up. This is how we strive back to harmony. This is why there are no cold fruits or vegetables growing in winter, when people should eat more animal food, such as meat and animal fat. This creates the energy needed to warm up the kidney Yang. There are many cold vegetables and fruits that grow in the summer, which can help cool us down when the heaven Yang descends with all its vigor and the dead winter earth is born into life. Because the live Yin energy of the earth is what fills up the plants and trees, the fruits and vegetable we eat contain an amount of Yin energy. This is why they are juicy. If one dries the fruit and vegetables, they become more Yang. Dry fruit, then, is not cold and can be eaten in the winter. The same is true with pickled fruits and vegetables.

During the winter, Yang is sparse and the earth is dead. Animals have a longer life cycle then one year. They eat large volumes during the thriving spring and summer seasons, storing it in their body as fat reserves for the winter. The animal fat is condensed Yang that is then released gradually, warming and nourishing the animal throughout the winter, and is actually an expansion of the Yang mechanism.

Because meat and fat are warming the Yang, we should eat less of it in the spring and summer and more of it in the fall and winter. This is the way to be harmonious with your diet. It has nothing to do with low fat and more veggies. The bottom line is that if you eat certain food at the right time, it is good; if you eat the same food at the wrong time, it is not. If you eat in accordance with the seasons, it will be beneficial for your health, but may not be beneficial for the food industry.

Our food must be regulated according to nature; to eat healthily, you must buy your food locally. The energy in the local farmer's produce is the best for your health, and is worth the extra few dollars you may pay.

Today's transportation and globalization, gives rise to many problems in our diet. There is wide consumption of a product referred to as soy protein, which acts as a substitute for meat.

It is consumed by Westerners who should not eat it because it is often highly processed. Such a food can seriously offset Yin and Yang.

The second most important element in traditional diet is the food quality. It is not just that the additives and chemicals added to food are harmful, but the quality of the food itself is. If the food is of a good quality and unadulterated, the energy within is abundant. This will improve health and fertility substantially.

Many people lack the confidence in the food they are eating unless it is sold in a major chain food store. This is the wrong way to obtain food. You need to find out for yourself if what you eat is safe or not. You, not the store manager, must be in charge of your safety.

FRUITS AND VEGETABLES – BE SEASONALLY CORRECT

Vegetable and fruits are generally healthy if grown locally and in season. Consumption of fruits and vegetables in winter should be reduced and limited unless dried or pickled. Vegetable oils are not the same as vegetables. Because they are unsaturated, if fried, they tend to oxidize and can be very harmful to your health and fertility. Unfortunately, many vegetable oils are already highly oxidized when purchased. For cooking, it is best to use saturated fat, such as chicken fat, lard or butter. A few vegetable oils are good, but only if cold pressed, organic, and used cold in salad dressing. It is important to read labels. Avoid food with vegetable oil listed as an ingredient. Processed fruits and vegetables with added chemicals, colors and preservatives are not healthy.

MILK AND DAIRY – STRAIGHT FROM THE COW

Milk and cultured dairy have been consumed for many generations in different parts of the world. What has made milk and other dairy products healthy has always been the health and natural diet of the animal, as well as its ability to roam free.

In the modern dairy, however, it is quite different. Animals are confined, eat grains, corn, or abnormal materials such as cardboard. They rarely see the sun and never exercise. When these animals produce milk, the quality is poor and often even dangerous to drink.

The overall cost of milk can be reduced drastically by the process of pasteurization. However when boiled off, does the milk remain good? Although the harmful bacteria are eliminated, bad milk stays bad. Even if safe to drink, it will result in illness.

Real milk – namely fresh, high quality and unadulterated milk from healthy cows – is the product consumed for generations. Modern, commercial milk purchased in stores has not been around long at all. Many states, unfortunately under pressure from the milk industry, passed laws prohibiting the sale of real milk to the public. However, other states kept the right of the public to make its own decision. In Connecticut, where I live, sale of real milk is legal and supervised by the state. The cases of people becoming ill from consuming this milk are practically non-existent, and in fact, the number of cases of illness from pasteurized milk is actually greater.

The problem with real milk arises in states where its sale is prohibited. This gives rise to poor quality milk which can be dangerous. The benefits of real, unadulterated milk are numerous and require a whole separate book. For further reading, I recommend **The Untold Story of Milk** by Ron Schmid. This explains the many aspects of milk, including the politics behind it and the reason people are so afraid of it today. You can also visit the Weston A. Price Foundation websites at www.westonaprice.org and www.realmilk.com.

There are two reasons to drink real milk. (1) It contains all the good bacteria, enzymes, and naturally occurring vitamins; (2) it ensures that the milk you are drinking is from healthy, happy cows. It is interesting to note that pasteurization extends the shelf life of the milk, thus making more money for the industry. Ultra pasteurization can even extend the shelf life of milk to several months, without refrigeration.

The other problem with commercial milk is homogenization: the process of blasting the fat molecules in the milk so that the fat will not rise to the top. When the milk fat rises, it clogs the top of the containers after just a few days, shortening shelf life. When homogenization was first introduced in the 1940s and 1950s, many people refused the modified product because they felt something must be wrong with it.

Even more startling is the attack against fat. The public has been lead to believe that it is harmful to the heart, leading to the popularization of fat free milk. Ironically, however, opposite the 1%, 2% and fat free milk on the supermarket shelves are cheeses, creams and butter full of fat. The food industry has essentially removed the fat from milk and transferred it to cultured products.

When it comes to yogurt and cheeses, it is even more important to consume products made from fresh milk. Raw milk cheeses are widely available in stores throughout the country, even in states where the sale of fresh milk is prohibited. Nevertheless, the preferred method to obtain these items is to make your own yogurt, kefir, and cheese. To make fresh yogurt, simply add half a cup of commercial yogurt to a half gallon of fresh milk, warm it on the stove until luke warm, then stir to melt the commercial yogurt. Place it in an oven at 115 degrees for six to eight hours. The result will be a pot full of home made yogurt. To make soft cheese, place the fresh yogurt in a cheese cloth and hang it for several hours to drain the liquid away.

The results of a study were recently released showing that women who drink whole milk are more fertile than women who drink fat free milk.

EGGS AND POULTRY – FROM CHICKENS THAT EAT A NATURAL DIET

I believe we should strive to eat as naturally as possible, insuring optimal nutrients. Eggs that come from free-range chickens, for example, are more nutritional. Free range means chickens that are free to roam, enabling them to eat worms and insects. Most organic growers feed organic grains to their chickens. Although this is preferable to genetically modified grains used by the mainstream poultry industry, it does not compare to free-range chickens. The result is seen in the eggs and yolks. The egg yolks from free-range chickens will be dark yellow or dark orange.

Eating premium quality eggs will support nutrient intakes, especially the egg yolks. Another good source of nutrients is to eat the chicken livers and bone marrow. The Chinese diet includes the entire chicken with the bones, skin and head, not just the meat. When the chicken is raised humanely in a healthy way, this is an excellent source of Yin and Yang energy.

MEAT AND FAT – SPARE THE GROWTH HORMONES

It is of great importance for consumers to know the source of the meat and animal fat they are consuming. Similar to chickens, healthy cows, sheep and goats will produce healthy meat and fat. The key to raising healthy animals is to maintain their natural habitat and diet. The fat and organ meat from grass fed beef is much healthier then that of an animal that is fed grain, receiving growth hormones or antibiotics. Liver from grass fed beef is especially recommended.

THE FOUR LEVELS OF THE HUNYUAN METHOD

While Chinese herbs and acupuncture are decisively not "do-it-yourself" modalities, I have long thought it would be beneficial to introduce a home program based on this ancient wisdom. With the Hunyuan method, I divide my treatment protocol into four levels. Approximately 25% of all pregnancies resulting from the Hunyuan Method are reached due to the first two levels of treatment. Approximately 75% of pregnancies result from all four levels. However, these include strong, potent herbs that are not recommended for home remedies as they can only be taken under strict supervision of a practitioner. Therefore, these potent herbs have been left out of the home program in favor of kitchen-based, mild herbs that carry no risk. The efficacy, of course, will not be the same as it would be if the patient visited an acupuncturist. However, to help improve the results of the mild herbs, I will explain additional methods of acupressure, Qigong exercises, and diet and lifestyle modifications. Again, this do-it-yourself protocol is not a substitute for visiting a health care professional or an herbalist, but it is your first step towards success.

It is recommended that each level be practiced for one month before proceeding to the next. However, if the patient does not suffer from any symptoms listed under Level 1, she should proceed to Level 2 immediately. If the patient is in the midst of levels two through four when a Yang illness or blockage arises, she must return to level 1 (or level 2 if level 1 is not applicable). When she has re-balanced the three Yang spheres at level one, within three days she may return to the level where the blockage began.

LEVEL 1: BALANCING THE THREE YANG SPHERES; TAI YANG, SHAO YANG, YANG MING

Before Yang meets Yin – before the Tai Yang life force connects with the Yin energy force within the body – it is imperative that the three Yang life force energy spheres come into balance.

The remedy for disharmony in the Tai Yang, Shao Yang and Yang Ming spheres must conform to the laws of nature: it must follow a natural modality of treatment such as offered by Chinese, Ayurvedic or American Indian folk medicine. With Chinese medicine, the remedy consists of diet, herbs, acupressure, Qigong (therapeutic movement and/or breathing), emotional balancing and lifestyle modifications.

TAI YANG ILLNESS – RECOGNIZING THE LIFE FORCE ENERGY IMBALANCE

Tai Yang illness occurs when the Yang mechanism – where the life force exits the body – is blocked from opening. The symptoms can be one or more of the following: chills, fever, runny or blocked nose, stiff neck, general body aches and exhaustion.

Although these symptoms do not appear to constitute a serious Western medical illness, they are serious from a Chinese fertility perspective. If not treated, the disharmony can travel deep into the Shao Yin, possibly damaging fertility prospects.

REMEDYING THE IMBALANCE – CLEAR THE CHANNEL

Modern cold remedies must be avoided, as these treat only the symptoms. It is possible that the remedies will force the illness to an inward place, becoming more serious.

DIET – LOSE THE DAIRY, EAT BLAND

Consumption of any dairy product, as well as oily, deep fried, spicy, and/or salty food, can obstruct the Tai-Yang energy force. Cold food and beverages will dampen the heat of the Tai-

Yang fire.

Bland foods are recommended, such as sprouted bread, eggs, lightly cooked vegetables, and chicken soup. It is best to eat small quantities rather than large meals so as not to further exacerbate the obstruction.

HERBAL – SPREAD THE FIRE

Add 3 teaspoons Cinnamon twigs (not cinnamon powder), 3 slices fresh ginger, and 2 teaspoons of maple syrup to two cups of water. Boil the mixture for 20 minutes.

In the early afternoon, drink one cup on an empty stomach, followed by a bowl of rice soup. Afterwards, lie down in a relaxed position under blankets. Help the life energy move through your body by imagining fire spreading from the heart to the extremities. Remain in this position until light perspiration forms on the skin.

ACUPRESSURE – STIMULATE ENERGY MOVEMENT

Use fingers to lightly stimulate the area around acupressure points GB 20 at the back of the neck, and Stomach 40 at the mid shinbone on the lateral side (see diagram on next page). It is not necessary to locate the exact points. Rub these areas three times per day.

QI GONG – RUB IT DOWN

When the Yang energy is blocked, it is advantageous to rub down the four extremities.

Stretch both hands in front of you, fingers pointing forward and away from the body. Insert the right thumb under the left armpit with four fingers hugging the top of the upper arm. Rub all the way down your arm and hand. Repeat the process twelve times. Switch to your right arm and do the same.

Use both hands to encircle your right upper thigh, close to the crotch, and rub down your leg and right foot. Repeat the process twelve times and then switch to your left leg.

EMOTIONAL – LEAVE THE STRESS BEHIND

Pensiveness means to think, think, think. This over-thinking restricts the Tai Yang from opening. Ease both the mind and body by retiring to bed and forgetting about everything. This will allow the life force to flow smoothly, uninterrupted.

LIFESTYLE – JUST HANG-OUT

Do not exercise

Do not work

Avoid exposure to wind along the neck and nape.

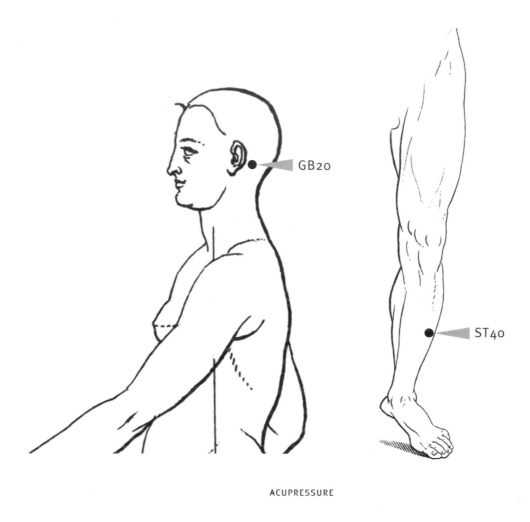

ACUPRESSURE

SHAO YANG ILLNESS

Shao Yang illness occurs when the Yang energy fails to warm up, and the Tai-Yang is unable to ignite the fire.

RECOGNIZING THE IMBALANCE

The main symptoms of the Shao Yang illness are dry eyes, bitter taste in the mouth, slight nausea, a general feeling of discomfort in the chest and abdomen area, headaches on one side of the head or behind the eye, decreased appetite, an upset emotional state, and a wiry pulse.

REMEDYING THE IMBALANCE

DIET – AVOID SUGAR STAGNATION

Stay away from sweets such as chocolate and jams. These foods create stagnation and drain the heat needed for the Shao Yang.

Include slightly cool spicy, salty, and sweet flavors, and moderate seasoning of all food. Recommended: Beef soup with cilantro and mint

HERBAL – A TRIP TO THE GARDEN

Add 8 teaspoons rosemary, 3 pieces of fresh ginger, 2 tablespoons cut licorice root, and 9 dandelion leaves to three cups of water. Boil the mixture for 30 minutes. Drink one cup at room temperature after morning breakfast.

ACUPRESSURE – IMPROVE YANG ENERGY CIRCULATION

External stimulation of the body can improve the circulation of the Yang energy. Relax both hands to the sides of the body. Clench fists lightly and place the eye of the fists (thumb and index finger) at GB 31 along the sides of thighs. Tap on GB 31 with your fists' eye 24 times. Repeat the process 8 times per day.

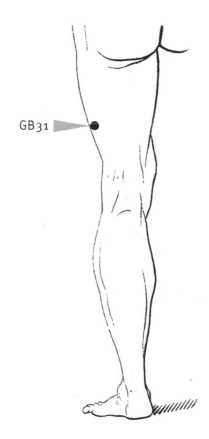

GB31

QI GONG – RADIATE THE LIFE FORCE

Use thumbs and eight fingers to brush through the hair from the forehead backwards toward the neck. Brush back on the sides of the head, returning to the forehead. Use slight force so as to feel the Yang energy traveling to your face. On waking in the morning, rub the scalp with medium force from front to rear 24 times, radiating the life force.

EMOTIONAL – DON'T WORRY, BE HAPPY

Avoid anger and frustration. Add joy to your day, helping to kindle and sustain the Shao Yang fire.

ACUPRESSURE

LIFESTYLE – STRESS-FREE MORNINGS

The morning is when the Shao Yang is most active. Stressful mornings must be avoided in order to give the Shao Yang the balance it needs to do its work.

YANG MING ILLNESS

The body's life force needs rest. Yang Ming illness occurs when the Yang mechanism that facilitates the entrance of the life force back into storage cannot do so. The life force overstays its welcome.

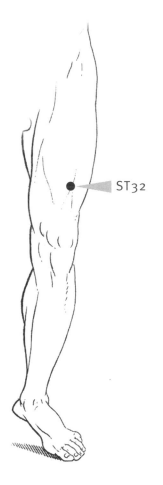

ST32

ACUPRESSURE

RECOGNIZING THE IMBALANCE

When The Life Force cannot close down, symptoms include overheating, increased thirst and desire for cold drinks, constipation, constant hunger, red face, increased perspiration, strong and rapid pulse.

REMEDYING THE IMBALANCE

DIET – KEEP IT COOL

Avoid bread, rice, milk and other constipating foods, as well as greasy and/or deep fried foods.

Include: Raw and leafy vegetables such as spinach and cabbage.

If you are suffering from heat symptoms, or you are craving cold beverages, you may add cold drinks to your diet, but this should be discontinued once heat symptoms subside.

HERBAL – TASTES GREAT

Add 2 teaspoons of organic honey and 1/4 teaspoon grated fresh ginger to one cup of hot water. Cool the beverage and drink late in the evening before going to sleep.

ACUPRESSURE

While in a sitting position, use the base of the palms to rub the point Stomach 32 forward and backwards 36 times. Apply four times a day.

QI GONG – UNLOCK THE GATES

This exercise helps to unlock the Yang Ming. The Yang is finally able to retreat into storage.

Layer palms on each other, placing them on top of abdomen. In a circular motion rub entire abdomen with medium pressure from the lower abdomen to the left side to the upper abdomen to the right side. Repeat for 36 rotations. Change direction for 24 rotations.

EMOTIONAL – GET THAT SMILE OFF YOUR FACE

Joy and laughter will increase the warmth around Tai Yang. It is best to keep the mind in an even mood of peacefulness.

LIFESTYLE – CUT DOWN ON EVENING STIMULATION

Excitement and stimulation during the evening hours will prevent the Yang Ming from closing down, the fire persisting. It is best to eat a light dinner and to go to bed early. Television and other stimulants should be avoided, although listening to soft music may calm your mind.

LEVEL 2: STRENGTHENING THE TAI YIN SPHERE

As opposed to the Yang spheres, the Yin spheres are inside the body, from the cellular level to the organ level. The three aspects of the Yin—the Tai, the Shao and the Jue   compose the body's Yin energy. They contain the storage of old energy, the death of old energy, as well as transformation and rebirth of new energy.

The three Yin are the source of life and the root of fertility. The Tai Yin is the pure Yin, representing the earth as the mother of all things. As the Yang energy comes in from the outside (the sun radiating upon earth, the food we eat), it begins to move the Yin energy within, specifically at the spleen and lungs. The Yang energy causes the life force to be separated from the physical, the resulting damp mist joining up with Yin energy as it ascends to the lungs and descends into the large intestines. This separation and the coming together of Yin and Yang is the root of life and fertility, and is where infertility healing begins.

TAI YIN ILLNESS

RECOGNIZING YOUR IMBALANCE – THE YIN ON HOLD

When an illness or blockage occurs in the Tai Yin, the Yang no longer reflects into the earth and therefore cannot stir up the Yin. Symptoms include feeling cold, fullness of abdomen, decreased appetite, loose bowels, craving for sweets, pale and thick tongue, tiredness, weak and slippery pulse, and gradual weight gain despite exercise.

REMEDYING THE IMBALANCE

DIET – STAY WITH WARM AND COOKED

Consumption of cold energy will decrease the Yang in the Tai Yin and will move you away from fertility and a healthy pregnancy. Avoid cold foods and drinks such as ice water, ice cream, or frozen desserts. Avoid water at room temperature, as well as raw fruits and vegetables.

Recommended: Beef, lamb, and slightly cooked or steamed fruits and vegetables

HERBAL – YOUR NATURAL MORNING COCKTAIL

Add 2 teaspoons cinnamon powder or sticks, 7 slices sun dried ginger, 1 teaspoon cloves, 2 teaspoons sliced licorice, 5 pieces Bai Zhu, 5 pieces Fu Ling and 1 piece ginseng root (or 1 teaspoon of ginseng extract) to 3 cups of water and boil for 30 minutes.

Drink 1 cup after morning breakfast every day for one month.

ACUPRESSURE – BELOW THE BELT

Use fingertips to rub Stomach 36, located below the knee and one-half inch lateral to the shinbone for five minutes. Continue by rubbing Spleen 6, located 3 inches above the ankle inner bone on the medial side of the leg, for five minutes. Repeat the exercise five times per day.

QI GONG – SPREAD HEAVEN'S ENERGY INTO YOUR UPPER BODY

A peaceful state of mind is crucial for success in overcoming this illness. The environment should be clean, with ample fresh air and preferably close to nature.

Wearing loose fitting clothes, and either standing or sitting down, place both hands to sides, calm the mind and regulate breathing. Close the eyes and attempt to listen inwards to the heartbeat for one minute.

Inhale deeply and exhale slowly. Raise hands above the head and stretch toward the sky. Still relaxed, imagine the hands becoming longer and longer as they reach into the heavens.

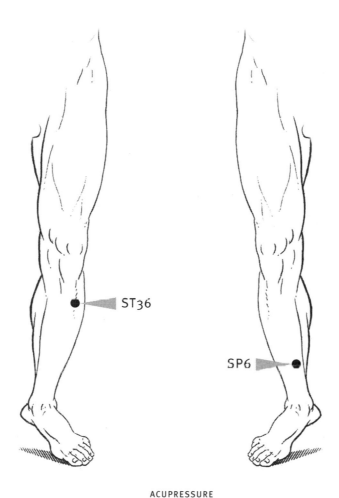

ACUPRESSURE

Begin lowering hands, palms facing body, while imagining that heaven's energy is coming down into your head, moving down your throat, and into your chest. Place your palms on your chest and slide to lower abdomen area, heaven's energy now spreading throughout your upper body. Your palms still placed below the naval, keep your intentions and thoughts on the lower abdomen for about thirty seconds. Repeat this exercise ten times.

It is best to practice this exercise upon waking in the morning, but other times during the day will also be of benefit.

EMOTIONAL – USE MEDITATIVE HEALING TO AVOID ANGER

Avoid anger and fear as much as possible, especially over infertility issues, as these emotions damage the Tai Yin. A daily meditation just before bedtime is recommended. The meditation can be as short as one minute or as long as an hour. Begin by closing the eyes and emptying the mind. Visualize the following sentences on a big screen inside the head: *The world is constantly changing. Infertile today is fertile tomorrow. Not pregnant today is pregnant tomorrow.*

LIFESTYLE – KEEP THE TEMPERATURE MODERATE AND THE AIR FRESH

Because external cold impairs the Yang from moving inwards and stirring the Yin, avoid cold temperatures caused by overactive air conditioners in home or office. If nothing can be done about a cold office, dress warmly. Stay out of damp environments as much as possible, and make sure that clothes, house, vehicle and office are dry, clean, and full of fresh air.

LEVEL 3: BUILDING A SHAO YIN RELATIONSHIP

With a Tai Yin illness, the Yang energy from the outside is unable to stir the Yin within the body. Here, in the Shao Yin, the Yang from outside the body cannot transform the Yin inside. Yang mixing with Yin is the beginning of the new life energy, the two components needed to make a baby. They interact within your body, between you and your husband and between heaven and earth. If the Yang cannot transform the Yin, conception will not occur.

RECOGNIZING THE IMBALANCE

The Shao Yin illness in your body displays itself with the following symptoms: cold hands and feet, thin weak pulse, pale white tongue. Some patients, however, manifest this illness by feeling too warm, or by feeling hot but then cold. Other patients may feel hot at night and suffer night sweats, but feel cold during the day.

REMEDYING THE IMBALANCE

DIET – BRING ON THAT CHOLESTEROL

Avoid cold food and drinks.

Include foods condensed with nutrients and energy, especially saturated fat of premium quality.

Recommended: Organic butter (preferably raw), whole raw milk, raw cream and raw cheeses from grass-fed, naturally-raised animals. (Availability of raw milk and cheeses varies due to state laws; visit www.realmilk.com for answers). It is of the utmost importance that supermarket quality saturated fat not be substituted for premium quality saturated fat. It could mean the difference between success and failure.

HERBAL – A POTPOURRI FOR YOUR DAILY USE

Incorporate cinnamon, licorice, dry ginger, jujuba dates and Yin Yanghuo leaves into teas or soups every day for one month. Bai Zhu, Sha Ren and Cang Zhu can also be added.

Caution: Although aconitum is traditionally the primary herb used to heal the Shao Yin, do not take it at home. It is potent and should only be taken if recommended and monitored by a professional to avoid any possible complications.

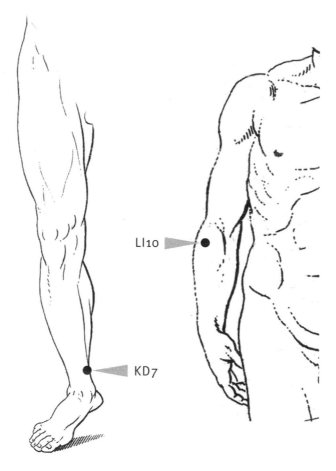

LI10

KD7

ACUPRESSURE

ACUPRESSURE – USE INTENTION AND IMAGINATION TO BRING ACTION

Use finger tips to massage Kidney 7 and Large Intestine 10, rubbing in energy with great intention and imagination, six times per day.

QI GONG – ESCORT THE LIFE ENERGY INTO YOUR LOWER ABDOMEN WITH YOUR PALMS

Place the left palm on the center of the chest, covering the heart. Place the right palm on the lower abdomen, covering the pubic hair area. Imagine the energy emitted from the palms as filling up the chest cavity and lower abdominal cavity.

Carry out this exercise at night while lying in bed before falling asleep. Attempt to fall asleep in the same position. On waking during the night, resume the position. On waking in the morning, change to a sitting posture on the side of the bed. Place the back of the hands on the lower back, rubbing the kidney area up and down 25 times (up and down considered to be one rub). Breathe calmly, and slowly wake up to the new day.

EMOTIONAL: BALANCE FEAR AND JOY IN HARMONY

Avoid fear and experience joy. Fear harms the heart's ability to radiate fire. It blocks the Yang energy. Joy allows water to absorb the Yang, enabling the life force.

Fear and joy share the same root, in that fear is the fear of death and joy is the joy of life. In the Shao Yin sphere, fear and joy are both very necessary but must remain in balance. If in disharmony, they can harm life.

Accepting joy attracts Yang energy – the life energy of the heart. Rejecting joy blocks the Yang energy from absorption by the kidneys. Joy is the acceptance of life's energy. Fear is not the fear of failing nor is it of remaining childless. Fear is the rejection of the life force – of our fate. It is denial. It is not accepting what is happening to us. When denial is strong, or when true fear is strong, the heart's joy, expressed as fire, cannot spread and radiate to the entire body.

In the Shao Yin, the goal is to bring the joy back we experience in childhood and minimize the fear we acquire as adults. We need to dispel the fear and rid ourselves of rejection. We must stop feeling sorry for ourselves, accept our circumstances and our future. Accepting the joy frees the kidneys to spread water energy. Rejecting the fear allows the heart to spread fire energy.

LIFESTYLE MODIFICATIONS – START (OR ENHANCE) A DAILY MEDITATION PRACTICE

In Shao Yin, the interaction of water and fire is problematic. It affects the physical body, energy, emotions and subconscious. The biggest obstacle in these two energies coming together is the distractions in our everyday lives.

When the mind is distracted, the Yang is scattered and unable to nourish the fire and water energies. We have many distractions in our life including our careers, the media, gossip and social events. This distraction of the mind harms the Shao Yin. The reason that meditation has been so highly valued in Chinese and other Asian cultures is because of its calming effect on the mind and the harmony that comes with it. When, by meditation, the mind is put at ease, the interaction between water and fire is facilitated.

Begin a meditation practice. If you already do practice meditation, attempt to increase the time you spend meditating. Do not keep your mind busy. Keep your mind empty.

LEVEL 4: BREAKING THE JUE YIN OBSTACLE.

In the Jue Yin, the Yang wants to break apart from the Yin. A new life cycle wants to be born.

RECOGNIZING THE IMBALANCE

The symptoms of Jue Yin illness are thirst, a pounding heart, and hunger with no desire to eat.

REMEDYING THE IMBALANCE

DIET – EAT THAT LIVER AND ONIONS

Follow recommendations in the Tai Yin and Shao Yin sections, but in addition add organ meats (liver, heart, kidneys, brain) to your diet to strengthen the Jue Yin function of transforming the old cycle into a new one.

HERBAL

Add one teaspoon hide gelatin, 30 Goji berries, 5 slices dry ginger, 2 teaspoons cinnamon twigs, 1 piece ginseng, 2 teaspoons fennel seeds to 3 cups of water and boil for 25 minutes. Drink 1 cup early in morning after breakfast for one month.

ACUPRESSURE

Use left fingertips to stimulate Conception Vessel 1 (at the bottom of the trunk between the scrotum and anus), and the right palm to stimulate area of Governing Vessel 20 (top of the crown of the head).

QI GONG – BRING NATURE'S ENERGY IN

While standing-up, stretch both hands forward with palms open, and away from the body. Clench the fists and imagine grasping the energy in front of you. With eyes closed, take a deep breath while pulling the clenched fists to the sides of the body, then up to the chest. While

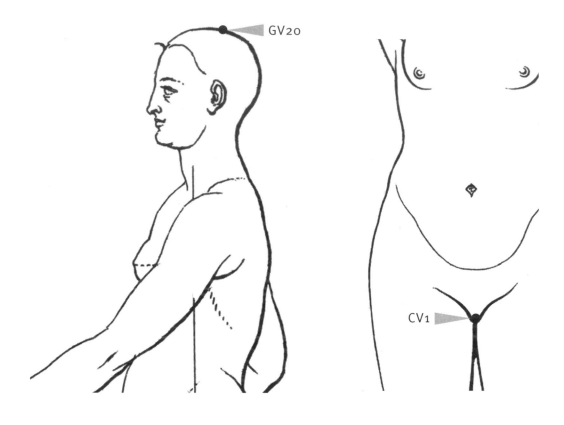

ACUPRESSURE

doing so, imagine yourself pulling nature's energy from in front of you and into your chest cavity. Hold your breath in for five seconds while feeling the newly introduced energy in your body. With medium force, thrust your arms and hands forward, exhaling in a loud voice while abruptly opening your eyes wide. Repeat this exercise 16 times every morning for one month.

EMOTIONAL – SOMETIMES ANGER CAN WORK

Sadness is the obstacle of Jue Yin. In a 24-hour cycle, sadness begins in the evening and in an annual cycle, it begins in the fall. Nature is in decline and the Yang energy is descending.

When night comes in the daily cycle, and when winter comes in the yearly cycle, sadness ends, transforming to fear and pensiveness. Fear assists in the rejection of death and pensiveness helps to plan the next move of rebirth. If sadness fails to transform to these other emotions, the Yang life force energy in Jue Ying cannot break out and form a new cycle.

To cure this obstacle, anger is necessary. Anger is Yang energy bursting upwards. It is the opposite of sadness which drains energy. If we understand nature, we learn that each emotion has the right time as a natural and useful tool for creating and prolonging life. At the wrong time, an emotion is a destructive tool that shortens life and the ability to create it. Jue Yin needs anger, but not trivial anger over mundane things. Jue Yin needs true anger. True anger is an enormous desire to live. It is crying out loud "nobody can stop me from getting pregnant!" This is the anger needed in Jue Yin.

Since mundane anger, sadness and resentment over trivial daily affairs are counter-productive, it is important to take actions of forgiveness and to let go of resentments. Balance the emotions in your heart.

LIFESTYLE MODIFICATIONS – A BALANCED EXERCISE PROGRAM

If not engaged in an exercise program already, it is time to begin. If overdoing it with exercise, now is the time to slow down. Exercise should be completed in the morning as it helps the Yang to open up. Do not go to the gym in the evening under any circumstances.

Stephanie was told that her egg quality was poor. Not ready to use egg donation, she looked for alternatives and came across the Hunyuan website. Deciding to give it a try, both Stephanie and her husband began a herbal regiment. The Hunyuan assessment by Yaron was that the Shao Yin male-female bond was broken under the psychological pressure of 'poor egg quality'. Yaron says that by commencing treatment together, it helped solve this problem and Stephanie conceived within six months.

········· 7 ·········

CASE STUDIES

A WORD ABOUT CASE STUDIES

When a patient comes into my office, I ask about her symptoms, pains and aches, as well as her health history. I check her pulse and look at her tongue and facial complexion. When I analyze all the data, I decide on the pattern she presents and accordingly I choose the appropriate herbs or herbal formula.

Many patients come to me after they have read other books about infertility and Chinese medicine, and have already self-diagnosed multiple problems, with every symptom falling under a different category. A low level physician with little education sees things similarly. With case studies, we not only learn about the different disharmonies causing infertility, we can also learn the thinking process behind the art. We're able to then decide which one of these many patterns is the real cause and which ones are not. It is the thinking process behind Chinese medicine that makes it so unique and powerful.

The case studies will list the patient's Western diagnosis when applicable, although it is irrelevant from a Chinese medicine perspective. Modern practitioners, who will go so far as to claim that a specific Western medicine diagnosis, (ie: endometriosis) equals a specific diagnosis in Chinese medicine (ie: Qi and blood stagnation), are making a big mistake. I will categorize the patients according to one main symptom to show how the analysis can vary.

It is also important to know that the description of a case study is only applicable for a certain point in time. When the pattern and symptoms change, the needs change, and the recommended herbs must change. In fact, for herbs to be appropriate in Chinese medicine, they should be adjusted every two weeks.

Even though all patients, except four, from the following case studies conceived naturally with the Hunyuan treatments, when you identify your infertility condition with one of the cases listed below, do not rush to use the same herbs or acupuncture points. The case study section is just a guiding tool to explain the thinking process behind Chinese medicine. The real cause of a patient's infertility is hidden within their particular pattern of disharmony. When we balance the disharmony with herbs and acupuncture, the ill symptoms disappear and fertility returns. This is how patients become pregnant with the Hunyuan method. The difficult part is to identify the true cause of a disharmony among conflicting symptoms. This is what ultimately determines success or failure.

NIGHT SWEATS

Patient 1:

Female, 39, western diagnosis: poor egg quality

MAIN COMPLAINT: infertility

HISTORY: Menstrual cycle day 7, feels cold since teenage years, has cold hands and feet, heavy night sweats since last IVF of about one month. No thirst and low appetite. Facial complexion is pale. Feels tired during the day even though she sleeps for seven to eight hours every night. The pulse is thin and weak and slightly rapid. The tongue is pale, thin white coating with slight teeth marks on the sides.

PATTERN: kidney and spleen Yang deficiency

PATTERN ANALYSIS: When the patient feels cold for many years, and the hands and feet are always cold, the kidney Yang is low. Fertility drugs typically extract original Yang from the kidneys and the Yang loses its root in the water. When the Yang can't root or go into storage at night, it floats. The skin pores open and body fluids are pushed out in the form of night sweats, the body tries to get rid of excess Yin. When the kidney Yang is exhausted, the spleen Yang is weakened and the appetite decreases and there is no thirst. Even though the pulse is slightly rapid, it is thin and weak, which is a declined Yang pulse of the Shao Yin.

HERBS: Fu Zi, Zhi Gan Cao, Sheng Jiang, Sha Ren, Bai Zhu, Huang Qi

ACUPUNCTURE POINTS: stomach 36, spleen 6, kidney 7, large intestine 10

HERBS AND ACUPUNCTURE ANALYSIS: The first three herbs strengthen the kidneys' original Yang while the latter strengthen the spleen Yang. The acupuncture points strengthen the same.

Patient 2:

Female, 35, western diagnosis: unexplained infertility

MAIN COMPLAINT: infertility

HISTORY: Menstrual cycle day 12, has cold feet but not cold hands, in the winter feels a little colder, night sweats during and shortly following the menses, some light headedness, seeing floaters or spots in front of her eyes, the hair and skin feels dry, slight thirst, when standing up fast feels light headed, the menstrual bleeding is light with one day of flow and two days of spotting, pulse is thin, weak and slightly rapid, the tongue is pale and the coating is missing at the front of the tongue. Under the tongue the veins are slightly dark in color.

PATTERN: liver blood deficiency

PATTERN ANALYSIS: Weak pulse shows blood deficiency, cold feet but not hands show a liver blood deficiency and less so kidney Yang deficiency, dryness, light flow of period shows blood deficiency.

HERBS: Dang Gui, Bai Shao, Sheng Dihuang, Chuan Xiong, Gan Cao, Bai Zhu, Huang Qi

ACUPUNCTURE POINTS: kidney 7, liver 8, stomach 36, large intestine 10

HERBS AND ACUPUNCTURE ANALYSIS: Strengthen the blood by tonifying the spleen. The first four herbs build the blood and the latter three strengthen the spleen. This helps build up blood. Using Sheng Dihuang and not Shu Dihuang will prevent obstruction of the spleen and will nourish the blood more effectively. Acupuncture kd 7, st 36 and Large intestine 10 strengthen the spleen while liv 8 helps the liver blood. **The Yellow Emperor** says that when the Yang grows, the Yin flourishes. This is why we strengthen the spleen Yang to produce blood (blood belongs to Yin).

Patient 3:

Female, 43, western diagnosis: high FSH

MAIN COMPLAINT: infertility

HISTORY: Menstrual cycle day 6, night sweats around 5 AM. Since last IVF two months ago, the patient feels warm during the day but has no thirst. After lunch, the patient feels tired. Patient felt cold and had cold hands, feet and nose for many years, but in the last two months she doesn't feel cold anymore, urination is frequent every hour, pulse is thin and deep and feels slightly tight, tongue coating is missing and the tongue seems pale on top but red underneath.

PATTERN: kidney Yang deficiency with acute Yin deficiency

PATTERN ANALYSIS: Underlying cause for infertility is the kidney Yang deficiency presented in long-term cold hands, feet and nose. In addition, fertility drugs have concentrated heat in the liver, causing the liver Yin to become deficient and resulting in night sweats. The tight pulse and red under tongue show a heat pattern in the liver despite the chronic Yang deficiency. The Shao Yin true Yang is deficient, which causes infertility, however an acute Jue Yin shortage will prevent the Yang from going out into a new cycle. This will create heat within the Yin and the Yin will dry out. During the very early AM hours, the Yang wants to open into a new day but it can't. The heat concentrates in the liver and the body fluids are steamed outward as early AM sweats.

HERBS: Sheng Dihuang, Mu Danpi, Hong Zao, Hei Zhima, Gou Qizi, Nu Zhenzi, Sheng Gan Cao, Sha Ren

ACUPUNCTURE POINTS: kidney 3, liver 7, spleen 9, large intestine 11

HERBS AND ACUPUNCTURE ANALYSIS: Even though the Yang is the cause of infertility here, the acute Jue Yin heat overrides it, which is why the patient no longer feels cold. From one original problem, we now have two. The first step is to clear the liver heat and nourish its Yin. At the same time we have to preserve the spleen Yang energy, otherwise the liver Yin will not be able to recover. The Tai Yin spleen needs Yang energy to steam the earth. This allows the Yin in Shao Yin and Jue Yin to transform (refer to chapters 2 and 4). The first six herbs cool the liver heat and nourish liver Yin; the latter two herbs protect and nourish the spleen Yang energy. The acupuncture points kd 3, liv 7, nourish liver Yin and with large intestine 11, cools the heat. Spleen 9 protects the spleen.

COLD FEELING

Patient 4:

Female, 44, western diagnosis: poor egg quality.

MAIN COMPLAINT: recurrent miscarriages

HISTORY: Menstrual cycle day 17, the patient feels cold for many years, has cold hands and feet, feels thirsty and wants to drink warm drinks. Appetite is low and the bowel movement is at times loose, after meals feels very full with some indigestion, some shortness of breath after exercise, the hair seem to fall out in recent months, pulse is large but feels hollow and slightly slow, tongue is pale and the coating seems slightly thick, white and dry.

PATTERN: spleen Yang Qi deficiency leading to blood deficiency

PATTERN ANALYSIS: The spleen Tai Yin needs Yang energy to steam the earth into dampness. When the Yang or Qi are deficient, the earth Yin is cold dry (refer to chapter 2), the patient feels cold and the stomach earth is dry. The patient is thirsty but desires only hot drinks (water + Yang energy). When the spleen Yang Qi is missing, the separation of nutrients from food is not sufficient and the bowels become loose. The Tai Yin has two organs: spleen and lungs. When the spleen is deficient of energy, the lungs have difficulty breathing. When the spleen is deficient, the blood production is impaired, as verified by the hollow, body-less pulse and the loss of hair. It is then mainly a spleen deficiency with traces of blood becoming deficient. This is often the cause for miscarriages.

HERBS: Fu Zi, Gan Jiang, Zhi Gan Cao, Bai Zhu, Dang Guiwei, Huang Qi

ACUPUNCTURE POINTS: kidney 7, spleen 9, stomach 36, large intestine 10

HERBS AND ACUPUNCTURE ANALYSIS: The first four herbs strengthen the spleen Yang, while the latter two herbs strengthen the spleen production of blood. The acupuncture points strengthen the spleen and stomach. After ovulation, we avoid the use of acupuncture point spleen 6 as it can cause a miscarriage. Spleen 6 before ovulation will be a better option instead of spleen 9. The patient is on day 17 (past ovulation) so we use spleen 9 instead.

Patient 5:

Female, 43, western diagnosis: PCOS

MAIN COMPLAINT: infertility

HISTORY: Menstrual cycle day 24, patient has cold hands and feet for several years but she doesn't feel overall cold. There is thirst with craving for cool drinks, at times the patient has headaches, the menses are very painful, the pulse feels tight and somewhat rapid, and the tongue has pink red color with thin white coating. The tongue body appears thin, around ovulation the patient experiences sharp pains around the ovaries.

PATTERN: heat trapped in the Shao Yang and gall bladder syndrome

PATTERN ANALYSIS: Cold hands and feet are normally caused by Yang deficiency, however there are other causes too. The Shao Yang warms the opening of the Yang mechanism (refer to chapters 2 and 4). When the Shao Yang heat does not spread the way it should, it accumulates in the center of the body. It prevents clear Yang energy from reaching the hands and feet. This causes cold hands and feet. The patient craves cool drinks, testifying for the trapped heat, the tongue redness shows heat too.

HERBS: Chai Hu, Bai Shao, Zhi Shi, Sheng Gan Cao

ACUPUNCTURE POINTS: gall bladder 42, gall bladder 34, liver 3, three heater 5

HERBS AND ACUPUNCTURE ANALYSIS: the four herbs aim at removing gall bladder Shao Yang stagnation. When the stagnation is removed, the heat is dissolving by itself. The acupuncture points aim at removing the same Shao Yang Qi stagnation.

Patient 6:

Female, 41, western diagnosis: blocked fallopian tubes

MAIN COMPLAINT: infertility

HISTORY: Menstrual cycle day 5, the patient feels cold since she began preparing for college examinations 20 years ago. Her hands and feet feel cold to the touch, but the patient doesn't recognize her hands and feet as feeling cold. Sleeping at night is not great and urination is frequent. Sometimes there are night sweats, but not on a regular basis. The patient hears a constant high pitch ring in her ears, the mouth is dry but the patient is not very thirsty. The skin feels dry, the hair has split and its roots have turned gray over the past three years. The eye sight has also diminished over the same period. The patient feels tired during the day.

PATTERN: kidney Yang and Yin deficiency

PATTERN ANALYSIS: Starting with excessive thinking, the spleen Yang is strained and the kidney Yang becomes deficient. This has caused the patient to feel cold for the past 20 years. When the Shao Yin Yang energy (the Yang in the water) is deficient for a long period, the water becomes deficient as well. **The Yellow Emperor** says that when the Yang is dying, the Yin shrinks. If the Yang is deficient for a long period, the Yin aspect of the body's energy, which connects to the body tissues, is weakening. This is also called essence deficiency. The symptoms of ear ringing, gray hair, dry mouth, and splitting hair are all related.

HERBS: Fu Zi, Sheng Dihung, Rou Gui, Shan Yao, Shan Zhuyu, Ze Xie, Gou Qizi, Hei Zhima, Huang Jing, Fu Ling

ACUPUNCTURE POINTS: spleen 6, stomach 36, large intestine 10, Ren 6, bladder 23

HERBS AND ACUPUNCTURE ANALYSIS: Both herbs and acupuncture help strengthen the kidneys' Yin and Yang. We use a total of ten herbs to go through the spleen and stomach and to descend to the Kidney Yin and Yang. The principle herbs are Fu Zi and Sheng Dihuang. The first strengthens the kidney Yang, while the latter strengthens the kidney Yin. Gui, Yao, Zhuyu help strengthen the liver Yang, while Qizi, Zhima and Ze Xie strengthen the liver Yin. Huang Jing and Fu Ling strengthen the spleen. In this strategy, we strengthen both Jue Yin and Tai Yin to reach a whole around support for the Shao Yin. This is one of the ways of reaching a recovery from a chronic kidney Yin and Yang deficiency.

EXHAUSTION

Patient 7:

Female, 40, western diagnosis: high FSH

MAIN COMPLAINT: infertility

HISTORY: Menstrual cycle day 35, patient complains of day-long exhaustion for the past several years. The menstrual cycles are 40-45 days. Symptoms include slightly dry mouth with no apparent thirst, achy legs during the menstruation, full bleeding for three to four days at commencement of menstruation, followed by three days of light spotting. Appetite is deficient, and the patient suffers slight headaches some mornings which feel like they come from deep inside the head. Pulse is thin, weak and slow, and the tongue is pale and thick-bodied with no coating.

PATTERN: kidney Yang deficiency, Shao Yin deficiency with impact on Tai Yang

PATTERN ANALYSIS: When the Yang is weak, there is no energy during the day and the patient feels tired. The Shao Yin Yang energy, which is the same as kidney Yang, is the root of the Tai Yang. When the Shao Yin is deficient during the night, then the Yang is deficient during the day, hence the patient is tired. **The Yellow Emperor** says that if the Yang does not store well in winter, the patient will experience a warm disease in the spring. The same happens during a daily cycle. If the Yang does not store well during the night, then a warm disease will be experienced in the morning, meaning that the Yang is unable to function at normal capacity but instead floats or flickers, resulting in the patient experiencing the occasional dull headaches in the mornings. Spotting at the end of the period shows the weakness of the Yang. Chinese medicine describes this symptom as 'the Yang can't hold the blood in the vessels'. The bleeding should have stopped after 4-5 days but it continues to spot.

HERBS: Fu Zi, Gan Jiang, Zhi Gan Cao, Sha Ren, Yin Yanghuo, Du Zhong, Cang Zhu, Ban Xia, Huang Qi, Gui Zhi

ACUPUNCTURE POINTS: kidney 7, stomach 36, large intestine 10, du 20

HERBS AND ACUPUNCTURE ANALYSIS: the first three herbs warm the kidney Yang. Ren, Yanghuo, Zhong assist the Yang in descending to the kidneys. Cang Zhu and Ban Xia harmonize the middle heater and the spleen and stomach, while Huang Qi and Gui Zhi help the Tai Yang open up. The acupuncture points combinations helps strengthen the Yang and make it rise in the Tai Yang.

Patient 8:

Male, 44, western diagnosis: low sperm count

MAIN COMPLAINT: male infertility

HISTORY: Patient has no apparent illnesses but sperm count is low. In the evening, he feels tired and sleeps "like a rock," urination is frequent and the libido is low, patient complains of sore lower back, thirst with craving for cold drinks. Pulse is thin, tight, has force and is rapid, the tongue appearing slightly red with missing coating.

PATTERN: kidney Yin and essence deficiency

PATTERN ANALYSIS: Even though tiredness is mostly the result of Yang deficiency, in some instances the Yin is the cause. When the Yin is deficient, the Yang has no roots and the body's function declines and tiredness occurs. On the other hand, sleeping shows that the Yin is well, but at times sleeping heavily "like a rock" shows a Yin malfunction. The key here for the analysis is thirst. When the Yin is deficient, there is craving for cold drinks. Cold water will improve the Yin ability to anchor the Yang. Even though at times cold energy will harm the Yang, at other times it can help.

HERBS: Sheng Dihuang, Bai Shao, Sheng Gan Cao, Bai He, Sang Piaoxiao, Sang Jisheng

ACUPUNCTURE POINTS: spleen 4, kidney 3, kidney 6, heart 7

HERBS AND ACUPUNCTURE ANALYSIS: The first 4 herbs improve the kidney Yin and essence, while the last two herbs improve the libido and sexual function of the male genitalia. The acupuncture points improve the kidneys' control of the sex organs and the harmony between the Yin and the Yang in the Shao Yin sphere.

Patient 9:

Female, 38, western diagnosis: PCOS

MAIN COMPLAINT: infertility

HISTORY: Menstrual cycle day 11, patient feels tired from the middle of the day until the evening. Sleep is sound, however the patient wakes up around 1:00 AM and then falls back asleep. Patient experiences cold hands and feet, and occasional dizziness. She has craving for sweets, likes warm drinks, and has a slightly dry mouth. The menses are light and the blood is dark brown. The pulse feels strong and slightly rapid. The tongue is pale, with teeth marks on the sides, and the veins under the tongue are dark.

PATTERN: spleen Yang deficiency causing blood deficiency and blood stagnation

PATTERN ANALYSIS: Blood deficiency and stagnation will impact the liver in a negative way, causing 1:00 AM insomnia. However, the dominant pattern with this patient is of a spleen

Yang deficiency. The Tai Yin has insufficient Yang to transform the earth. The earth is still and the blood is frozen. The normal production of blood is the result of Yang energy, which is added into the earth to create transformation. **The Yellow Emperor** says that when the Yang is born the Yin flourishes. The earth uses Yang energy to separate the nutrients from the food and drinks and these are the building blocks of the blood. The pulse is strong because the blood stagnates and it is the ovulation time. Even with premature ovarian failure, when there is no physical ovulation, the liver energy still surges around the ovulation time. The craving for sweets is the key here for understanding the true cause behind the blood stagnation, which is a spleen Yang deficiency. Other symptoms which also point to this are the pale tongue with teeth marks.

HERBS: Huang Qi, Dang Guitou, Bai Zhu, Fu Zi, Zhi Gan Cao, Chuan Xiong

ACUPUNCTURE POINTS: spleen 10, spleen 3, large intestine 6, liver 5

HERBS AND ACUPUNCTURE ANALYSIS: The first two herbs help the spleen recover its blood production, while Zhu, Fu and Cao recover the Yang function of the spleen. Chuan Xiong helps relieve the acute blood stagnation present in the liver. Emphasis with the herbs is the heavy use of honey fried Gan Cao to prevent Fu Zi from flaring fire in the blood and aggravating the blood stagnation. Sp 3, 10 help recover spleen blood production, large intestine 6 helps Tai Yin absorb Yang energy, while Liv 5 will help the liver blood stagnation.

CONSTIPATION

Patient 10:

Female, 33, western diagnosis: unexplained infertility

MAIN COMPLAINT: infertility

HISTORY: Menstrual cycle day 22, patient has chronic constipation for the past ten years, bowel movement once every three days. She also feels cold, has cold hands and feet, and no thirst. Menstruation is regular every 28 days and the bleeding lasts 4-5 days, appetite is normal, sleeps well and the energy is good during the day. Pulse is normal but slightly slow, tongue has normal pink color and thin white coating (which is normal).

PATTERN: kidney Yang deficiency

PATTERN ANALYSIS: when the Shao Yin is in a disharmony, the heart fire does not descend and the kidneys' water does not ascend. The water remains at the bottom, and with no Yang, it becomes dry (refer to chapter 2). Dry water below, signaling a deficiency in the Yang energy, causes the bowels to slow down, resulting in constipation but no pain or other acute symptoms. The cold hands and feet confirm this diagnosis.

HERBS: Fu Zi, Zhi Gan Cao, Sheng Jiang, Rou Gui, Gui Zhi, Suan Zao Ren

ACUPUNCTURE POINTS: bladder 23 and 25, heart 5, kidney 7

HERBS AND ACUPUNCTURE ANALYSIS: The main focus is to warm up the kidneys. The first four herbs warm up the kidney Yang, while the latter two will warm up the heart Yang and cause it to descend. The acupuncture points invigorate the connection between the heart Yang and kidney water.

Patient 11:

Female, 36, western diagnosis: high FSH, diminished ovarian reserve

MAIN COMPLAINT: infertility

HISTORY: Menstrual cycle day 30. Chronic constipation in the past two years, following a series of IVFs and fertility drugs. The patient feels warm at night and thirsty with cravings for cold drinks. She is hungry with good digestion. Bowel movement is once per day but difficult to move. The pulse is strong and rapid, the tongue is red and the coating is thin yellow and dry.

PATTERN: heat in the Yang Ming with dryness in body fluids

PATTERN ANALYSIS: Fertility drugs have caused localized heat in the Yang Ming. The heat dries the fluids in the bowels and it impairs the Yang Ming descending action (refer to the Yang Ming section). If the Yang Ming is obstructed, the Yang energy of Tai Yin and Shao Yin cannot be healthy and fertility cannot happen.

HERBS: Ren Shen, Zhi Mu, Sheng Gan Cao, Shi Gao, Geng Mi

ACUPUNCTURE POINTS: large intestine 11, stomach 44, stomach 25

HERBS AND ACUPUNCTURE ANALYSIS: The herbs and acupuncture points help reduce the heat in the Yang Ming. Emphasis is on the use of Ren Shen (ginseng) that helps nourish the body fluids. Even though kidney Yang is in the core of fertility, for this patient cold herbs must be used to allow the normal Yang function.

Patient 12:

Female, 39, western diagnosis: tilted uterus

MAIN COMPLAINT: infertility

HISTORY: Menstrual cycle day 3. Patient suffers chronic constipation for approximately ten years, suffers insomnia for approximately the same period. Bowel movement is once every 2-3 days but not difficult. Patient has tendency for light headedness. Menstruation is very short – one day of light bleeding and one day of spotting. Vision is at times blurry and in the past patient has fainted from dehydration. Mouth is dry and patient experiences slight thirst. Skin and hair are dry. Pulse is thin and weak, while tongue is pale with no coating. At times the patient has vivid dreams with heart palpitations.

PATTERN: liver and heart blood deficiency

PATTERN ANALYSIS: Blood deficiency causes infertility and in the above case it is very prevalent. Symptoms of dryness, light headedness, light periods all testify to a blood deficiency. When the blood is deficient, the bowels are dry and chronic constipation follows. Blood deficiency depletes the reproductive system of its essential fluids and pregnancy becomes difficult. In this case, the blood of the heart and the blood of the liver are both deficient, accounting for symptoms such as dreams, and heart palpitations along with a thin, weak pulse.

HERBS: Shu Dihuang, Bai Shao, Dang Gui, Chuan Xiong, Ren Shen, Bai Zhu, Zhi Gan Cao, Huang Qi, Yi Mucao, Long Yanrou

ACUPUNCTURE POINTS: spleen 6 and 10, large intestine 10, kidney 3, heart 7

HERBS AND ACUPUNCTURE ANALYSIS: the first four herbs help build the blood, while Shen, Zhu, Cao, Qi strengthen the spleen production of blood. Mucao and Yanrou help build the heart blood. When the blood is full, the heart and liver blood is naturally full. Fertility can take place without obstructions. The acupuncture points spleen 6, 10, and large intestine 10, invigorate the spleen to build blood. Kidney 3 and heart 7 help the heart blood. The famous gynecologist Chen Ziming in his book **The Great Compendium of Gynecological Prescriptions** explains that blood is of the foremost importance when it comes to fertility and pregnancy. Blood is produced by the spleen and lungs in the Tai Yin sphere, it is controlled by the heart in the Shao Yin sphere and it is stored by the liver in the Jue Yin sphere. The patient must keep her blood in her body and be scarce with giving away blood, such as with unnecessary blood tests, unless it is most necessary. Losing blood decreases fertility.

HOT FLASHES

Patient 13:

Female, 40, western diagnosis: endometriosis

MAIN COMPLAINT: infertility

HISTORY: Menstrual cycle day 8. Patient complains of severe hot flashes during the day and night during the past five months, following two medicated cycles of IUI. Although the hot flashes are severe, the patient feels very cold immediately afterward. There is no thirst, the pulse is thin, weak, and slightly rapid, and the tongue is pale and moist.

PATTERN: severe Yang deficiency caused by fertility drugs

PATTERN ANALYSIS: Fertility drugs extract the true Yang from the kidneys, thus causing its root to sever. The Yang has no place to root and it floats to the surface of the body. This is the feeling of a hot flash. At times, the Yang rising to the surface abruptly pushes the body fluids outwards and causes sweating. As soon as the Yang surfaces outwards, a cold follows. The body's true Yang, which is supposed to be inside to warm the body, is no longer there.

HERBS: Fu Zi, Zhi Gan Cao, Gan Jiang, Rou Gui, Cang Zhu, Sha Ren

ACUPUNCTURE POINTS: kidney 7, stomach 36, spleen 6, large intestine 10

HERBS AND ACUPUNCTURE ANALYSIS: The herbs and acupuncture both aim at saving the Yang and helping it root again. The more severe the hot flashes, the more Fu Zi needs to be used.

Patient 14:

Female, 47, western diagnosis: diminished ovarian reserve and menopause

MAIN COMPLAINT: infertility

HISTORY: Menstrual cycle day 70. Patient complained of severe hot flashes after stopping hormone replacement therapy one year ago. Hot flashes appear more severe in the afternoons and nights with heavy sweats occurring. The patient is chronically constipated, as well as thirsty with a craving for iced drinks. Menstruation has become irregular in the past year, sometimes as long as 80 days or as short as 16 days. The pulse is strong and rapid and the tongue is red with no coating.

PATTERN: heat accumulating in the Yang Ming

PATTERN ANALYSIS: Heat in the Yang Ming and dry bowels can cause hot flashes with sweating. Craving for iced drinks displays the true nature of the flashes, namely heat flares from the Yang Ming. These flashes are not the result of menopause or hormones, but rather localized heat at the wrong time at the wrong place. The Yang Ming time is in the evening and at this time the patient experiences aggravation of the flashes. This is clearly a Yang Ming disharmony.

HERBS: Ren Shen, Zhi Mu, Shi Gao, Sheng Gan Cao, Geng Mi, Mai Dong, Tian Huafen

ACUPUNCTURE POINTS: stomach 44, large intestine 11, spleen 6

HERBS AND ACUPUNCTURE ANALYSIS: This is a cold herbal formula to clear heat from Yang Ming and nourish the body fluids. The points stomach 44 and large intestine 11 clear heat from Yang Ming, while spleen 6 strengthens the spleen. Within the herbs, Geng Mi (rice) has the function of protecting the spleen from an herbal cold injury. When the flashes stop, the patient must stop taking these herbs or else the spleen becomes weak. As long as there is heat trapped in Yang Ming, the cold herbs benefit the patient's health.

Patient 15:

Female, 27, western diagnosis: uterine fibroids

MAIN COMPLAINT: infertility

HISTORY: Menstrual cycle day 9. Patient experiences hot flashes mainly in the morning hours after getting out of bed. The patient suffers mild headaches on and off with no consistent pattern, and sometimes becomes very dizzy. The periods are regular every 26 days but very painful with nausea accompanying the pain. Bleeding is normal for 4-5 days, the pulse is strong, tight, and rapid and the tongue is normal pink with thin white coating.

PATTERN: Shao Yang Qi stagnation

PATTERN ANALYSIS: The Shao Yang helps the Tai Yang to open up by warming up the Yang energy. When the Shao Yang energy is stuck, the Tai Yang can't open up smoothly and hot flashes may occur. Testimony for the Shao Yang stagnation are the headaches, tight, strong pulse and the painful periods with nausea. These symptoms follow the Shao Yang and Jue Yin disharmony. The Shao Yang is above the Jue Yin and their relationship is exterior-interior. When the Shao Yang minister fire is impaired, the Jue Yin wind wood becomes impaired too, resulting in painful periods and nausea.

HERBS: Chai Hu, Bai Shao, Zhi Shi, Sheng Gan Cao

ACUPUNCTURE POINTS: gall bladder 42, liver 2, pericardium 6, liver 8

HERBS AND ACUPUNCTURE ANALYSIS: The herbs aim at relieving Shao Yang stagnation. Chai Hu causes the energy to rise in the Shao Yang and Tai Yang, while Zhi Shi causes the energy to descend in the Yang Ming. Shao Yang is the pivot of the Yang mechanism. When one herb rises and another descends, the pivot becomes lubricated and functions properly. Bai Shao and Gan Cao nourish the Yin. When the Yin is well nourished, the Yang mechanism is smooth. **The Yellow Emperor** says that sweet and sour flavors can transform the Yin. Bai Shao is sour and Gan Cao is sweet. Together they are the preferred formula for transforming Yin.

INSOMNIA

Patient 16:

Female, 44, western diagnosis: poor egg quality, one tube removed

MAIN COMPLAINT: infertility

HISTORY: Menstrual cycle day 17, patient complains of insomnia for the past two years. She can fall asleep easily but she wakes up two or three times during the night and has difficulty falling back to sleep. During the day, her concentration seems to be impaired and she tends to forget things, she feels a little cold and the hands and feet at times feel cold as well. Occasionally, she experiences shortness of breath and the heart seems to race, the pulse is small, thin, deep and slightly slow. The tongue is slightly purplish with missing coating at the front.

PATTERN: Shao Yin heart Yang deficiency

PATTERN ANALYSIS: The heart stores the spirit and together the heart and the spirit are the Emperor Fire. When the heart fire can't nourish the kidney Yang, infertility may result. When the heart Yang is impaired, the spirit can't "rest" at night and the patient experiences insomnia because the Yang can't go into storage. So during the day, the Yang opening action is weak and the patient has a slight cold feeling, shortness of breath, a rapidly beating heart, and forgetfulness. Critical for the analysis here is the small pulse. **Yellow Emperor – Discussion on Pulse Essentials:** *When the pulse is long, the Qi is in control and when the pulse is short, the Qi is ill.* A small pulse means that the Yang energy does not extend from bottom to top (from toes to head). The heart and the lungs are in the chest, which is the upper section of the body. When the Yang cannot extend enough and nourish upward to the chest and head, the symptoms will include difficulty in breathing, heart palpitation or rapid beating, forgetfulness and insomnia.

HERBS: Fu Zi, Zhi Gan Cao, Sheng Jiang, Yin Yanghuo, Sha Ren, Fu Shen, Gui Zhi

ACUPUNCTURE POINTS: heart 5 and 7, kidney 3 and 7

HERBS AND ACUPUNCTURE ANALYSIS: The first four herbs strengthen the kidney true Yang, as well as the spleen and heart Yang. Fu and Gui combination helps the heart Yang to descend into the kidneys. The acupuncture points help to harmonize the heart and the kidneys in the Shao Yin.

Patient 17:

Female, 37, western diagnosis: repeated miscarriages, genetic abnormalities

MAIN COMPLAINT: infertility

HISTORY: Menstrual cycle day 2, patient complains of insomnia, which is 'really bad' in the last two days. She falls asleep around 10 PM and wakes up around 1:00 AM and cannot fall back asleep until the morning around 5:00 AM. The bleeding during the period is light for 2-3 days. The patient feels slightly light-headed when standing up fast, and has slight thirst and dry skin. At times she has headaches that feel a little dull but stay the whole day or until she takes over-the-counter pain medication. The pulse is faint and slightly rapid, the tongue pale with a red tip.

PATTERN: liver blood deficiency

PATTERN ANALYSIS: The liver stores the blood and releases it to the body as needed. When the body moves fast, such as in exercising, it needs more blood and when it is resting, it needs less blood. During rest, the blood is stored in the liver. If one shifts quickly from rest to movement and becomes light headed, this signals a blood deficiency in the liver. The Jue Yin time, or the liver time, is 1:00-5:00 AM. When the liver blood is deficient, the Yang cannot go into storage. The patient wakes up and can't fall back asleep. This, of course, will impact fertility directly. Testimony for a blood deficiency is that the insomnia becomes worse during menses, where the body loses more blood, and that the bleeding is light.

HERBS: Dang Gui Pian, Bai Shao, Sheng Dihuang, Chuan Xiong, Bai Zhu, Zhi Gan Cao, Dang shen, Huang Qi

ACUPUNCTURE POINTS: liver 8, spleen 6, stomach 36, large intestine 11

HERBS AND ACUPUNCTURE ANALYSIS: The first four herbs invigorate the blood circulation and help the liver storage, while with the latter four, they also strengthen the spleen and improve the blood production. The acupuncture points help improve spleen blood production.

Patient 18:

Female, 35, western diagnosis: ovarian cysts

MAIN COMPLAINT: infertility

HISTORY: Menstrual cycle day 13, patient complains of waking up around 1-2 AM with an inability to fall back asleep for approximately an hour, and that this has been the case on and off for about a year. In the last two days, she has been suffering from headaches that feel sharp on the side of the head and left eye. She also feels sharp pains in the lower abdomen that make her believe she is ovulating. The periods have full flow for 3 days and light blood flow for 2 more, but the first day of the period is always extremely painful. The pulse is strong and tight. The tongue is light pink with thin white coating.

PATTERN: Shao Yang Qi stagnation

PATTERN ANALYSIS: The Shao Yang and the Jue Yin are internally-externally linked. The Jue Yin wind wood is the beginning or the origin of the Shao Yang minister fire. The one cannot do without the other. When the Shao Yang stagnates or doesn't operate well, the Jue Yin is stuck too. As we approach the Jue Yin time at 1:00 AM, the Yang can't transition smoothly. The patient then wakes up. Since it is not a Jue Yin principle problem, the patient can fall back asleep after a short time. The key for the analysis are the headaches. Compared to patient 1, 7 the headaches here are sharp, the periods are painful and the ovulation is painful. **The Yellow Emperor** says: *If the energy stagnates there is pain.* The menstruation bleeding shows that the blood is not yet affected, rather it is still normal.

HERBS: Chai Hu, Bai Shao, Sheng Gan Cao, Zhi Shi

ACUPUNCTURE POINTS: gall bladder 42, liver 2, three heater 5, lung 9

HERBS AND ACUPUNCTURE ANALYSIS: the four herbs help ease gall bladder and liver Qi stagnation. The acupuncture points gallbladder 42 liver 2, three heater 5, ease gallbladder Qi stagnation, while lung 9 strengthens the lungs. The lungs belong to metal and metal will help control the wood, which is the gall bladder and liver.

PAINFUL MENSES

Patient 19:

Female, 39, western diagnosis: endometriosis

MAIN COMPLAINT: infertility

HISTORY: Menstrual cycle day 20, for 20 years, the patient suffered severe menstrual cramps, but then the pain subsided for a few years while taking oral birth control pills. Six years ago, upon discontinuing the birth control pills, strong pain has returned, now reaching down to the lower back. Nausea and vomiting often accompany the pain if western pain medications are not taken. The menstruation flow is dark red – almost brown – and full of blood clots. The pulse is strong, feels tight and is slightly rapid. The tongue is purple red with dark veins underneath. The patient often suffers severe headaches and also feels cold on occasion, primarily in the winter. Appetite and digestion are normal.

PATTERN: liver blood stagnation

PATTERN ANALYSIS: The infertility cause lies in the blood stagnation pattern, which is prevalent. **The Yellow Emperor** says: *If there is no smooth flow, there is pain.* At the time of the period, the excess Yin and blood need to flow out of the female body if there is no pregnancy (refer to chapter 3). If the liver function of smoothing the blood flow is impaired, the blood begins to stagnate, causing severe pain. Strong tight pulse and blood clots, as well as dark veins under the tongue, all confirm that blood is stagnating.

HERBS: Tao Ren, Hong Hua, Sheng Dihuang, Bai Shao, Chuan Xiong, Dang Guiwei

ACUPUNCTURE POINTS: liver 3, kidney 3, liver 5, three heater 5

HERBS AND ACUPUNCTURE ANALYSIS: the herbs aim at improving blood flow and removing stagnation. It is important to use Sheng Dihuang and not Shu Dihuang, as Sheng Di cools the blood better. When the blood stagnates, the energy can't flow well and it accumulates, creating heat in the blood. That's why the pulse becomes rapid during this blood stagnation. The acupuncture points help remove blood stagnation from the liver and nourish the Yin.

Patient 20:

Female, 34, western diagnosis: endometriosis

MAIN COMPLAINT: infertility

HISTORY: Menstrual cycle day 15, patient complained of very painful menstruation two to four days prior to the beginning of flow accompanied by headaches and nausea. Headaches feel sharp and are localized at the top of the head. The patient tends to become angry and anxious. The period flow is 3-4 days, which is normal, however at times spotting occurs 2-3 days prior. When the patient experiences diarrhea in the evening, she knows that the menstruation will begin the next day. Appetite is sometimes low and the patient feels tired. The pulse is thin but tight and the tongue is slightly purplish with thin white coating.

PATTERN: liver Qi stagnation

PATTERN ANALYSIS: The liver's energy allows the smooth flow of blood in the menses. Several days before the blood flow begins, the Jue Yin and the liver move into a transition mode, in preparation. With the new period, a new cycle begins. The last phase of the old cycle, also known as the transition phase, is Jue Yin. If the Jue Yin mechanism is obstructed, the menstruation pains begin the week before the period. Spotting before the period is common as well. The pains themselves are somewhat similar to patient 19 with blood stagnation. However, pains caused by Qi obstruction are different than that caused by blood obstruction. Qi stagnation pains can be sharp, but they can come and go as the Qi changes rapidly. Blood stagnation pains are sharp and persistent, and they do not come and go. Liver Qi stagnation can impair the spleen functions, causing diarrhea immediately preceding the period. The liver Qi stagnation and impaired spleen Qi will cause the patient to become tired.

HERBS: Gou Teng, Gou Qizi, Shu Dihuang

ACUPUNCTURE POINTS: liver 2 and 3, kidney 3

HERBS AND ACUPUNCTURE ANALYSIS: Gou Teng eases the liver Qi stagnation, while Qizi and Dihuang nourish the liver Yin. The liver Qi stagnates naturally to protect the woman from endless bleeding. That is why light cramping during the period is a sign of good health, and not, as many think, a bad sign. Light cramping is a sign that the liver Qi stagnates, as it should, to protect us. When the liver is, however, over-protective, then the cramping is severe. The liver Qi over stagnates when it perceives that the blood or Yin energy is not enough. Every little loss of Yin is perceived as a great loss. To relax the liver, we can use Gou Qizi and Shu Dihuang to nourish and build the liver Yin. When the liver Yin becomes stronger, the Qi stagnates less and the pain subsides. Dry herbs, used to strengthen the spleen, will further dry the Yin, while blood-invigorating herbs will aggravate the stagnation.

Patient 21:

Female, 41, western diagnosis: endometriosis

MAIN COMPLAINT: infertility

HISTORY: Menstrual cycle day 6, patient complains of strong pain during some periods, and mild pain during other periods. The patient feels cold, has cold hands and feet, and the menstruation bleeding lasts for 7-8 days. The patient feels sore in the lower back and weak in the knees. She has slight thirst and desires only hot drinks. Once, after drinking cold water, she felt chills for two days. The pulse is thin and slow and gradually becomes slightly rapid. The tongue is pale with no coating and some horizontal cracks.

PATTERN: kidney Yang deficiency causing cold in Chong and Ren meridians

PATTERN ANALYSIS: The Yellow Emperor says: *If it is obstructed, it is painful.* The Yang function is to warm and move the energy, blood and body fluids. When the Yang declines, the water freezes and becomes ice. Ice does not flow like water. Ice stands in place and stagnates, lifeless. When the blood wants to move out during menstruation, it is frozen in place and strong pains will follow. This freeze does not necessarily result in blood clots or dark veins under the tongue, which makes it different then patient 19-blood stagnation. With blood stagnation, heat is generated in the interior and the patient will not drink hot drinks. With Yang deficiency and cold, on the other hand, a patient will crave hot drinks. The pulse is thin and slow, and the tongue pale, showing that the Yang is deficient. When the pulse becomes slightly rapid it shows a recent loss of blood during menses.

HERBS: Fu Zi, Gui Zhi, Rou Gui, Gan Jiang, Bu Gu Zhi, Dang Guiwei

ACUPUNCTURE POINTS: spleen 6, stomach 36, large intestine 10, du 20

HERBS AND ACUPUNCTURE ANALYSIS: the first five herbs form and move the kidney Yang while Dang Guiwei help the Yang energy go into the blood and warm up the blood. The acupuncture points help warm up the Yang. Even though patients 19, 20, and 21 suffer endometriosis and painful periods, the cause and manifestation for each one is different. This is why the herbs and the acupuncture should be different in each case.

IRREGULAR MENSES

Patient 22:

Female, 38, western diagnosis: premature ovarian failure

MAIN COMPLAINT: infertility

HISTORY: Menstrual cycle day N/A – patient has had no periods for past 8 years since discontinuing birth control pill. The patient feels cold and has cold hands and feet. No thirst, but appetite is OK. The patient feels very sad. The pulse is thin and weak. The tongue is pale and moist.

PATTERN: Shao Yin-Yang deficiency

PATTERN ANALYSIS: **The Yellow Emperor** says: *At age 49, the Tian Kui dries out.* Tian Kui means the Yin aspect of heaven, or the Yin aspect of the Yang energy. **The Yellow Emperor** also says: *When the Yang is born, the Yin flourishes, and when the Yang dies, the Yin shrinks.* With this patient, the Tian Kui has prematurely dried out. The reason is the exhaustion of the true Yang of the kidneys (refer to chapter 3)

HERBS: Fu Zi, Zhi Gan Cao, Sheng Jiang, Bai Zhu, Huang Qi, Tu Sizi, Ban Xia, Chen Pi

ACUPUNCTURE POINTS: kidney 7, spleen 9, stomach 36, large intestine 10

HERBS AND ACUPUNCTURE ANALYSIS: This formula aims at strengthening the kidneys one true Yang. The acupuncture points help invigorate the Yang.

Patient 23:

Female, 33, western diagnosis: PCOS

MAIN COMPLAINT: infertility

HISTORY: Menstrual cycle day 11, patient menstrual cycle is irregular, 16-35 days long. Period flow is normal, 4-5 days. Overall, the patient feels cold, and has cold hands and feet. She prefers warm fluids and warm food. She experiences slight headaches in an irregular pattern, as well as some lower abdominal pains during mid-cycle. Her lower back and abdomen feel cold. The pulse is thin and weak, and the tongue is light pink with thin white coating.

PATTERN: Shao Yin-Yang deficiency

PATTERN ANALYSIS: The kidney true Yang is the root of the Chong and Ren meridians and it is the spring from which the liver receives its energy. Short and irregular menstrual cycles can be caused by several patterns; heat, stagnation, excess and deficiency. In this case, the main cause is Shao Yin true Yang deficiency. When the Yang is deficient in the Shao Yin, the heart emperor fire is lacking (refer to chapter 2). The emperor can't oversee the empire, so regulating the cycle to be on time is lost.

HERBS: Fu Zi, Zhi Gan Cao, Sheng Jiang, Bai Zhu, Huang Qi, Tu Sizi, Ban Xia, Chen Pi

ACUPUNCTURE POINTS: kidney 7, spleen 9, stomach 36, large intestine 10

HERBS AND ACUPUNCTURE ANALYSIS: The herbs and acupuncture strengthen the Shao Yin-Yang energy, helping the kidney and heart Yang in recovering their function. When the true Yang becomes strong, the body can regulate its menses. This has to do with the Shen Ji or spirit instrument (see Shen Ji Qi Li section in chapter 8). The menstrual cycle conforms to the moon and the Yin and Yang energies around us. When the Shen Ji is weak (because the true Yang is weak), the regulation of the body and its relationship with nature is impaired. This is why menstruation sometimes arrives early and sometimes arrives late.

Patient 24:

Female, 44, western diagnosis: Elevated FSH, early menopause

MAIN COMPLAINT: infertility

HISTORY: Menstrual cycle day 47. Patient's menstrual cycle is normally 50-70 days in the past three years following fertility drugs. The patient experiences some hot flashes but immediately thereafter feels cold. Her lower back is weak and she feels tired. She dislikes cold drinks, but rather prefers warm. She dresses heavily as she feels cold all the time. The pulse is faint and the tongue is pale.

PATTERN: Shao Yin-Yang deficiency

PATTERN ANALYSIS: Kidney Yang energy is deficient and the Chong and Ren meridians are both empty. The uterus suffers deficiency of energy and menstruation does not come on time. Symptoms all point to a Yang deficiency. Hot flashes followed by cold feeling signals the floating of the deficient Yang.

HERBS: Fu Zi, Zhi Gan Cao, Sheng Jiang, Bai Zhu, Huang Qi, Tu Sizi, Ban Xia, Chen Pi

ACUPUNCTURE POINTS: kidney 7, spleen 9, stomach 36, large intestine 10

HERBS AND ACUPUNCTURE ANALYSIS: The herbal formula and acupuncture are the same for this patient and patients 22 and 23. Even though the irregularity with the menses is different for each one, the underlying cause is the same Yang energy deficiency.

THIRST

Patient 25:

Female, 42, western diagnosis: poor egg quality

MAIN COMPLAINT: infertility

HISTORY: Menstrual cycle day 20, the patient feels very thirsty and experiences hot flashes which are of greater intensity at night. She has also suffered from occasional night sweats since two months after using fertility drugs. Overall, the patient feels cold and has had cold hands and feet for many years. Recently, the patient has felt warm and has craved cold water or iced soft drinks. The bowel movement is normal and urination is slightly too frequent. The pulse is thin and rapid and the tongue is pale and dry with red tip.

PATTERN: chronic kidney Yang deficiency with acute stomach Yin deficiency

PATTERN ANALYSIS: The underlying cause of infertility is the chronic kidney Yang deficiency, which displays the symptoms of cold hands and feet. Recent fertility drugs have caused the stomach Yin to become deficient and dry, causing night sweats, hot flashes, thirst for cold drinks and a warm feeling overall. This should not be mistakenly assessed as a recovery of the kidney Yang. It is rather a masking of the underlying condition.

HERBS: Fu Zi, Zhi Gan Cao, Sheng Jiang, Zhi Mu, Tian Hua Fen, Mai Dong

ACUPUNCTURE POINTS: stomach 44, large intestine 11, spleen 9, kidney 7

HERBS AND ACUPUNCTURE ANALYSIS: The true cause of infertility is kidney Yang deficiency. However, hot herbs alone will be unable to bypass the acute heat and Yin deficiency in the stomach (caused artificially by fertility drugs). That is why it is necessary to combine the two. The first three herbs strengthen the kidney Yang, while the latter three cool the stomach heat and nourish the stomach Yin. The acupuncture points stomach 44 and large intestine 11 clear heat from the stomach, while spleen 9 and kidney 7 strengthen the kidney Yang.

Patient 26:

Female, 36, western diagnosis: fibroids

MAIN COMPLAINT: infertility

HISTORY: Menstrual cycle day 9, patient feels dry mouth and thirst and likes room temperature drinks to keep hydrated. The appetite is rather low with some indigestion after food. The bowel movement is normally a little loose two to three times per day. The patient feels tired and desirous of staying in bed all day if she could. The pulse is weak and the tongue is pale with thick white coating.

PATTERN: spleen Qi deficiency

PATTERN ANALYSIS: The spleen transforms and transports the body fluids and the water we drink. When the spleen Qi is weak, the water is not transforming and it accumulates below, causing loose bowels and indigestion. When fluids are not distributed upwards, there is slight thirst or dry mouth without a desire to drink.

HERBS: Fu Zi, Gan Jiang, Zhi Gan Cao, Bai Zhu, Fu Ling, Huang Qi, Sha Ren, Cang Zhu

ACUPUNCTURE POINTS: spleen 6 and 9, stomach 36, lung 7, large intestine 10

HERBS AND ACUPUNCTURE ANALYSIS: This herbal formula helps dry up the spleen and strengthen the spleen and kidney Yang energy. The spleen receives its Yang energy from the kidneys, so we strengthen the kidneys as well as the spleen. Tai Yin (spleen) likes Yang energy to transform the earth, otherwise the earth is a frozen earth or a dead earth. The warm herbs add the Yang energy into the Tai Yin and the earth becomes alive. The earth strives for harmony. If it is too cold, it strives for warmth and if it is too wet, it strives for dryness. If it is too dry it strives for moistness and if it is too hot it strives for coolness. The herbs need to balance the scale. The acupuncture points help recover the spleen Yang.

Patient 27:

Female, 31, western diagnosis: thin uterus lining

MAIN COMPLAINT: infertility

HISTORY: Menstrual cycle day 21, patient feels very thirsty and likes to drink cold drinks. Patient is prone to migraines that come once or twice every month. The bowel movement is normal and urination is very yellow. The menstruation is painful and the blood is dark red. The eyes at times become red and feel hot. The feet always feel ice cold and the patient feels she must sleep wearing socks. The pulse is tight, strong, and rapid; the tongue is slightly purple with patchy white coating.

PATTERN: heat accumulating in the liver blood

PATTERN ANALYSIS: Yang energy is most important for our health and fertility, however the Yang has to be distributed correctly. When the Yang accumulates at one place, it will become deficient at another. If the Yang accumulates in the Jue Yin sphere, it heats up the root. The root of the Yang energy is the blood. The blood is the substance of the Yin. **The Yellow Emperor** states: *The pulse is the mansion of the blood.* When the blood is heated up, the pulse becomes strong and rapid as the Yang energy in the blood pushes it faster. Dark red blood and painful menses also suggest the Yang is accumulating in the blood. Thirst for cold drinks indicates the body's craving to cool off the interior. Red eyes that feel hot suggests that the heat in the blood has reached the liver, as the liver opens into the eyes.

HERBS: Sheng Dihuang, Xuan Shen, Ju Hua, Sang Ye, Mai Dong, Gou Qizi, Gan Cao, Hong Zao, Sheng Jiang

ACUPUNCTURE POINTS: liver 2 and 3, stomach 44, large intestine 11, spleen 4

HERBS AND ACUPUNCTURE ANALYSIS: The first four herbs clear heat from the blood and liver, while Gou Qizi and Mai Dong nourish the Yin of the liver and stomach. Cao, Zao and Jiang protect the spleen and the Tai Yin from the cold herbs. The acupuncture points liver 2, 3, stomach 44 and large intestine 11 clear heat from the blood, while spleen 4 helps protect the spleen from the cold.

Cold herbs will normally harm fertility, however when the time is right, as with this patient, cold herbs will nurture fertility. In reality, there are no good or bad herbs. It is only a question of what it is that the patient needs.

ANXIETY

Patient 28:

Female, 43, western diagnosis: ovarian cysts

MAIN COMPLAINT: infertility

HISTORY: Menstrual cycle day 9, patient suffers general anxiety, which has aggravated considerably in the past four years since trying to get pregnant. She also suffers recurrent stomach pain when she is anxious or tired. The bowel movement is normal but at times there is diarrhea, which is not linked to food. During PMS, 4-5 days prior to menses, the anxiety levels increase considerably. The period is painful and the bleeding is normal for 4-5 days. The pulse feels tight, strong and slightly rapid. The tongue is slightly red and the coating is slightly yellow and there are some teeth marks.

PATTERN: liver Qi stagnation

PATTERN ANALYSIS: The liver regulates the smooth flow of Qi. The liver is in the core of Jue Yin sphere and together with the pericardium (heart muscle) they act as the axis of the Jue Yin energy and functions. When the liver Qi stagnates, the energy in the Jue Yin and pericardium stagnates. In return, when the energy around the heart stagnates, the patient feels anxious. Anxiety is a natural body response to uncertainty and discomfort. It causes the body and spirit to desire 'change.' This is in contrast to feeling calm and comfortable. When the Qi stagnates, the patient cannot be calm, because Qi stagnation indicates that functions will begin failing. As a defense mechanism, the body and spirit are on the alert. This is called anxiety. The Chinese word for anxiety is **Fan,** which literally means that the head is on fire. The liver stagnation can cause painful menses and diarrhea as we have seen in previous patients. It also causes the pulse to become strong, tight and rapid and the tongue red. This is because Qi stagnation causes localized heat at the wrong place and at the wrong time.

HERBS: Chai Hu, Long Gu, Mu Li, Bai Shao, Sheng Gan Cao, Pipa Ye, Dang Shen

ACUPUNCTURE POINTS: liver 2 and 3, heart 7, lung 7, ear point shen men

HERBS AND ACUPUNCTURE ANALYSIS: Chai Hu raise the Qi, while Long Gu and Mu Li cause the Qi to descend. The three herbs together help ease the rising liver Qi stagnation. Bai Shao and Gan Cao nourish the liver Yin, which in turn eases the stagnation as well. Pipa and Dang Shen strengthen the Tai Yin. The Tai Yin has two organs: the lungs and the spleen. In the five elements cycle, the lungs control the liver and the liver controls the spleen. Since the liver is in excess, both the lungs and the spleen need to be strengthened. The lungs will restrain the liver stagnation and the spleen can recover from the excess control of the liver. Excess control of the liver on the spleen causes bouts of diarrhea. The acupuncture points liver 2 and 3 ease liver Qi stagnation, heart 7 and ear shen men ease the spirit, while lung 7 strengthen the lung control over the liver.

Patient 29:

Female, 38, western diagnosis: endometriosis

MAIN COMPLAINT: infertility

HISTORY: Menstrual cycle day 29, patient complains of anxiety, which has aggravated since the last IVF failed six months ago. The patient feels cold and has cold hands and feet, the urination is frequent and the sleep is "not that great." The patient becomes easily bloated after meals and has to restrict her diet from dairy and sweets. After lunch there is a general tiredness feeling that improves around 7-8 pm. The pulse is thin, weak and slightly rapid, and the tongue looks pale with red tip. The patient feels dry mouth and thirst and prefers warm drinks.

PATTERN: kidney Yang deficiency

PATTERN ANALYSIS: Yang deficiency causes anxiety when it is in the Shao Yin sphere. In the Shao Yin, the heart fire is at the upper part of the body and must descend to the kidneys. The kidneys are at the bottom of the trunk and the kidney water must ascend to the heart. The reason water can ascend is because it contains an abundance of Yang energy. When the water Yang is deficient, the water cannot ascend to the heart. The heart fire then flares upwards, causing the "head to be on fire" or in other words, anxiety. Since fertility drugs have further exhausted the kidney Yang, the anxiety has intensified since the last failing IVF cycle. The spleen receives its Yang energy from the kidneys and naturally becomes weak as well. Symptoms such as indigestion and feeling bloated are related. However, dry mouth and thirst with desire for warm liquids show that water accumulates at the bottom at the kidneys and not in the center of the body at the spleen. When water or damp accumulate in the center, there is no thirst. The problem is Shao Yin, not Tai Yin, related. Treating the spleen alone will not be wrong, but will not be as accurate as treating the kidneys with the spleen.

HERBS: Fu Zi, Zhi Gan Cao, Gan Jiang, Gui Zhi, Fu Shen, Sha Ren, Hou Po

ACUPUNCTURE POINTS: kidney 7, spleen 9, stomach 36, heart 5

HERBS AND ACUPUNCTURE ANALYSIS: The first three herbs strengthen the kidney Yang. Gui Zhi and Fu Shen help the heart fire descend into the kidneys, Sha Ren and Hou Po invigorate the spleen water metabolism and thus help the kidney Yang recover. Kidney 7, spleen 9 and stomach 36 help the kidney and spleen Yang, while heart 5 helps the heart descend.

Patient 30:

Female, 31, western diagnosis: unexplained infertility

MAIN COMPLAINT: infertility

HISTORY: Menstrual cycle day 18, patient complains of feeling anxious for many years, with occasional insomnia and frequent dreams. She has experienced problems concentrating, and has felt occasional heart palpitations around menstruation. The period has two full days of blood flow, then it stops for one day and continues on day four and five. The pulse has an irregular beat and it seems to halt every few beats, baffling western physicians as to the cause. The patient has no reported heart condition. The tongue is pale with peeled coating at the tip of the tongue. The patient generally feels a little cold and has cold hands but not cold feet.

PATTERN: heart Yang deficiency

PATTERN ANALYSIS: The heart is the emperor. It controls the blood in the vessels and the blood circulation. When the heart Yang is deficient, the emperor function of overseeing the reproductive system and the blood circulation is impaired. Insomnia, heart palpitations, halting pulse and menstruation irregularity are all a testament to heart deficiency. When the Yang is deficient above, the hands will feel cold and when the Yang is deficient below, the feet will feel cold. **The Yellow Emperor** says that when the Yang is born, the Yin flourishes, so if the heart Yang is deficient, the heart blood will naturally decline. The emperor (the commander in chief) has lost command, and therefore control, over the liver in terms of when to begin and when to stop the bleeding.

HERBS: Fu Zi, Rou Gui, Gui Zhi, Dang Gui Tou, Huang Qi, Bai Zhu, Gan Cao, Ban Xia, Fu Ling, Ze Xie

ACUPUNCTURE POINTS: heart 5 and 7, large intestine 10, spleen 3

HERBS AND ACUPUNCTURE ANALYSIS: the first three herbs warm the heart Yang, adding Dang Gui and Huang Qi, which assists the heart blood. Huang Qi, Bai Zhu and Gan Cao strengthen the spleen Yang and blood production, thus helping the heart. Ban Xia helps the stomach descend, while Fu Ling and Ze Xie remove excess water from the bottom, which indirectly improves the heart Yang. Heart 5, 7 and large intestine 10 improve the heart Yang, while spleen 3 connects the spleen and stomach and assists in the up and down movement of energy in the center of the body, so the heart Yang can descend and the kidney water can ascend. The stomach and spleen are in the center of the body, also called the middle heater. The stomach descends and the spleen ascends. Together they are the axis of the energy in the body, allowing the Qi to travel from top to bottom and from bottom to top.

HEADACHES

Patient 31:

Female, 45, western diagnosis: poor egg quality and old age

MAIN COMPLAINT: infertility

HISTORY: Menstrual cycle day 15, patient complains of severe headaches in the past year since beginning fertility drug regiment. The headaches are sharp and localized at the top and sides of the head. The patient feels warm throughout the day and has night sweats at night, which at times can be so heavy that the patient is forced to change her clothing. Sometimes when the head aches, the patient feels dizzy as if the room is spinning around her. Western testing has revealed no physical explanation for these symptoms. The patient feels thirsty at night and keeps a glass of water by the bed. The pulse is thin, tight and rapid. The tongue is red and has no coating. The patient feels very tired in the morning and finds it hard to get out of bed.

PATTERN: liver Yin deficiency with Yang rising

PATTERN ANALYSIS: Fertility drugs often exhaust the Yang in the water, but sometimes they dry the water too. The Jue Yin and the liver are the last stop in the storage phase of the Yang energy. From here, the Yang opens up evenly, enabling the ability to feel the morning energy upon waking-up. During the night, the Yang is stored in the water, and then in the wind wood of the Jue Yin as it prepares for departure. The Jue Yin is the last Yin anchor to hold the Yang in storage. When this Yin is dried out, the Yang cannot anchor and it loses its momentum, resulting in a slower then normal opening of the Yang in the morning, making it more difficult to wake-up. Later on in the day, the energy picks up, the energy flowing in four directions; up and down, and in and out of the body. The liver Yin function is to monitor and smooth out the energy flow in each direction. The wood energy grows upward and roots downward, branching outward and strengthening inward (the tree trunk). This quality of wood allows the energy flow in each direction, connecting the top with the bottom and the inside with the outside. However, when the wood is dry (no Yin), the roots are not connected to the branches. The Yang energy wants to go up to heaven and separate from the heavy earth, resulting in separation of Yin and Yang. In the body, the dry liver cannot root the Yang down and the Yang rises pathologically, causing headaches. When severe, the Yang's abrupt movement causes vertigo or dizziness with a feeling that the room spins. At night, when the Yin should be strong and should embrace the Yang, the separation of the two causes body fluids to surface outward, which induces heavy night sweats. When the patient loses body fluids in this manner, thirst rises and she needs to drink to compensate for the loss. The red tongue with no coating shows the dryness of Yin fluids.

HERBS: Shu Dihuang, Shan Yao, Shan Zhuyu, Mu Dan Pi, Gou Qizi, Mai Dong, Nu Zhenzi, Hei Zhima

ACUPUNCTURE POINTS: liver 3 and 8, kidney 3, large intestine 11

HERBS AND ACUPUNCTURE ANALYSIS: Dihuang, Dan Pi, Qizi, Dong, Zhenzi, Zhima nourish the liver Yin, while Shao Yao and Zhuyu strengthen the kidney Yang (the Yang is born, then the Yin flourishes). It is important to strengthen the kidney Yang or else the Yin cannot transform and the spleen will become obstructed. There is no need to suppress the Yang, since the reason for its ascent is the dryness of Yin. Liver 3, 8, kidney 3 and large intestine 11 nourish the liver Yin.

Patient 32:

Female, 37, western diagnosis: PCOS

MAIN COMPLAINT: infertility

HISTORY: Menstrual cycle day 11, patient complains of chronic headaches over many years, experienced when tired at the end of the day. Overall, she feels cold and has cold hands and feet, she is not thirsty and the appetite is decent. The bowel movement is regular and urination is frequent. The pulse is forceless and slightly rapid and the tongue is pale with moist coating and slight teeth marks on the sides.

PATTERN: kidney Yang deficiency

PATTERN ANALYSIS: The Yang energy is responsible for circulating the Yin and the body fluids. When the Yang is deficient below, the water is accumulating above. When the Yang is deficient above, the water accumulates below. When the water accumulates, the Qi becomes obstructed and the person experiences pain. If the water accumulates below and the Yang wants to separate upwards, the headaches can come randomly throughout the day. However, if the water circulates normally throughout the body during the day, until the patient becomes tired in the evening, then it will stop midway in the upper part of the body and the headaches will commence. After rest or sleep, the water travels back to the bottom, in its natural place, and the headaches stop. Regardless of water at the top or at the bottom, the cause for both is kidney Yang deficiency.

HERBS: Fu Zi, Zhi Gan Cao, Gan Jiang, Fu Ling, Cang Zhu, Ban Xia, Chen Pi, Rou Gui, Gui

Zhi

ACUPUNCTURE POINTS: Du 20, stomach 36, spleen 6, kidney 7

HERBS AND ACUPUNCTURE ANALYSIS: The herbs tonify the kidney Yang and cause it to rise to the head. This results in a drop in water circulation. The acupuncture points cause the Yang energy to rise so the water can go down. It is important to differentiate between headache types and to avoid the automatic assumption that a headache is a Yang rising situation. The whole picture needs to be considered.

Patient 33:

Female, 36, western diagnosis: one blocked fallopian tube, stage 1 endometriosis

MAIN COMPLAINT: infertility

HISTORY: Menstrual cycle day 7, patient complains of strong headaches mainly localized at the forehead and behind the eyes for about three months since taking fertility drugs. For many years, the patient has experienced cold hands and feet. Previously, she was not overly thirsty, but in the last three months, she feels very thirsty and craves cold drinks. Urination is very frequent and she feels pain in the center of the back. The pulse is thin and very rapid, the tongue is pale and the center of the tongue coating seems thin and dry compared with the front and rear.

PATTERN: acute stomach heat and chronic kidney Yang deficiency

PATTERN ANALYSIS: This is a common situation for infertility patients who use fertility drugs. There is often both a chronic condition and a drug related acute condition. The chronic condition was previously the true cause for the infertility, but now the acute syndrome is an additional cause for infertility. The chronic condition here is a typical kidney Yang deficiency. The patient feels cold, cold hands and feet and urinates frequently. The artificial heat introduced into the body is accumulating in the stomach in this particular case, causing the patient to feel very thirsty and have strong frontal headaches. The front of the head is where the stomach meridian is distributed, and heat along this channel will cause the front of the head to ache. Pain in the center of the back shows that heat is accumulating in the stomach organ and not only in the stomach channel.

HERBS: Zhi Mu, Mai Dong, Sha Shen, Hei Zhima, Gan Cao, Hong Zao, Dang Shen

ACUPUNCTURE POINTS: stomach 44, large intestine 11, kidney 3 and 6, spleen 6, moxa on Du 4

HERBS AND ACUPUNCTURE ANALYSIS: This condition, like many post-fertility drugs conditions, is very delicate. The pathology develops in an abnormal way. Normally, a patient who suffers kidney Yang deficiency is very unlikely to develop heat in the stomach. This is because the overall Yang is missing. With drugs, the situation is different. You can have Yin deficiency and overnight feel very cold, or you can have Yang deficiency and all of a sudden experience heat syndrome. For this patient to become pregnant, the kidney Yang needs to recover, however accessing the kidneys with hot herbs is obstructed. The herbs all enter into the body through the stomach and the stomach now suffers heat. Any hot herbs going into the stomach will aggravate this heat and will not reach the kidneys. This is a drawback for the patient. We now must clear the heat slowly and only after the stomach heat is gone are we able to warm the kidneys. If we clear the stomach heat quickly, the kidney Yang will collapse. Basically, there is no short way here. Before the stomach heat, the treatment should have been 3-6 months, but now it will be 6-9 months instead. This is why I recommend trying the Hunyuan first and moving on to other modalities later.

Joanne and her husband could not get pregnant for seven years. They tried four IVF cycles and two additional IVF cycles with donor eggs. They then heard of the Hunyuan Method and wanted to try it. After six months of treatment, conception was still eluding them. Yaron Seidman recommended they try IVF again, this time with a stronger, healthier body. The IVF treatment worked and Joanne carried to term. Two years later, Joanne decided to go for another IVF treatment, yet it failed again. Frustrated, she remembered that the previous IVF cycle succeeded only after taking herbs for six months. She told her husband "I think that the last IVF worked only because of the Chinese herbs. We must try it again". Joanne received herbal treatment for two months and she continued taking herbs throughout the IVF cycle. This time it worked and she conceived twins. Joanne continued with the herbs for the first five months of pregnancy and later carried to term. She says that had they only known that the Hunyuan method and the herbs could help the IVF succeed, they could have had a baby many years back. Joanne says that the herbal treatment made all the difference.

8

IMPROVING YOUR CHANCES

EXERCISE THE RIGHT WAY

While trying to get pregnant and after you are pregnant, it is important to exercise in a sensible way. The goal of exercising is to restore and improve health. It is not to burn calories or to lose weight. The guiding principle for exercise is to avoid doing too much of it, or too little.

Exercise should be done gently with minimum impact on the body. Over straining the muscles and ligaments is not healthy. High impact exercises should be avoided as they damage the joints and tendons, which in turn will cause the liver to deteriorate. The liver nourishes the tendons and will be over-taxed. The liver is the first organ to support the embryo, and if the liver is weak, the embryo will not develop or will not implant. Heavy perspiration during exercise and exhaustion of the muscles will cause the spleen to deteriorate; it is the spleen that nourishes the muscles. If the spleen is tired, the Yang energy cannot rise in the body and a pregnancy cannot stick. On the other hand, light exercise stimulates the tendons and muscles, as the liver and spleen are encouraged to circulate energy. This in turn will improve fertility and pregnancy rates.

So how much is too much? Heavy sweat, sore muscles and achy joints are indications of too much. How much is too little? No sweat at all, stiff joints, and no feeling of an increase in energy indicates a lack of exercise.

Tai Chi and Yoga, which are more body friendly and involve learning breathing and relaxation techniques, can improve the body, energy, and spirit. These disciplines are beneficial when it comes to trying to conceive, as well as during pregnancy. It is important to find an experienced teacher who can guide you through.

TIMING CONCEPTION – OPEN YOUR OWN WINDOW

Every woman has a window of fertility in the middle of the menstrual cycle which lasts approximately ten days. This window can shift depending on the length of the cycle. In a regular 28-day cycle, it is from days nine to 19. In a short menstrual cycle of 24 days, it is from days five to 15. In a long menstrual cycle of 40 days, is from days 21 to 31.

To calculate your fertility window, take the number of days of your last menstrual cycle and subtract 14 to reach your mid-fertile point, the middle of the window. Then subtract five from the mid-fertile point to pinpoint the window's first day, the first day to begin having intercourse. From the mid-fertile point, add five days to identify the last day of the window, when intercourse should stop.

In our example, if the last menstrual cycle is 28 days, the mid-fertile point is day 14 of the cycle, the beginning day for intercourse is day nine, and the end day of the fertile window is day 19. Let's say that the last menstrual cycle is 40 days long, the mid-fertile day is day 26 (40-14=26), the beginning day is day 21 (26-5=21), and the end day is day 31 (26+5=31).

This calculation method is only good for women who have a regular cycle. If the cycle is irregular, modern techniques of detecting ovulation will be necessary.

BEST TIME FOR INTERCOURSE – DON'T DEPLETE THE HUBBY

Once you have established your fertile window, you should establish a rhythm of one intercourse session every other day. Daily intercourse will deplete your husband's resources. The best chances for conception come with intercourse which occurs in the morning when the body is most rested and when the Yang energy opens up to become more active. As noted previously, the Jue Yin, when the Yin comes to extinction and the new Yang is born, extends from 1 AM to 7 AM. It is a time of "war" between Yin and Yang, when the liver, which is the Jue Yin organ, is the "general" who calls the decisions. Even when intercourse occurs at 4 PM the prior day, conception and implantation will occur during Jue Yin time in the early morning hours.

COMMONLY-OCCURRING MISTAKES AND HOW TO AVOID THEM

In modern medicine, conception is a mechanical event. The egg meets the sperm and they create an embryo. When we follow this line of thinking, then timing the ovulation is the essence of fertility treatments. However, in Chinese medicine, conception involves the heaven and earth and the male and female energies. When the energies are aligned correctly, then the egg and sperm will perform their natural function with ease. We are therefore most concerned with disturbances to energy, mind, and spirit.

Most common modern recommendations to time ovulation are counterproductive. Ovulation kits and measuring basal body temperatures increase the female and male anxiety and thus create energy obstructions. When the woman anxiously awaits ovulation, she transmits this message to her male partner, the liver energy becomes stagnant, and the Jue Yin suffers. When the Jue Yin can't break apart the Yin and Yang, then conception cannot happen. The "general" is restrained and can't lead this war into a victory.

Using the fertility calculation above is preferable to ovulation kits because it does not involve stress and anxiety. The only exception is when the menstrual cycle is very irregular and must first be regulated in order to detect the fertile window.

Two common myths that should be shattered when it comes to attempting to conceive are

PI

the notions that couples should attempt to have intercourse in a variety of strange positions, and that the woman should stay lying in bed for a period of time after intercourse. The path to successful conception is the natural way, with heaven on top and earth below, meaning the man is on top and the female is below. The Pi hexagram has the earth and Yin below and the heaven and Yang above. This hexagram is demonstrating "bad luck," the Yin moving downward and the Yang moving upward. The end result is the separation of Yin and Yang into the pre-heaven state before the creation of life. The father and mother must go into this pre-heaven state in order to create new life and a new post-heaven. This is the Yin Yang principle of nature. The dead of winter must come first before spring shows up.

After intercourse, the female stands up and the vertical line inside her uterus becomes horizontal. On the vertical line we call Jing that connects heaven and earth, the newly formed embryo has changed its position from horizontal to vertical, or from Wei to Jing. The newly conceived life has just changed from a pre heaven state (lifeless) to a post heaven state which is full of life.

The father on top and the mother below can make this pre heaven vertical (Jing) line inside the uterus prepare for conception. Thereafter the mother changes position and stands up so the embryo has its first change from Jing to Wei, from vertical to horizontal. Although in the modern era, men and women have intercourse in a variety of positions, the traditional position is lying down with the male on top and the female below. This is because it is the energetical state needed for conception.

Patients often tell me that through on-line research they have come upon four requirements for successful conception. In addition to staying in bed after intercourse, the others include placing a pillow under the hips during sex, elevating the feet in the air immediately thereafter, and not bathing or showering for at least one day. None of these actions will have any affect whatsoever on fertility.

BELIEVE IN YOURSELF

When we understand that we were created from heaven and earth and that heaven and earth are around us all the time, we can also understand that our body is capable of becoming pregnant naturally. This is what I call "Hunyuan." We all have within us this connection to heaven and earth. We have this connection to nature from before our birth throughout our life. We know how to bring the female and male energies together to create the next life. If, however, we fall into the trap of modern science, where our life is only physical and there is no heaven and earth, male and female, or Yin and Yang, then our Hunyuan is lost.

Your first step toward successful conception is to know and believe that you can do it. Believing that you can't do it, or visiting clinics that encourage you to believe that you can't do it, will harm your chances. The only question that should matter is how to restore a heaven-earth balance that is out of synch.

BECOME ONE WITH YOUR PARTNER

After you believe in yourself, the next most important step is to unite with your partner. To bring heaven and earth together, the husband and wife must unite. That doesn't mean you should get together to go for a consultation at the IVF clinic, it rather means that you must be in it together all the way from beginning to end. Disharmony of heaven and earth is always a disharmony of the male and female. In contrast to modern medicine, which pinpoints the blame on the wife or the husband, in Chinese medicine it is always the couple's disharmony that needs to be restored. "Getting pregnant" is a man and woman coming together and "infertility" is a man and a woman who can't come together.

Although the remedies given to men and women may be different, the goal of the mutual remedy is to allow their unification. Otherwise, the unification is broken, and a new relationship begins; doctor-wife or doctor-husband. The intervention of the doctor between husband and wife does not exist with Chinese medicine. With IVF, for example, the doctor assumes the role of the husband, intervening at the time of conception by delivering the sperm to the egg. The male heaven is not there, even if his sperm is there. The time of the Jue Yin is fragile and delicate, and it needs the perfect harmony of heaven and earth to allow the Yin to close and to allow the Yang to be born. Instead, the physician is intruding into the female body in a seriously disharmonious way, creating great difficulty.

If the husband and wife are healthy, then heaven and earth come together in harmony. During the course of treatment, it is important for me to locate the disharmony with the husband as it relates to his wife, and the disharmony with the wife as it relates to her husband; then both husband and wife receive the necessary herbs. Each of the herbal formulas aims at harmonizing the couple by bringing them closer to each other. In addition, I use acupuncture for the wife, because the female is Yin and acupuncture can bring the Yin outside to meet the Yang. At other times, I use only herbs with both partners.

HARMONY WITH NATURE

The Yellow Emperor: *The emperor asked: 'What defines the star constellations and what is the meaning of the eight sections?' Qibo answered: 'The star constellations are harmonizing the movements of the sun and the moon. The eight sections host the eight pathological winds and at the right moment and time the pathological winds surface. The seasons are divided into spring, fall, summer and winter. When you harmonize the seasons well, the pathological energies of the eight sections are blocked and cannot surface. However, when the body is deficient and it meets a deficient energy from heaven, both deficiencies cause pathological Qi to penetrate the bones and harm the five Yin organs. The doctor's work is to rescue the patient and not allow him harm. This is why you must know the prohibitions of heaven.'*

Knowing how to harmonize with nature may seem easy, but in reality it is quite complex. Every one of us strives for harmony with nature, each at his own level. Some of us like to eat natural, organically raised food, others take vacations in nature, and some do what it takes to stay away from chemicals. We also try to keep in tune with nature every time we hear the weather forecast.

In Chinese medicine, staying in harmony with nature is all-encompassing. Our energy is derived from nature; our life force is the result of the interaction between heaven and earth. This is not just in a metaphorical sense, but rather in a very physical day to day sense.

The Yellow Emperor first addresses the broad categories of the seasons. It is clear to the naked eye that the summer is hot and that the winter is cold. We can also see that the spring is about birth and the fall energy is about decline. Logically, in the summer we should keep ourselves cool to a certain degree and in the winter we should keep ourselves warm. In the spring we should become more outgoing, while in the fall we should turn our emotions inward. The same principle applies to our diet, exercise, sleep and other activities.

To understand this on a deeper level, we must consider that the seasons are not exactly the same every year. A particular date, say April 15, may be cloudy and cold one year and then clear and warm the next. Why are some winters warmer than others? Why is there a widespread flu outbreak in February one year, and in October the next? The answer lies with the six heavenly energies and how they project themselves onto earth.

I have decided to include this chapter into this book because, despite its complexity, it has great value in helping you, the reader, harmonize with nature, and it will assist you in foreseeing and preventing difficult times when your body might become ill. I will teach you in this section how to calculate the year according to Chinese medicine and how to understand the energies around you. When you know that a difficult time is coming, you can prepare yourself and keep healthy. **The Yellow Emperor** says *"when the body is deficient and it meets a deficient energy from heaven, both deficiencies cause the pathological Qi to penetrate the bones and harm the five Yin organs."* If you find it too confusing, simply take your time and get back to this chapter later on.

The 28 star constellations have a direct impact on the earth's energy because they affect the behavior of the sun and the moon, which create the play of Yin and Yang. Specifically, the ancients noticed certain patterns reappearing every so often in the skies that cause a specific impact on the energy on earth. When this energy is good, there is less illness, and when it is negative, more people become ill, such as with a widespread flu outbreak.

The scholars of Chinese medicine were able to analyze the skies and systemized a uniform code for calculating how these patterns will repeat. They observed the five brightest stars in the sky; Mercury (Shui Xing/ Water star), Venus (Jin Xing/ Metal star), Mars (Huo Xing/ Fire star), Jupiter (Mu Xing/ Wood star) and Saturn (Tu Xing/ Earth star). Because of the different distances of the stars from the sun, the completion of an orbit around the sun varies in length for each star. In 60 years, the earth rotates around the sun 60 times. In the same 60 years, Mercury travels 240 orbits around the sun, Venus travels 96, Mars 30, and Saturn just two. Every 60 years, the five bright stars and the earth will align onto one straight line with the sun. This repetition of star alignment is similar to the repetition of the four seasons. It allowed the sages to establish a code or a relationship between the stars and the earth, between the skies and our health.

The sages created 10 heavenly bodies they named **Tian Gan** and they defined 12 earthly branches they named **Di Zhi**. Together they are known as **Tian Gan Di Zhi**. Each heavenly body determines the overall energy of the year, while each earthly branch determines the energy in the six segments of the year. When we combine the 10 heavenly and 12 earthly, we

GREGORIAN YEAR	CHINESE YEAR
2008	Wu Zi
2009	Ji Chou
2010	Geng Yin
2011	Xin Mao
2012	Ren Chen
2013	Kui Si
2014	Jia Wu
2015	Yi Wei
2016	Bing Shen
2017	Ding You
2018	Wu Xu
2019	Ji Hai
2020	Geng Zi
2021	Xin Chou
2022	Ren Yin
2023	Kui Mao
2024	Jia Chen
2025	Yi Si
2026	Bing Wu
2027	Ding Wei
2028	Wu Shen
2029	Ji You
2030	Geng Xu
2031	Xin Hai
2032	Ren Zi
2033	Kui Chou
2034	Jia Yin
2035	Yi Mao
2036	Bing Chen
2037	Ding Si

get 60 unique combinations of energy that repeat themselves every 60 years.

The Tian Gan: **Jia, Yi, Bing, Ding, Wu, Ji, Geng, Xin, Ren, Kui.**

The Di Zhi: **Zi, Chou, Yin, Mao, Chen, Si, Wu, Wei, Shen, You, Xu, Hai.**

For easy reference, to the left is a table of the years in the Chinese calendar for the next 30 years.

If you know the heavenly body, then you know the element of the year and you can also tell if this element will be excessive or deficient in that year. So, for example, in the year Jia Zi,

The heavenly bodies correspond to the five elements: earth, metal, water, wood and fire. Two heavenly bodies occupy one element, one excessive and one deficient. Below is a table for easy reference:

	EXCESSIVE	DEFICIENT
Earth	Jia	Ji
Metal	Geng	Yi
Water	Bing	Xin
Wood	Ren	Ding
Fire	Wu	Kui

the heavenly body is Jia, which is the excessive earth element. We know that the earth element is excessive in the year Jia Zi. If we take the year Wu Zi, which is 2008 on the western calendar, we can see that the heavenly body is Wu. Wu belongs to fire and it is in excess. Wu Zi (2008) has an overall excessive fire characteristic.

After we have learned how to recognize the overall energy of the year, we need to learn how to dissect it and find the energy in each one of the year's six time segments, each segment two months long. The six yearly periods are determined by the twelve earthly branches. The earthly branches correspond to: Tai Yang, Shao Yang, Yang Ming, Tai Yin, Shao Yin and Jue Yin. These are also known as the six energies of heaven. The Tai Yang is cold and water (refer to chapters 2 and 4), the Shao Yang is minister fire, the Yang Ming is dryness and metal, the Tai Yin is dampness and earth, the Shao Yin is emperor fire, while the Jue Yin is wind and wood. These six heavenly energies act upon the earth and they determine the energies around us all the time. The energies change constantly and that is why the temperature is not the same every day.

The first of the six periods begins two weeks prior to the Chinese New Year and it lasts for two months. The second period begins the next day and lasts for two months, and so on. Each period of the year will have different characteristics, including two different energies. The one energy is the core energy, while the other is guest energy. The core energy creates and follows the pattern of the seasons and never changes. This is why there is a four-season pattern that repeats itself every year.

For simplification purposes, let's call the six segments of the year first period, second period, third period, etc…

You can see that the core energies follow the pattern of the seasons. The early spring is characterized by wind and birth. The late spring becomes warm and the summer hot. The late summer is characterized by dampness and the fall by dryness, and finally, the winter becomes very cold.

YEAR 2009	FIRST PERIOD	SECOND PERIOD	THIRD PERIOD	FOURTH PERIOD	FIFTH PERIOD	SIXTH PERIOD
Core Energy	Wind Wood	Emperor Fire	Minister Fire	Dampness Earth	Dryness Metal	Cold Water
Guest Energy						

Next we must calculate the guest energies, which will determine if these two months will be easy or difficult on your body. I remember a conversation I had with one reproductive endocrinologist who stated that in his practice he finds that there are periods of time when no patient becomes pregnant with IVFs, and other times when it seems like everyone is getting pregnant. This is related to the guest energies.

To calculate the guest energies, we use the "Heavenly Axis" (Si Tian) which sets the energy tone in the first half of the year. To calculate the year, we need to find the Heavenly Axis.

The following table shows the 12 earthly branches and their corresponding Heavenly Axis energies:

HEAVENLY AXIS		
1. Shao Yin Emperor *Fire*	Zi	Wu
2. Tai Yin Dampness *Earth*	Chou	Wei
3. Shao yang Minister *Fire*	Yin	Shen
4. Yang Ming Dryness *Metal*	Mao	You
5. Tai Yang Cold *Water*	Chen	Xu
6. Jue Yin Wind *Wood*	Si	Hai

As we learned, each year is composed of one heavenly trunk and one earthly branch. The earthly branch in each year is the "Heaven Axis." For example, in the year Wu Zi (2008), Zi is the earthly branch and it determines the "Heaven Axis." The "Heaven Axis" in this year is Shao Yin Emperor Fire. Within the six segments of the year, the "Heaven Axis" is always in the third segment.

The fourth segment contains the guest energy that follows the "Heaven Axis," while the second segment includes the energy that precedes the axis. In the table above, you can see that Tai Yin Dampness Earth follows the Emperor Fire, while Wind Wood precedes it. The fifth segment guest energy is Shao Yang Minister Fire and the sixth segment guest energy is Yang Ming Dryness Metal. The six energies follow a sequential order backwards or forwards from the "Heavenly Axis."

In summarizing the entire year Wu Zi (2008), we have the following:

Year overall energy – Wu, excessive fire

The core and guest energies as follows:

YEAR 2008	FIRST PERIOD	SECOND PERIOD	THIRD PERIOD	FOURTH PERIOD	FIFTH PERIOD	SIXTH PERIOD
Core Energy	Wind Wood	Emperor Fire	Minister Fire	Dampness Earth	Dryness Metal	Cold Water
Guest Energy	Cold Water	Wind Wood	Axis is Zi Emperor Fire	Dampness Earth	Minister Fire	Dryness Metal

When we combine the three together, we find times that are better than others for us to become pregnant, and there are times that are less optimal in which we need to take much better care of ourselves. For example, in the year Wu Zi (2008) the overall energy is excess fire, the third segment core energy is fire and the guest energy is fire. This is a time when the Yang energy is very aggressive and many people can become ill with heat-like symptoms (nausea, headaches, dizziness, etc). It is beneficial to stay cool and away from hot drinks. Hot, stimulating drugs are very harmful at this time and patients taking them will experience more intense side effects than normal. Even the use of hot herbs should be restricted. This is why **The Yellow Emperor** says in two separate chapters that those who do not know the additions of every year, and those who don't know the decline and excess of energy, cannot serve as healers.

To understand the meaning of each combination of core and guest energies, it is best to review chapters 2 and 4 and to attempt to understand their true meanings. Then it will not be difficult to decode the energy chart you have calculated. If you know the energies of the year, your life can become much more harmonious with nature. Your chances of becoming pregnant are dramatically increased. If you receive Chinese medicine treatment from a practitioner who knows the yearly energies, you are in much luck.

I can share with you a story that occurred in my practice in May of 2008, a year of Wu Zi, representing excess fire. The months are at the third phase of the year, where the core energy is Shao Yang minister fire and the guest energy is Shao Yin emperor fire. This is the period in the 60-year cycle where the Yang energy is the strongest. Five patients who had tried to become pregnant for years with IVF and herbal treatments became pregnant. These patients were the most Yang deficient patients I'd had in a long time, yet they all conceived, some without any assistance at all.

SHEN JI AND QI LI

The Yellow Emperor: *The Emperor asked: "In some years, there is great fertility while in others there is infertility. It is hard to control. What energy causes this?' Qibo answered: 'The six heavenly energies and the five species have mutual control and restrictions. If the energy is conforming, fertility will flourish and if it differs, fertility will decline. This is the Dao of heaven and earth. It is the normal state of birth and transformation. This we call 'the root is in the core of the species'. There is also a root outside of the species, which also has five kinds. This is why the creation of the five species is different. The creation on earth has five smells, five colors, five species and they are all mutually suitable.'*

The emperor asked: 'what is it called then?' Qibo answered: 'When the root is inside the species core, we call it Shen Ji (spirit instrument). When the spirit departs, the instrument stops (the species dies). When the root is outside of the species core, we call it Qi Li (energy existence). When the energy stops, transformation ceases and there is no more.'

This quote is very important in that it helps us understand that our lives and our fertility are connected to heaven and earth. From ancient times, the sages recognized that at some times there were periods of more fertility among the five species, while at other times there was less fertility. The five species, also called the five worms, are **Mao** (animals with fur), **Yu** (with feathers), **Lin** (with fish scales), **Jie** (with shells) and **Luo** (none of the above). The human being belongs to the Luo species. The two instruments that connect us to heaven and earth are the Shen Ji and the Qi Li. The Shen Ji means the God-giving life that we have. With every breath we take, our spirit stays alive. Our spirit, or Shen Ji, is not independent from heaven and earth. The six heavenly energies and the five earthly elements directly impact our spirit. In the modern world, most of us falsely believe that we have complete control over our lives, or at least we want to believe that. Otherwise, the situation feels very unstable. In reality, we are getting our life force from somewhere when we are born, and this life force is returning to its origination point when we die. This is the definition of Shen Ji.

The Shen Ji is impacted by the earthly five elements, namely the five emotions we feel, the five flavors we eat, the five colors we see and the five odors we smell. The Shen Ji is also influenced by the six heavenly energies, namely Tai Yang Cold Water, Yang Ming Dryness Metal, Shao Yang Minister Fire, Tai Yin Dampness Earth, Shao Yin Emperor Fire and Jue Yin Wind Wood.

The Yellow Emperor says: *If the energy is conforming fertility will flourish and if it differs,* *fertility will decline.* This means that if the six heavenly energies and the five earthly elements are positively impacting your Shen Ji, your fertility will increase, while if these energies are negatively impacting your Shen Ji, then your fertility will decline. This is of course the same for your overall health. If your Shen Ji is in harmony with nature, then health increases, and if not, then health decreases. Health and fertility are not two different things, they are rather one and the same. When Shen Ji is well nourished and healthy, then there are no diseases and no infertility. How do we nourish our Shen Ji? We harmonize with nature. We don't try to take control of it and go against it.

The Yellow Emperor: *The Yellow Emperor asked: 'There are years where there are no prevalent diseases and the energy of the five Yin organs doesn't follow the earthly five elements energy. How is that so?' Qibo answered: 'This is because the six heavenly energies control the five earthly energies (elements), then the energy of the five Yin organs must follow the heaven'.*

Zhang Zhicong, a famous Yellow Emperor commentator, remarks on this quote: *This segment explains that heaven has five transformations and the earth has five directions. On top of this, there are the six energies and the 'Heavenly Axis' (Si Tian) and the 'Spring Origin' (Zai Quan). These are all interacting together and controlling each other. When The Yellow Emperor says that a year has no prevalent diseases, this means that there are no diseases caused by the heavenly transformations or the earthly five directions.*

This section explains again that the energies around us can affect our fertility and cause diseases, such as a flu epidemic, to surface. It is thus very important to understand the energies of any particular year, and then to devise a strategy as to how to conform to them so we can stay healthy.

How can we understand Qi Li then? **The Yellow Emperor:** *When 'entering and exiting' stops. the Shen Ji dissolves and dissipates. When the rising and descending ceases, the Qi Li is alone in danger. Because of this, if there is no 'entering and exiting,' there is no birth, growth, maturing, old age and natural death (human cycle). If there is no rising and descending there is no birth, growth, transformation, decline and storage (nature's four seasons cycle). Because this is so, each one (Shen Ji and Qi Li) has controls and restrictions, and each one has birth and formation. As the saying goes: if you don't know the additions of each year, the sameness and differences among energies, you can't really understand birth and transformation. This is the essence of it all.*

The Qi Li has to do with the rising and descending of energy. "Rising" means the rising energy of the earth and "descending" means the descending energy of the heavens. Human beings live in between heaven and earth, or in other words, we all live in between the descending and rising of the heaven and earth energies. They impact our body positively or negatively. The Shen Ji is impacted by exiting and entering, the heaven and earth energies going in and out of the body to create and nourish the Shen Ji. The spirit instrument is created and nourished by the heaven and earth's energies which connect to the core of one's body. Qi Li has a different mechanism. The heaven and earth interact among themselves. This mutual interaction of heaven and earth influences the body. Li Yangbo says that Qi Li is like a secret code determined by the position of the stars at the time of birth. This determines how the rising and descending energies will impact us throughout life. The heaven-earth interaction, which is different every year, will impact the Qi Li differently. This is why we are all different, and in a flu epidemic some will contract the virus and others will not.

The Yellow Emperor says: *When the rising and descending ceases, the Qi Li is alone in danger. Because of this, if there is no rising and descending there is no birth, growth, transformation, decline and storage."* If your Qi Li code is compromised you can't adjust to the environment and seasons, and if the seasons or environment's energy is negative or ill, your Qi Li will be impaired. Either way, be it your Qi Li or the environment around you, if there is no harmony between the two it will lead to the decline of your health and the decline of your fertility.

When we talk about allergies for example, if you alone have an allergic reaction to the environment, it is because your Qi Li is compromised. If, however, many people suffer from an allergy simultaneously, it is the environment, or heaven-earth energies, that are ill and causing your Qi Li to be impaired.

SPECIAL ALLOPATHIC INFERTILITY CLINIC

In as much as I am passionate about classical Chinese medicine, sometime surprises come to me in very unexpected ways, and once it came from Western medicine.

As part of my doctoral program specializing in Chinese medicine for infertility, I chose to spend several hundred hours in a Western fertility clinic. I approached Dr. Karol Chacho, who accepted me for the rotation and internship at his clinic. His motto is: "Don't do IVF if you don't have to and don't take drugs if they are not necessary."

When I visited his office for the first time, I was more than a little taken aback. I am extremely familiar with the general procedure at most IFV clinics, where doctors see patients for two to three minutes at a shot, most often telling them they are too infertile to conceive naturally and should begin IVF procedures as soon as possible. Here, I found something entirely different. Patients are treated warmly in a low-key setting. Although Dr. Chacho is a superior surgeon who offers cutting edge IVF technology, his goal is to help the patient conceive in the least invasive way, even if that translates to less money making potential for him. I was thrilled to see that some doctors in the infertility business still administer real medicine to their patients. Real medicine, in my mind, is when the doctor's motivation for healing the patient comes from his heart.

Chinese medicine and Western medicine both have limitations. A patient who has tried Chinese medicine and is still not pregnant, should consider all her options. If IVF is chosen, then Dr. Chacho's clinic, or one like his, is the best hope. He offers many procedures long forgotten by most other clinics, including a test for mycoplasma, which is infertility impaired by bacteria, and post coital tests to find out if the cervical mucus is obstructing the sperm. He will also do natural inseminations without the use of drugs.

Dr. Chacho, unlike many other RE'S, encourages his patients. After fixing a small problem, he often tells them to go home for six months to try to conceive on their own before moving onto the next step. In fact, many of these women do conceive with no additional help, much to Dr. Chacho's delight.

YOUR BABY IS WHAT YOU EAT

Prior to visiting my office, a 39-year-old patient had conceived naturally. Unfortunately, an ectopic pregnancy resulted, the fallopian tube removed. Thereafter, the patient became convinced that IVF would be her only option. Even though IVF does not eliminate the possibility for an ectopic pregnancy, it does nevertheless decrease its probability.

After two failed IVFs, I recommended to the patient that she try an herbal course. The patient politely declined while stating the following reason: *I had a DES exposure while in my mother's womb, and because of that, I am certain that only IVF will be appropriate.*

Why am I bringing up this story? Because I believe it characterizes our entire modern society. Although her mother used artificial hormones which actually caused the patient's problem, the patient was still confident that using modern hormones and drugs today would have no negative impact on her baby in the future.

To expand on the importance of parental choices with regard to the health of their offspring, let us turn to a book by a prominent gynecologist from the Qing Dynasty (1644-1911), Zhang Yao Sun's **Pregnancies, Labor and Delivery Collections.** In Chapter 3, 'Appropriate actions during pregnancy,' he wrote: *When the baby lives in his mother's womb, the mother's Qi is his Qi, the mother's blood is his blood and the mother's breath is his breath. When the mother's* *heart is virtuous, her Qi and blood harmonize well and the baby will grow to be of great health. When the mother's heart is poor, her Qi and blood are in chaos and the baby will suffer. It is important to remember that the mother's Qi being pure or turbid, or her heart being virtuous or poor, are all affected by the seasons and everything else with which she comes in contact.*

The Qi is controlled by the heart. The heart's spirit rules the interior of the body and it reacts to the exterior. Whenever the body comes in contact with the exterior, the spirit moves and the Qi follows. When the mother comes in contact with 'Virtuous,' the Yang energy moves and the Qi becomes pure. When she comes in contact with 'Poor,' the Yin energy moves and the Qi becomes turbid. Because of that, the pregnant woman must be cautious of what she comes in contact with. As soon as the baby is conceived, it digests myriad things. These myriad things are all what the mother ingests and digests. In ancient times, the pregnant woman will not lay or sit in an awkward place, she will not ingest any evil flavors, she will not eat anything which is not by nature. Oh! Pregnant woman, know that you can teach your fetus to become like a king or to become a beautiful nobleman.

It is for every woman to consider what she injects into her blood stream in terms of how it will impact her baby. As Confucius said: *Only doing it before is wisdom, while doing it after is foolish. The reason for that is before birth, the truth, even tiny, already manifests itself, and the affair seems small but it is actually grand. For the heart of the knowledgeable person knows the truth and so he makes changes in his life accordingly.* Making your child healthy after he is born cannot equal making your child healthy before he is born.

Susie and Stephen could not conceive. Deciding that drugs and IVF treatments were not for them, they grew convinced that the best approach was to become healthy first. They reached out to Yaron Seidman and the Hunyuan Method, and within 30 days conceived naturally.

9

CULTURE GIVES BIRTH
TO MEDICINE

A visitor called, clad in his best robes, and awaited the arrival of his host in the reception room. A rat, which had been disporting itself upon the beams above, insinuating its nose into a jar of oil which was put there for safe keeping, became frightened at the sudden intrusion of the caller. It ran away, and in so doing upset the oil jar, which fell directly on the caller, striking him a severe blow and ruining his elegant garments. Just as the face of the guest was purple with rage at this disaster, the host entered. When the proper salutations were performed, the guest proceeded to explain the situation: 'As I entered your honorable apartment and seated myself under your honorable beam, I inadvertently terrified your honorable rat, which fled and upset your honorable oil jar upon my mean and insignificant clothing, which is the reason for my contemptible appearance in your honorable presence'.

This is a story told by the Swedish sinologist and philologist Bernhard Karlgren (1889-1978) to describe a culture fundamentally different then ours in the West. It is a culture rooted with moral values dating back 4500 years where a guest must always esteem his host and humble himself, regardless of the circumstances.

The medicine sage Sun Simiao in the 7th century A.D. wrote in his book **Emergency Prescriptions Worth a Thousand Gold**: *To have Da Yi (great physician or great medicine), one must be versed with the ancient classics. Why is this so? Because if one does not know the five classics, he will never know virtue and compassion.* Known as 'The Confucius Classics' for the past 2500 years, they are: **Yi Jing** (Book of Changes), **Liji** (Book of Rites), **Shiji** (Book of Odes), **Shujing** (The Book), **Chunqiu** (Spring and Autumn Annals), compiled and edited by Confucius at the age of 43.

For us Westerners, to understand the intrinsic value of Chinese medicine, we need to understand the fertile soil out of which it grows. As with the story we just read, why would an angry man call his host repeatedly 'honorable' even when he is furious? The "Confucius classics," dealing with such questions, were edited and compiled in the Sixth Century B.C., however the information written in them dates back as far as the Xia and Shang dynasties (24th century B.C.-12th century B.C.).

Chinese culture was rich in social morals and behaviors back as far as 4000 years ago. The Chinese written language developed as a language of symbols, first as ancient script on oracle bones as part of imperial divination, and later on as a sophisticated system of symbols used by the common people. In this chapter, I will introduce the Confucian classics so we can get a better feel for the medicine and its motives.

Book of Rites – Conveyance of Rites: *What a person most desires is food, drink and sex. What a person most fears is death and hardship.*

For us to truly understand the greatness of Chinese medicine, we need to discuss the Confucius classics. They explain the culture and societal values in the 2000 years preceding **The Yellow Emperor** classics of medicine, from 2400 B.C. to 400 B.C. During this time, the harmony between heaven and man was absolute. The codes by which people lived their lives were indeed inspirational. Even to this day, Chinese people and many Westerners spend an extraordinary amount of time learning the Confucius classics in order to better themselves and their harmony with nature, i.e. their health. I have placed this chapter at the end of the book because it signifies closing a circle. After reading and digesting this chapter, you should reread the book. You will no doubt pick-up more the second time around.

Confucius was born in 551 B.C. in the small town of Zou in the state of Lu (today Shandong Province). Becoming one of China's most celebrated philosophers, he believed that a comprehensive education makes a complete man, and he emphasized the study of morals and virtue in addition to literature. He advocated justice, filial piety, courtesy, benevolence, righteousness, loyalty and trustworthiness. He sought a just treatment of the people from the government and rulers and every so often elaborated on the examples of Emperors Yao (2300 B.C.) and Shun (2200 B.C.), who were known to be benevolent rulers of the "golden" ancient times. While he died in 479 B.C., the six classics he compiled (the five mentioned before plus the book of music) have lived ever since in the hearts and minds of endless generations.

Emperor Kang Xi, who ruled China from 1736 to 1795 A.D., named Confucius "The Grand Master of All Ages." The philosopher Zhu Xi (1130-1200 A.D.) rearranged the Confucian classics and created what is known today as the "four books and five classics". The four books are: **The Great Learning, Doctrine of the Mean, Analects** and **The Book of Mencius.** The first two were originally part of the book of rites, and the Analects are a record of speeches by Confucius and his disciples. Mencius (372B.C.-289B.C.) was a philosopher who lived after Confucius and followed his way.

THE NOBLEMAN

The Great Learning: *The path of the great learning is by understanding the obvious virtue. It is by a good demeanor. First you know demeanor and then you become stable. Stable and then you become quiet. Quiet and then you become peaceful. Peaceful and then you can think. Think and then you can attain."*

In the Chinese traditional education system over the past 2000 years, there were two kinds of learning; "small learning" and "great learning." The small learning was the way children learned. They memorized classical texts without really understanding the essence. When a child grew into adulthood, he moved onto the "great learning," where the goal was to understand the essence in these same texts.

In this quote, it is explained that the way to enter this realm of "great learning," is to first behave in an appropriate manner, allowing for a stable and mature character. Once mature, an individual can begin the path of self contemplation and meditation. Self contemplation then allows for peace in his heart, and once there is peace, then it is possible to truly think about life and its meaning. Once practiced in this kind of thinking, then it is finally possible to head down the path of the great learning, which is understanding the obvious virtue (**Ming Ming De**).

When we learn literature today, the information is always outside of our body. We read it, we think about it, but it never becomes part of us. Confucius explains that the "great learning" is different than the "small learning." In the small learning, we memorize texts or 'it', but in the great learning, 'it' is not coming from the outside but rather from the inside. In order to do so, we take the steps listed above of controlling our behavior, becoming stable, etc. We must follow this procedure or we will not get there.

Our "everyday" thoughts are concerned with the desire for food, drink and sex, and the fear of hardship and death. When our heart is truly at peace, our thoughts are more profound. This is very fundamental for the understanding of Chinese culture and medicine. Only when the heart is in a state of true peace can one accept the circumstances of life. Only then will the true meaning of life be revealed, and only then can one enter "the great learning."

We live in a very impatient world and we expect instant results. The pace of life is fast, information from the Internet comes fast, modern medicine acts fast, we fly from place to place fast, and we call each other between continents fast. This can give us the false impression that we accomplish a lot very quickly. But in reality, do we? How is it that in ancient times, a 20 year-old could be ready to enter into the "great learning" and today even 50 year-olds are not yet ready? I believe it is because the demeanor or our society as a whole has deteriorated to a point where stability and contemplation become impossible. How is it possible to be stable and contemplative when life runs at hundreds of miles an hour? How can the heart become peaceful?

The good news is that it is never too late to start and age does not matter. Again, the first step is to have an appropriate demeanor. Confucius describes a well demeanored person as a nobleman (Jun Zi) . As a sage of Chinese culture who leads endless generations into cultural prosperity because of his teachings, we can only aspire to learn from his example. His thoughts about what it takes to be a nobleman are the tool we need to take the first step toward defining our demeanor.

ANALECTS - CHAPTER 1: *To practice again and again what you have learned, isn't it pleasure? To have study friends come from afar, isn't it happiness? To be not appreciated by others and still feel fulfilled, isn't it a nobleman?*

A nobleman enjoys practicing appropriate behavior and demeanor again and again. This allows him to fulfill his first step toward virtue. Next, the nobleman is always happy to have friends come from afar to study appropriateness and demeanor with him. Lastly, the nobleman does not learn and practice his demeanor for the sake of appreciation by others. He practices good demeanor to attain virtue (Ming Ming De). When we want to learn the nobleman's way, this motivation is crucial.

ANALECTS - CHAPTER 15: *Confucius said: making a mistake and not correcting it, this is called a real mistake.* If our life is very fast paced thus far, and we couldn't find time for the right demeanor, cultivation, thoughts and virtue, it is not too late. We can always correct it and thus it was never a real mistake. Only if we stay with the wrong demeanor and never bother to correct it, can we call it a real mistake. This oftentimes happens in our old years, when we reflect back and correct our demeanor. But this does not have to happen at the end of our life but rather, as was in ancient times, when we enter "the great learning."

ANALECTS - CHAPTER 16: *Confucius said: 'The nobleman respects three things; heaven's destiny, great men and the words of the sage. The petty man doesn't know about heaven's destiny so he can't respect it. He thus looks down at great men and makes a mockery from the sage's words.'*

If we want to learn something from anyone, we have only two options; either to learn from a great man or from a petty man. A great man (or woman) is someone who first and foremost understands life (heaven's destiny). How did this great man understand life? He followed the words of the sage.

The petty man makes fun of the sages and their words. This is because he does not understand life and he cannot even realize how much he does not understand. Unfortunately in our modern society many mock our traditional cultures and sages, because we are educated to think that new is better then the old.

THE GREAT LEARNING: *When the sages wanted to understand the virtue under heaven (Ming Ming De) they first ruled the country well. When they wished to rule the country well, they first organized their family well. When they wished to organize their family well, they first cultivated their own self. When they wished to cultivate their own self they first corrected their heart. When they wished to correct their hearts, they first allowed their intentions to become honest. When they wished their intention to become honest they first attained knowledge. They attained knowledge from studying the phenomena of nature around them. You study nature around you and then you attain knowledge. You attain this knowledge and then you can become honest. When honest you can correct your heart. When your heart is upright you can cultivate your self. When you cultivate your self, you can organize your family well. When you organize your family well, only then can the country be ruled well. When the country is ruled well, only then is there peace under heaven.*

The text continues: *The cultivation of oneself is the root for everyone from the son of heaven (emperor) to the common people. If this root is in chaos, the whole society is in confusion.* According to the sage's words, it all starts and ends with me. It is not that I should want the president to be better or the government to do a better job. It is not that I should want the schools and the teachers to be better, the doctors to understand life or my neighbor to behave nicer. It is all about me and my own "self." When I can cultivate myself then I can organize my family. When my family is organized, then my town, state, county, and country are influenced. When all of the above are impacted then there can be peace under heaven. Some people might immediately say: *What does it matter what I do? There will always be other petty men who don't do as I, so the country can never be ruled well and there is never peace anyhow.* However, Confucius says that fear and desire are not the way of the nobleman. The nobleman thinks about heaven's destiny, life, and the words of the sage. He does not look for other people and he does not look for their appreciation. Thus...

ANALECTS – CHAPTER 4: *Confucius said: 'When you see a virtuous man, think how to match him, but when you meet a not virtuous man, then just examine yourself.'* In our demeanor, it is important to follow great men and not petty men. If we follow petty men then we become petty ourselves. Instead, when we come upon petty men, we should examine ourselves. When we know of great men, we follow in their footsteps.

ANALECTS – CHAPTER 15: *Confucius said: 'The nobleman always examines himself, while the petty man always blames others.'*

To accomplish our first step in improving our demeanor, we go through self-examination. We must be critical of our own behavior even when it seems that the "other" person is to blame. If we blame others we can never become better, and if we criticize the "other" person, he or she will not change either.

It is said in **BOOK OF RITES – CONVEYANCE OF RITES:** *Since it is so, when the nobleman makes his actions clear, it is not clear to the ordinary people. When he nurtures, he doesn't nurture the ordinary people. When he handles affairs, he doesn't handle the affairs of the ordinary people. If his actions are clear to the people, then there is always a mistake in his doings. If he nurtures the people, his nurturing is always not enough, and if he handles the people's affairs, he always loses his noble position.*

This quote, as previously explained, emphasizes that the nobleman's actions are for himself and not for the people. Nevertheless, he is selfless, not selfish. His motives stem from understanding the obvious virtue of heaven (**Ming Ming De**) and not from fear and desire. Thus in his actions he does not fear what other people say and he does not strive for fame and power. However, since he has attained virtue he must speak.

ANALECTS – CHAPTER 14: *Confucius said: 'When a man has virtue he must have words to tell others, but when one has words to speak, he doesn't necessarily have virtue. When a man is benevolent, he must have courage, but when one has courage he is not necessarily benevolent.* Humans have the natural ability to speak and be courageous, however virtue (act with justice) and benevolence (helping others) are the two heaven qualities which differentiate humans from animals.

BOOK OF RITES – RULES OF PROPRIETY: *People today possess no rites (etiquette and manners), even though they can speak words, but in their hearts are they really different from animals? Only animals have no rites. Because of this, the sages created the rites to teach men. When men have rites they have the knowledge to differentiate themselves from the animals.*

Animals, plants and humans were all created by nature. However, for good or bad, humans were created differently from animals. Humans can possess virtue and benevolence, enabling them to "save the world," but they also possess fear and desires, causing them to "destroy the world." Animals and plants simply live in the world. This is why humans can become noblemen or petty men. The difference between the two lies in the acceptance of "the great learning" or the rejection thereof.

So how does the nobleman behave and self-examine? **BOOK OF MENCIUS – CHAPTER 8:** *Mencius said: 'The nobleman is different from the common people by storing things close to his heart. The nobleman takes benevolence and keeps it dear to his heart. He takes the rites and keeps them* *dear to his heart. Being benevolent means to love people and possessing rites means to respect others. When he loves people, people forever love him and when he respects people, people forever respect him. Even with such noble behavior, some petty people will still go against him. He will then self-reflect: "I am not sufficiently benevolent and my rites are not enough." After self-reflection he'll become more benevolent and have better rites. Petty men will still go against him. The nobleman will self-reflect, thinking "I am not loyal enough," and he will become more loyal. Because it is so, the nobleman to his last day will be worried about doing wrong. In his worries, he will think: Emperor Shun (a well-known nobleman) was a man. Me, I'm a man too. Shun established the nobleman rules under heaven so they can be handed down to later generations. Me myself, I am devoted to my fellow villagers, so I am worried. How worried am I? Like emperor Shun. If a true nobleman has a day of no worries, then he dies. He cannot do deeds without benevolence and he cannot act without rites. If there would be one morning when everyone is at ease, the nobleman still cannot be at ease.'*

As we see, the nobleman is full of expectations and demands from himself. He wants to be the best, but not the best compared to other people, rather the best advocate of heaven's virtue (Ming Ming De). He wants to fulfill heaven's virtue as it is dear to his heart. Born as a human being, his choice is between petty fear and desire, and noble benevolence and justice. With the first, he will help destroy the world, and with the latter, he will help to save it.

As practitioners, we examine ourselves so as not to harm the environment, kill animals for no reason, abuse power or harm patients. I myself am far from noble, but I aspire to walk this path.

ANALECTS - CHAPTER 5: *Confucius asked his disciple Zi Gong: Who is better, you or disciple Hui? Zi Gong answered: how can I compare to Hui. Hui hears one sentence and he can understand ten things out of it. I hear one sentence and merely can understand two things. Confucius said: you can't match him, but in reality I can't match him either.*

The way of the nobleman is simply wanting to become better. It doesn't mean that we are better than others, but rather that we want only to better ourselves. We are not competing as to who is a better nobleman and there is a prize attached to it, but rather there is no prize, only hard work. To be a healer, doctor, or acupuncturist one must be a nobleman. This is why Sun Simiao, quoted in the beginning of this chapter, claims that to be a great doctor one must know well the Confucian Classics. One must become a nobleman wanting to help others and not necessarily wanting self gain.

ANALECTS - CHAPTER 13: Confucius said: *One should not desire speed and should not seek small gains. When he looks for speed he never arrives at his destination, and if he seeks small gains, big affairs can never be accomplished.*" If the doctor does not take time to self-examine, better himself, and become a nobleman, he can never attain heaven's virtue (Ming Ming De) and if he looks for small gains, meaning the fees received from the patient, he will never accomplish the true call of medicine, which is also heaven's virtue (Ming Ming De). The years invested in education by acupuncturists or medical doctors belong to the "small learning" and not the "great learning." The "small learning" is the process of learning information outside of your heart or "it." The "great learning" is the process of self cultivation and bettering one's heart.

Understanding the obvious virtue (Ming Ming De) leads us to another Confucian classic,

ZHONG   YONG

Zhong Yong, which I previously referred to as "Doctrine of the Mean," the common translation which in reality doesn't do it justice. To understand the meaning of Zhong Yong, we need to explore some of its contents. Zhong Yong states: *When the gamut of human emotions – happiness, anger, sadness and pleasure has not discharged yet, this is called Zhong (center). When the emotions have discharged and they are proper and just (Zhong Jie), this is called harmonious. 'Center' is the root for every thing under heaven. 'Harmonious' means to attain the Dao under heaven. Reaching 'harmonious center' and then heaven and earth can assume their proper position. Only then are the myriad things born.*

ZHONG

Zhong (center) is the place where human emotions emerge. Before they emerge they are even, so they cannot be seen. We can see that the word Zhong (center) is used in two different ways. It is the place where emotions have not yet discharged, and it is also the place we're at after the emotions have been released in a harmonious fashion (Zhong Jie). And as we learned in an earlier chapter, the character Zhong shows a human mouth and a vertical line going through the human which connects to heaven above and earth below.

So when we think of human emotions, we realize the link between man, heaven and earth. Our emotions, released or not released, come from our connection to heaven. We do not feel emotions because of chemical and electrical stimulation of brain cells and nerve endings. The reason that we have these emotions from heaven is that it enables us to make the choice between the nobleman and the petty man, between saving the world and destroying the world. The ability to make this choice is called the Dao of man. So the text says: *When the emotions have*

ZHONG JIE

discharged and they are proper and just (Zhong Jie), this is called harmonious. 'Center' is the root for everything under heaven. 'Harmonious' means to attain the Dao under heaven. We need to have emotions in order to attain the Dao of man, but these emotions need to be harmonious. They are harmonious when they are proper and just or Zhong Jie. When we become excessively sad or angry, or even over joyous at the wrong time for the wrong reasons, then the emotions are not proper and we cannot attain the Dao of man. We cannot walk the path of the nobleman. Then we are left with the path of the petty man.

YONG

The word Yong in the title Zhong Yong means "the common place." It is the normal place where Zhong (center) should find itself. Zhong Yong thus means our emotional connection with heaven and its normal place in our lives. When we talk about Ming Ming De, or understanding the obvious virtue of heaven, it does connect directly to Zhong Yong. Ming Ming De means the ability of the nobleman to make the right choices we explained earlier (self-examination, cultivation, think of others and not self etc). The nobleman has this ability to call right from wrong because his emotions, when discharged, are proper (Zhong Jie) and when still, are centered (Zhong). So it is said in **The Great Learning**: *The path to enter the great learning finds itself in Ming Ming De (understanding the obvious virtue).*

So what do we mean by "understanding obvious virtue?" The three components – "understanding," "obvious" and "virtue" – refer to the abilities of the nobleman. He can truly understand life, things are obvious to him, and he can attain the heavenly virtue. So for example, when Christian missionaries arrived in China several hundred years ago, they knew the Chinese called it "Zhong Guo," or the country of the center. The English translation then

ZHONG

became the "middle kingdom." Zhong, as we know, means "center," but the meaning of center in Chinese culture far outreaches what we call center in the West. For us, center means the midpoint between A and B. In Chinese, Zhong means a man standing between heaven and earth with a line going through him which connects him to both sides. Life comes down from heaven, breathing life into man at the pivot point. He is not the center of the universe, and because of this, he must obey the heavenly rules we call Dao.

The centerline Zhong is also the connection of heaven's lifeline and our emotions, i.e our ability to choose between right and wrong. When Zhong is in harmony, we can attain the heaven's way or Dao we call nobleman's way. When it is in chaos, we become petty men (angry men are petty men, while even-hearted men are gentlemen).

In the West, the concept is different. The man is in the center of the universe. That is why when Westerners hear the name Zhong Guo, they called it the "middle kingdom" instead of what it really means, "the kingdom which obeys heaven." Obeying heaven means that a man doesn't consider himself the epicenter, he is rather receiving life from heaven. In return, he must obey heaven's virtue. He is thankful and feels he is in debt to pay it back by making the right choices and becoming a nobleman. In our modern world, where the man is the center of the universe, we can see that nature around us is rapidly destroyed. This is because many choose the 'comfortable' way of the petty man (fears and desires).

In the Confucius classics and in the traditional culture of China, a man aspires to moving closer to the centerline because it is his lifeline. This centerline is called Dao.

ANALECTS – CHAPTER 15: *Confucius said: 'A man can accomplish the greatness of Dao, it is not the Dao that accomplishes the greatness of man.'* The Dao is central, not man. The man aspires to get close to the Dao and not vice verse. This is called understanding the obvious virtue of heaven (Ming Ming De).

FOLLOWING HEAVEN'S VIRTUE (MING MING DE)

Before going on to explain the meaning of Ming Ming De we need to become familiar with a piece of Chinese history, which can be broadly divided into two periods. "Antiquity" spans from 2500 BC to 230 BC while the "Modern" period stretches from 202 BC until today. The reason I divide history in this way has to do with Ming Ming De. While in Antiquity, China was divided into small states. From 230-221 BC, a ruthless emperor, Qin Shi Huang (259 BC-210 BC), unified the whole of China to form one big country. He accomplished this task by killing many citizens.

Qin Shi's goal was to break off the ancient ways and to found a new civilization. He thus ordered the burning of the Confucius classics, as well as other classics. He systematically ordered changing the ancient script into what is known today as "The Small Seal Script." Much of the symbolism embedded in the ancient script was gradually changed into a practical way of writing.

In Antiquity, the rules of heaven were clear to all, from the emperor down to the poorest farmer. The emperor received his mandate from heaven and thus was obligated to nurture and take care of his people. He would simply follow the advice of the court historians as to the arrival of the seasons, and he would issue his orders in accordance with heaven. As Heaven's way is benevolence and virtue, so too was the Emperor's.

Qin Shi Huang was determined to break off from the rule of heaven and antiquity, and establish his kingdom with ruthless force. His reign of Qin was very short lived and was followed by the Han Dynasty, when a renaissance of scholarship emerged. Many were battling to explain how it could have happened that such a ruthless dictator received the mandate of heaven, even if it was for just a few years. How could a ruler kill so many of his own subjects and order to burn down all traditions? This gave birth to the "modern" era.

Where in Antiquity the harmony with heaven was well established and clear to all, post Qin Shi Huang scholars were occupied with reestablishing the rules of harmony with heaven. These needed to be relearned and re-taught in order to prevent a recurrence of disharmony. In Antiquity, writing and script were reserved for the imperial court as no one else needed it. One followed the emperor and heaven's rules and life was accomplished. People were connected to heaven naturally and without effort. In modern times, the break from heaven had already occurred with Qin Shi Huang and now the task was to aspire back to the perfect harmony of antiquity. This required more and more scholars to emerge and propagate their teaching in order to help the people reach the harmony of ancient times. This era of the Han dynasty became known as the era of the "hundred scholars" (Zhu Zi Bai Jia), and it gave birth to the following 2000 years of accumulated knowledge, including the vast knowledge of medicine. **The Yellow Emperor, Shang Hanlun**, and all other famous medical works stem from the Han era and the "hundred scholars" desire to return to antiquity. Confucius and Lao Tzi, 500-600 BC, belong to antiquity, thus later scholars of the "modern era" looked back and cherished their writings and teachings.

In the Han Dynasty era, 202 BC-220 AD, where **The Yellow Emperor** classics and Shang Hanlun crystallized, the connection to antiquity was very close in time and in space. Other scholars of the Han were all immersed in antiquity as it was such a short time since the burning of the books by Qin Shi Huang. Scholars such as Dong Zhongshu (179-104 BC) and Wang Bi (226-249 AD) set the stage for the Han dynasty and future dynasties to aspire back to antiquity. While in the previous section we mainly explained the antiquity of Confucius, in the following

MING MING DE

two sections I will introduce few ideas from these 2000 years ago "modern" masters and how they taught the people of their time return to antiquity and harmony'. Ming Ming De is the way to enter the great learning. As explained, the great learning is the learning of life itself; the significance

MING

DE

of life, where we are coming from and where we are going to in this world. In order to gain access to this kind of learning, we need Ming Ming De. Ming contains two parts, the left representing the sun and the right the moon. Together, they are the two brightest elements in the day and night skies. The entire meaning of the word is "clear". De means "virtue", the left part means "footsteps" and the right side means "heart connected straight to heaven." Together, the meaning is "the action of the heart following the actions of heaven." Ming Ming De literally means "clear, clear virtue". So why does the word "clear" repeat itself? To truly understand this, we need to understand the harmony of antiquity. We need to understand our job here as humans on this earth, where we are coming from, and where we are going. When we understand it, and then think about medicine and fertility, this will bring us a step closer yet again to solving it.

The Yellow Emperor said that if we know nature and harmonize with it well, disease will not arise. There will be no need for medicine as there will be no disease, infertility included. Harmonizing with nature and with heaven does not only mean the four seasons and hot and cold temperatures, but rather harmonizing with the Dao of heaven. **The Yellow Emperor** starts off by saying: *The men of antiquity knew the Dao, they followed Yin and Yang.* The Dao of heaven, as Confucius explained in antiquity, is benevolence and virtue. There is one time every day and one time every year where this benevolence and virtue of heaven becomes visible to all. If you blink and miss this particular time, then you can't see it. You might think that heaven is even-hearted; not good nor bad. In reality you need to catch this spectacular moment of heaven's virtue and benevolence. The time is early in the morning when the sun comes out and a new day is born. It is also the time when spring arrives and new life is born. Heaven's eternal benevolence and virtue is by giving life morning after morning and year after year. The heaven's deeds are so pure that there is not even a slim chance that the sun will be selfish or lazy and not rise the next day.

Dong Zhongshu writes in **Luxuriant Dew of spring and Autumn – chapter 33**: *Heaven and earth are the origin of the myriad things. They are the springing platform of our ancestry. Vast without limits, their virtue shining clear.* Heaven and earth is what we have to thank for our life. Everything in this world, as well as our fathers, grandfathers and ancient ancestry, come from heaven and earth. In chapter 56, he goes on to explain: *Heaven and earth gives birth to everything, yet there is nothing more precious then man. Man receives his life from heaven like all others, yet others can't perform benevolence and virtue, only man can.*

In chapter 29, Zhongshu explains these two abilities of man: *The way to benevolence is to love other people and not to love oneself. The way to virtue is to correct oneself and not others. Not correcting myself, and even if I can, correcting others, is not the way of virtue. Loving myself, and even if I can, love others is not the way of benevolence.* Man can act like heaven, while animals, stones and trees can't. This is why man is in a special place under heaven, with special privileges and obligations.

A man is like a candle. A candle has three parts; a body made out of wax, a wick, and a flame. Each one of the three has one or more functions. Even though different, they are all needed. Without the body's wax, the flame can't exist and without the wick the flame can't attach to the body. Man is like a candle. He has his body and he has fire that makes the body alive. Without this fire, it is a dead corpse. Our body is the tissues, muscles, bones and organs. Our fire is the energy that makes every tissue alive. However, to understand how our fire works, we need to look back and analyze the candle fire.

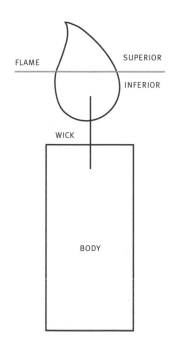

Even though the candle has one flame, we can divide the flame into two parts; an inferior fire and a superior fire. The inferior fire has two main functions; connection to the wick, thus being connected to the body, and burning the body's wax to sustain life. The more the candle lives, the more its body is consumed. The inferior fire burns the body until the body is no more, at which time the inferior fire can't exist anymore and ultimately will lead to the end of the superior fire. The superior fire, on the other hand, has two separate functions that give the candle a whole other meaning for its existence. The superior fire radiates heat and light outward and upward. Of course, the two fires are, in essence, one. The one cannot do without the other. Yet their function is different. The inferior fire burns the wax and elevates energy upward into the superior fire. The superior fire takes this energy and reflects it outward. The inferior fire's entire existence and purpose is to support and feed the superior fire. However, the superior fire's entire existence is to light outward to the benefit of others. The inferior benefits itself, while the superior benefits others.

Man has two fires, as we learned before, emperor fire and minister fire. In our body, the minister fire burns the wax, or it makes our body alive. It is the Yang energy allowing our daily life. The emperor function is to shed light and clarity over the entire kingdom. His fire is not for himself, but rather for helping others. His actions are benevolent.

Every man, as Dong Zhongshu explains, possesses this virtue of heaven. Every man has the emperor fire. Each and every one of us has an inferior fire and a superior fire – one fire to fuel our life and one fire to fuel others. The minister fire is the Shao Yang fire. The Shao Yang is the fire activity helping the three Yang spheres. The emperor fire is the Shao Yin fire, helping the three Yin, and as we learned before, is the fire that the father and mother hand down to the baby. The superior fire is what a "complete" parent hands down to the next generation.

BOOK OF RITES – SACRIFICIAL VIRTUE: *From all the greatness that heaven creates and the earth nurtures, there is no greater creation than man. The mother and father are complete and they give birth to it. The son is complete and it cares back to it. This is called filial piety. They don't harm their body and they don't shame themselves. This is called 'complete.'*

To become fertile, one must strive to be "complete." This has two aspects: not harming one's body and not shaming one's self. The first means that the inferior fire needs to be appropriate, not consuming the body too fast and not vanishing. In other words, our Yang energy and our lifestyle must harmonize with nature. On the other hand, the superior fire needs to be pronounced. This is called not shaming oneself and having filial piety. Both self shame and filial piety are toward heaven and not toward other people. Meaning, we have to follow the superior fire of heaven (benevolence and virtue) regardless of what other people think or tell us. Benevolence, or the obligation to help other people is not because we want recognition from them or returned favors, it is rather because we are in tune with heaven. To have inferior and superior fire is referred to as "to be complete." A man and a woman who want to have a baby need to be complete. A man (doctor) who wishes to heal other people needs to be complete. A man (patient) who hopes to heal needs to be complete. Superior and inferior fires must both be present in order for healing and recovery to take place.

Today is different from antiquity. The patient pays money and expects a cure, the doctor receives money and wants to heal. This is inferior fire. It should be there, otherwise the doctor cannot sustain his body (food to eat etc.). However with no light to radiate outward, how can the patient see the way? At the same time, if the patient has no light (superior fire) to radiate outward, how can the baby see the way?

We have explained it before as the Shao Yin original Yang that needs to go to the embryo. This fire above and superior to the body is connected to heaven, thus Dong Zhongshu says that the man, his father and ancestors receive life from heaven. Without this fire it is like a candle without a light. If a candle has only inferior fire that consumes itself, but no superior light to radiate outward, can we say that this candle has a use? Can we say that it is really alive? As Confucius said *A man without benevolence and virtue is like the animals.*

Dong Zhongshu, in chapter 35, goes farther: *The human body having life energy and emotions is like the heaven having Yin and Yang. If words describe the physical body without its noble emotions, these are like words describing the heaven as having Yang with no Yin. One must know that for superior and inferior, the crucial part is its center.* If we look again at the candle, its center is the wick. In the previous section I have explained Zhong Yong, or the center, out of which the emotions come in and out. It is the center that connects us to heaven. The wick in the candle must be centered upright. If it is inclining to one side, the inferior fire will burn the wax faster, causing it to leak and finishing the life of the candle sooner. At the same time, the superior fire will decrease, projecting less light outward. Thus when Confucius spoke about benevolence, he compared it to archery, saying *archery is the way to benevolence. With archery, one must correct his body upright. Only when his body is upright does he discharge the arrow. If the arrow missed the target, one does not blame others for his failure. He then corrects his body again and that's it! The nobleman does not compete, unless it is archery. When called, he bows and steps up to the stage. Discharging his arrow, he steps down to have a gentleman's drink. His competition is of a nobleman.* The way for us to become complete is to continually correct our "uprightness." We don't look to blame others, but rather look into our own actions in order to better ourselves.

Book of Rites – Black Garments: *If the heart cherishes it, the body dwells in it…. The heart completes the body but it can also harm the body.* The heart aspires to stay in the center, for if it deviates from heaven and from the center, it will be harmed. In today's world, we only do or not do what is allowed, or not allowed, by law. If last year it was allowed to talk on a cell phone while driving, then we would do so. If this year it is against the law, then we do not. This is different from following the Dao of heaven, which does not change from year to year. Benevolence and virtue are human qualities from the beginning of time. We can deviate from them or we can follow them. If we follow them, we can become complete. This will strengthen the superior fire and the possibility of conception. If we only nurture our inferior fire, preoccupied with our needs and not helping others, this will lead to a rapid deterioration of our body as well as our fertility.

Ming Ming De means that the superior fire is clear to us and that the inferior fire is clear as well. Thus we have the repetition "clear, clear virtue." Virtue is represented by the center wick allowing our body to connect to heaven and be in tune with it and follow it as it was followed in antiquity. *The Dao of the great learning is clear, clear virtue* means just that.

Even though this is all quite philosophical, it is imperative to understand that philosophy and culture do give birth to medicine. Philosophy is the science of understanding life and nature, as Zhang Xichun (1860-1933) puts it. *The more one dwells into philosophy, the more one is able to comprehend how things work in nature. As a result, when things go wrong and disease arises, one can use understanding to solve it.*

Why are women often so "sick" during pregnancy? This has to do with superior and inferior fire. When a woman becomes pregnant, in the first trimester, she feels exhausted and nauseated and at times vomits from the mere thought of a certain food, or from seeing a food from across the room. In conception, the father and mother unite their superior fire and set aflame a new candle. But where is the fetus's candle wax and flame coming from? It comes from the mother, meaning that her candle has two flames to burn and she feels exhausted. The new embryo withdraws inferior fire from the mother until it has its own body and its own inferior fire.

When the mother's inferior fire is reduced, the superior fire is considerably reduced or at least disturbed. The superior fire is the pure Yang that comes out of our spirit in the eyes, ears, and head. When the superior Yang is not at ease, the pregnant woman can see a chicken leg or a tomato and perceive it as offensive. One can smell a fragrance and alarm the whole body.

The treatment is then not really to harmonize the stomach and drink ginger, which may be the cure if it was normal, non-pregnancy nausea. What needs to be done is to harmonize and strengthen the superior fire. If done through acupuncture, it will be Tong Li (heart 5) or Da Ling (pericardium 7), which can strengthen the heart fire. With herbs and diet, it will be hot and warming herbs and food. This is how philosophy developed medicine. In today's world, we view the world as purely physical and this is why modern medicine is all physical. If the society as a whole will change its view and philosophy to reflect our life and energy, then medicine will have to change with it and reflect that. Our job as patients is to start thinking about the philosophy of life, and then medicine will simply follow along. In my opinion, there is no Western medicine and Chinese medicine, mainstream and alternative. There is only good medicine and bad medicine. Be it Western or Chinese, good medicine follows the philosophy of life, bad medicine doesn't. This is why Chinese medicine needs to learn from Western medicine where life is saved. At the same time, Western medicine needs to learn from Chinese medicine where life is prolonged. Alongside each other they can benefit our entire society.

CULTURE OF SYMBOLS

Confucius said: *Listen carefully, search for the good in it and follow it. Watch carefully and know it.* In antiquity, man followed heaven, but in order to do so, he needed knowledge. In ancient times, knowledge was handed down via symbols. The book was called the Book of changes or **Book of Yi**. Initially the book was known as *Continuous Mountain Yi* (lian shan Yi) then *Returned to Storage Yi* (gui cang Yi), and finally it became the Zhou Yi or the Yi of the Zhou Dynasty (1100-256 BC). From early antiquity, the culture transmitted via symbols. These were the trigrams composed of Yin (broken) and Yang (solid) lines and it was also the entire writing system, which was composed of symbols.

In antiquity, the sage, knowing that his life came from the sun's energy, would face the sun (South) and attempt to put the experience into a picture or a symbol. The look of the symbol would depend on the season of the year and the time of day it was drawn. The sky was viewed as two halves, one half heaven and the other half earth. The days of the year were marked by placing a pole on the ground and measuring the length of the shadow emitted.

At night, the sage would turn to face north and watch the moon and the stars. The ancients divided the night skies into four sections/directions. Each direction had star constellations, totaling 28 star constellations in the sky.

The four directions of the night skies and the 365 degree motion of the day's sun gave birth to the understanding of "the heaven is round and the earth is square." The heaven Yang turns 365 degrees (days) during the year and the night skies (earth) have four directions. As Confucius said: *to understand life, we need to listen and observe carefully, then we can search for the good in it and follow it, only then can we know it.* "It" means to know how to live a long, healthy life.

The sages then watched nature carefully in order to know it. They watched the shadow of the pole grow and wane as the seasons changed. They put it in a symbol to transmit this knowledge, because only by observing deeply can one know it. When you observe nature diligently then you can know it, and when you observe a symbol representing nature then you can know it too.

Thus the ancients created trigrams made out of three Yin and Yang lines as symbols. Each symbol must be observed carefully to decipher the idea within. However, symbols at times are hard to understand, thus the sages attached words to them. **The Book of Changes** was thus formed. It has three levels; words trying to explain the symbol, the symbol itself and the idea hidden within the symbol. Wang Bi explained in his book **Brief Examples of the Zhou Yi**: *You use the words to reach to the symbol, but after the symbol reached, the words are discarded. You use the symbol to reach for the idea. When the idea is reached, you discard of the symbol. It is like a trap and a hare. When you catch the hare you forget about the trap. It is like the fish and net. When you catch the fish you forget about the net.*

The ancients used symbols to reach for the whys and whats of life. The famous physician Zhang Jingyue (1563-1640 AD) in his book **Additions to Lei Jing,** wrote: *Medicine equals the art of symbols. It contains the complexity of Yin Yang movement and stillness. Medicine equals the art of ideas. It joins with the Yin Yang mechanism of growth and decline. Even though **The Yellow Emperor** classic talks about Yin and Yang, there is nothing greater than the book of changes. It is said that heaven and earth unite into one principle of Yin and Yang. The Changes (Yi) and medicine share common origin, both dwell in the research of transformation. They are interchangeably dependent and their philosophies join as one. How can you become a doctor, then, and not know the Changes (Yi)?*

To know life means to know how to cure life when it is in disharmony. To not know life means to not know how to cure a disharmony when it arises. Zhang Jingyue explains that to become a doctor, one must understand how life works, and that the best path to this understanding is to study the **Book of Changes'** symbols and the ideas that come out of them. The trigrams contain three Yin or Yang lines, however to explain the many phenomena in nature, the ancients layered two trigrams on top of each other, creating 64 hexagrams. Each hexagram then contains six Yin or Yang lines and is composed of two trigrams. The mathematical formula used to express "ideas" was that Yin and Yang are in heaven, earth and man, thus representing Yin and Yang (2) has to be multiplied three times 2x2x2=8. This gave birth to eight trigrams they called **Ba Gua**. In addition, heaven, earth and man have the six spheres within them. The six spheres are Tai Yang, Shao Yang, Yang Ming, Tai Yin, Shao Yin and Jue Yin. Thus 2 has to be multiplied six times in order to describe all phenomena in nature 2x2x2x2x2x2=64. This

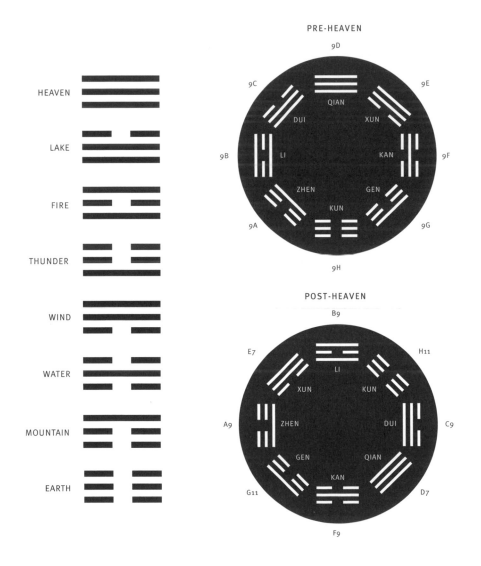

gave birth to the 64 hexagrams of **The Book of Changes**. Sixty-four, of course, also means that each one of the trigrams could have eight different trigrams on top of itself (including itself) and thus 8x8=64. Multiplying the trigrams or the six spheres gives the complete set of natural possibilities in nature: 64.

First, let's explore the idea of pre-heaven shifting into post-heaven. This explains the shift from before life into life. For us, trying to become pregnant represents the shift from before we conceive a new life to post conception. To grasp this idea, we must observe the symbols of the **Book of Changes**. In particular, we need to observe the pre-heaven trigram sequence and the post-heaven trigram sequence.

The first Ba Gua sequence represents the pre-heaven state of perfect harmony between Yin and Yang, but at the same time a state showing that Yin and Yang do not mix with each other. We can see that by using mathematics. A solid line is Yang, while a broken line is Yin. When we look at opposite trigrams, we see that they position in a perfect match. For example, if we compare A to E, the first line in A is Yang while the first in E is Yin. The second line in A is Yin while the second in E is Yang. The third line in A is Yin while the third in E is Yang. The opposing pairs B and F, C and G, D and H do match each other in the same way. This means that the lines crossing the eight directions (north-south, east-west, south-north, west-east, NE-SW, SE-NW, SW-NE, NW-SE) reflect trigrams that mirror each other. The trigram fire of the east, for example, is the exact opposite of the trigram water in the west. The trigram heaven in the south is the exact opposite of earth in the north.

Each Yang line represents the number 1, while each Yin line represents the number 2 because it is broken into two lines. In the pre-heaven Ba Gua, the sum of opposite trigram line count is nine for all pairs. So when we envision, by the use of numbers, the state of affairs in this sequence, we can see the idea that the pre-heaven Ba Gua, even though in "perfect harmony", is not moving. The sum of each direction is 9, shifting from one direction to the other always equals 9. This will equal an unthinkable scenario where the sun is always in the middle of the sky, morning, noon, afternoon and night. The sun will always hold steady in the middle of the sky and not set and rise. It means that when we progress in time the situation is always the same, or in other words, that there is no change. Of course, the sages using the number 9 is not coincidental. Nine represents the last number of possible changes 1,2,3,4,5, 6,7,8,9. It represents pure Yang energy, or energy not attached to a physical body.

When we add the line count in a trigram, the total number reflects a Yang trigram if the number is odd 3,5,7,9,11, and the trigram is Yin if the count is even 4,6,8,10,12. When we add the lines in each opposite pair of trigrams, we find out that in each pair one trigram is Yang and one trigram is Yin. For example, d has 3 lines and is Yang, while h has 6 lines and is Yin. This means that Yin and Yang oppose each other and are not mixed together. Another idea representing the separation of Yin and Yang in the pre-heaven Ba Gua is the sequence of the trigrams. Counting the line always from bottom upwards, we can see that the Yang increases on the left, while Yin increases on the right. Trigram A has 1 Yang, B and C have 2 Yang lines, D has 3 Yang lines. This puts Yang growth to the left. On the right, E has 1 Yin, F and G have 2 Yin lines, while H has 3 Yin lines. Again, it is like perfect harmony to the left and right, but the idea behind it is that Yang is to the left and Yin is to the right. They each hold their position but do not want to mix with each other. This is the perfect harmony before life.

In the pre-heaven Ba Gua harmony is very clear. The Yin has its place and the Yang has its place. Yin is Yin and Yang is Yang. They sit across from each other separated, so they are very easy to differentiate. However, this state of perfect harmony has no life, no movement and no change. It is as if we would say that to be in perfect harmony with nature, we must be dead or not have been born yet. Because before we are born and after we die there is no "change" anymore.

When we live, life is constantly changing. It is not possible that my south, SE, east, NE, north, NW, west, SW will all equal 9. The sun will not rise or set and the seasons will not change, I will not grow from childhood to adulthood to old age and die. The pre-heaven Ba Gua thus shows perfect harmony with no life. When we grasp this idea from the symbols and numbers, then we are half way through.

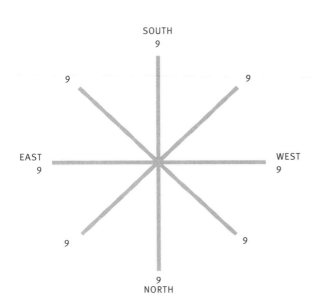

The post-heaven Ba Gua on the previous page represents the post-heaven state or the state of life after conception. It is the state where Yin and Yang are not separated, but rather mixed and entangled with each other. It represents a state of constant change. Looking at the post-heaven Ba Gua, we see no perfect match of opposite trigrams as we have seen with the pre-heaven Ba Gua. When we add the line count of opposite trigrams, we see an interesting story. Only the north-south and east-west add up to 9. Keeping in mind that the south is on top and north is at the bottom, the NE-SW line adds up to 11, while the SE-NW line adds up to 7.

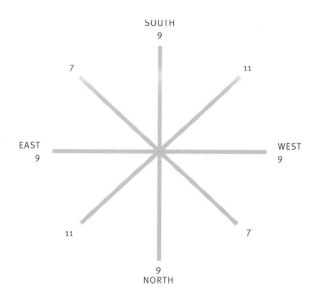

From our initial observation, we can see that the post heaven and pre heaven states represent different situations. As Wang Bi explained, we need to get to the idea in the pictures. The ancients used numbers and symbols to express a certain idea. They used a picture to convey an image. When our mind sees an image, we can have a good understanding of the idea. At the same time, the ancients used numbers to elaborate on the images. Numbers have a certain weight to them when we multiply, add or compare them. For example, let's say John bought three apples in the morning and four oranges in the evening, while Jay bought four oranges in the morning and three apples in the evening. Which one of the two has more apples and oranges? They are both the same. Even though John has 3+4, while Jay has 4+3, the weight of the numbers stays even though they are not exactly the same. In another example, Susan and her husband Joe take the bus to work every morning five days per week. Each one uses a bus ticket. Jody takes the bus to work and back home five days per week. Who uses more bus tickets per week? Susan and Joe use 10 (2x5), while Jody uses 10 (1x10) as well. We see that when we add and multiply the numbers, we can compare the weight of the numbers to find out if it is equal or not. The same is with the Ba Gua. When we add or multiply the number of trigram lines on each opposing trigram, we can find the weight of the numbers and the weight that the trigram expressed.

In the post-heaven Ba Gua we see that the weight of the four main directions – south, north, east, west – equal 9. This is the same 9 we had in all directions in the pre-heaven Ba Gua. This means that the main axis of Yin and Yang in the post-heaven scenario is firmly fixed. This is called Jing-Wei and is explained in chapter 2. We have also called it Ming and Xing. The original Yang, coming to us from our parents and represented by the north-south Jing axis, is called Ming. It is also the Yang energy in the three Yin spheres. On the other hand, the Yang energy used in daily life by the three Yang spheres is represented by the east-west Wei axis and is called Xing. Jing-Wei and Xing-Ming are all fixed parameters in the post heaven state. However, when we look at the oblique lines NE-SW 11 and SE-NW 7, we can see that the weight is different. The weight on the Yin-Yang scale is changing. So what is the idea behind it?

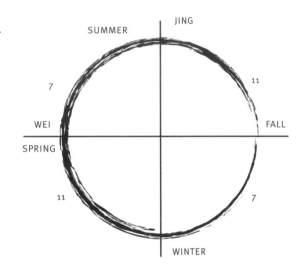

In the post-heaven scenario, where the Yin is changing into Yang and the Yang is changing into Yin, we need a weight different from 9. Let's take the four seasons cycle as an example; if each season equals 9 and the transitions between the seasons equal 9 as well, then how can we have a change? It remains static. Instead, in the post heaven world, which is our life as we know it, when the winter Yin (represented by 9) changes into the spring Yang (also represented by 9), the weight between the two is 11. However, when the spring Yang 9 changes into the summer Yang 9, the weight needed is 7. So when the Yin changes into Yang, the weight is 11, and when the small Yang changes into big Yang, the weight is only 7.

The same goes in reverse. When the Yang summer changes into the Yin fall, the weight in between is 11, but when the small Yin of fall changes into the big Yin of winter, the weight is only 7. In the four seasons chart of ancient times, the north belongs to the water element, south to fire, east to wood and west to metal. The four seasons fall under these elements as well. Summer is fire, winter is water, spring is wood and fall is metal. At the same time, earth is in the center of the seasons, meaning the whole sky is turning around the earth to create the four seasons.

In outer space, for example, there are no four seasons. The earth being in the center allows the four seasons to take place. This means that in order for one season to transform into the next season, we need earth in between.

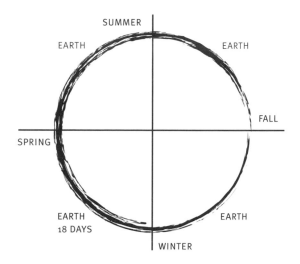

In a complete circle, we have 360 degrees, or for our purposes, let's say 360 days in one year. Each season occupies three months or 90 days. The sages, however, explained that the last 18 days of each season belong to the transformation of earth. Because of these 18 days, the season can shift from spring to summer to fall and winter. The number 18 has several meanings and a certain weight representing the earth and representing the place where Yin and Yang transform. When we divide the year of 360 days into the 5 elements, each equals 72 days. When we divide one season (90 days) into the 5 elements, each equals 18 days. This means that each of the five elements exercises its influence on the four seasons in 72 days. In winter, water has 72 days; in spring, wood has 72 days; in summer fire has 72 days; and in fall, metal has 72 days. Only earth has its 72 days divided equally among the four seasons. Each season receives its last 18 days from earth. Altogether, four seasons x18 days=72 days. The weight of the earth element equals the weight of each other element, but it is spread between the seasons or in the center of the seasons. Each transformation is controlled and influenced by the earth, and that is why there are no seasons in outer space, only here on earth. Going back to the post heaven Ba Gua, we can see that during the transformation period of the seasons, the weight of the added numbers are 11,7,11,7. The earth exercises a different weight on the winter changing into spring, then the weight it exercises on the spring changing into summer. The first is 11 and the latter is 7. 11=9+2, thus changing winter storage into spring's birth. The earth uses the fixed 9 and adds 2 to it. Yet, during the last 18 days of spring, the earth deducts 2 from 9 and adds only 7 to it (9-2=7). Between these two changes of a complete winter Yin storage to a complete summer Yang expansion, the weight exercised by the earth is 18 (7+11=18). The number 18 in ancient Hebrew means Chai or life, in ancient Chinese it means transformation. Yin and Yang are transforming, thus creating life.

This idea of transformation and life of the number 18 is presented in the growing and declining hexagrams (Xiao Xi Gua). Wang Bi in his book **Brief Examples of the Zhou Yi** wrote: *Each Hexagram is a description of a time period. Each line of the hexagram represents a transformation within this time period.* Life is a stretch of time, and within this stretch we have time periods in constant change. The big changes in our life are birth, childhood, adulthood, old age and death.

The small changes are every day changes – waking up, going to work and becoming active, relaxing in the evening and going to sleep at night. These changes happen every day to everyone. There is not one thing in nature that doesn't go through change. To understand this better, let's observe the 12 growing and declining hexagrams below.

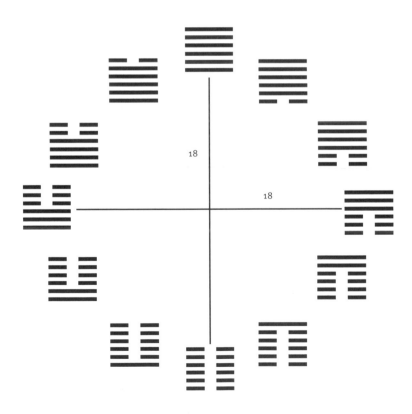

Each hexagram is composed of two trigrams totaling six lines. In the bottom, it is pure Yin or six broken lines representing the earth hexagram and at the top it shows pure Yang or six solid lines representing the heaven hexagram. Then, starting from the earth and counting from the bottom up, the first Yang line is born. The next hexagram has two Yang lines at the bottom, the third hexagram has three Yang lines etc… until reaching six Yang lines (pure Yang). Following the pure Yang hexagram of heaven, the Yin is born. The first hexagram has one Yin broken line, the second has two Yin lines, the third has three Yin lines, etc. until reaching the earth hexagram of six Yin broken lines. This ancient picture of growing and declining hexagrams demonstrates the gradual transformation of Yin into Yang and Yang into Yin.

Each one of these hexagrams has a meaning and is worthy of further exploration. However, at this point, let's only look at the addition of opposing hexagrams. In any direction, adding the Yin and Yang lines of opposing hexagrams, yields the weight of 18. This shows that the weight of changing the dial between Yin and Yang is 18. Eighteen representing change is the only number that contains two 9's. 9+9=18 and also adding left and right, 1+8=9.

Going back to the pre and post heaven Ba Gua (p. 258), let's multiply the opposing trigrams line count to see what kind of weight the numbers carry.

In the pre-heaven Ba Gua, we can see that 18 separates the trigrams in half. This means that the Yin and Yang are separated equally on both sides, not mixing with each other. This is called "perfect harmony" or "eternal peace," the state of affairs before we are conceived and after we die. This is unfortunately what modern Chinese medicine teaches as the balance of Yin and Yang, each occupying half and standing opposite to each other. Day is separated from night and hot is separated from cold. However, in the post-heaven Ba Gua, we can see again that Jing and Wei are equal to 20. This means that north-south, east-west weight is equal, but the four corners NE, SE, SW, and NW carry different weight. The change from north to east requires 30, while the change from east to south requires 12. Compared to the addition chart (p. 261) these same positions required 11

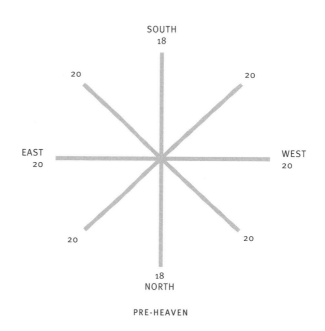

PRE-HEAVEN

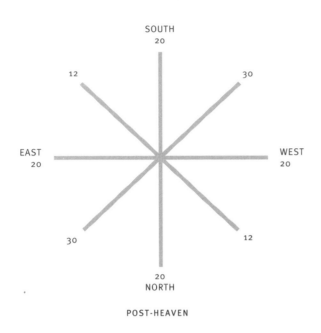

and 7 respectively. When we add the lines of opposing trigrams in the post heaven, change between the four directions needs 11 and 7, but when we multiply the lines in the same opposing trigrams, the change needed between the same directions is 30 and 12. This means that with additions of opposing trigrams 11+7=18 is the change weight of the earth, while in multiplications of the same trigrams, 30-12=18 is the same change weight of the earth. Only with additions does the earth weight add up to 18, while in trigrams multiplications the change weight is subtracted.

The calculations of the hexagrams in these pictures grow more and more complicated, but for us understanding the idea behind it is enough. The pre-heaven state of perfect Yin and Yang balance is a dead state either before we are conceived or after we die. In our lifetime, the Yin and Yang are in constant change. The Jing-Wei and Xing-Ming are constant, however the time elapsing every day, every season and every year carry a different weight, transforming our life into an active ever changing situation. What we strive for with medicine is to understand the weight in between the fixed positions in order to establish the correct weight for harmony. Chinese medicine is not the study of static Yin and Yang, it is rather the study of the weight influencing Yin and Yang. Yin and Yang are visible, however the transformation of the two is not. I can see the day and I can see the night, but I cannot see the change in between. I can see a live person and I can see a dead person, but I cannot see the change between the phases.

The same goes for fertility, conception and pregnancy. We can see the situation before the baby is conceived, namely the father and mother having intercourse. The baby's Yin and Yang are static. The Yang from the father is separated from the Yin of the mother. In other words, there is no embryo yet. Setting aside unnatural modern medicine procedures and equipment, we can see the baby after it comes out to the world, but we cannot see the development of the baby inside the abdomen of the woman. The post-heaven trigrams represent the life of the baby after it is born. For the rest of its life, changes will occur constantly until death. In between the two pre-heaven and post-heaven scenarios, we have the "change". This change is conception and pregnancy, the unification of the father and mother into a new life. It is the invisible change we cannot see with our eyes, yet we can measure its weight and meanings with symbols and numbers. Within the Ba Gua, where is the invisible "change" we call conception and pregnancy? It is within the steps of the trigrams. In the Ba Gua, we have 8 trigrams, of which four are Yang and four are Yin. In order for the pre-heaven Ba Gua to change into the post-heaven Ba Gua, each and every trigram in the pre-heaven scenario needs to make a move. Each move is measured by the number of steps taken by the trigram in order to reach its destination in the post heaven scenario. The picture below shows the steps of the Yang and Yin trigrams, while the trigrams themselves are invisible.

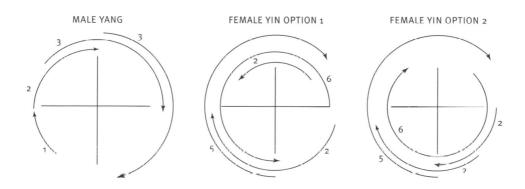

In the pre-heaven Ba Gua, the 4 trigrams on the left side are the Yang trigrams. In order to advance into the Yin side on the right, they make the following steps: 1+2+3+3=9. Adding all of the Yang steps together equals the Yang representative 9. The Yin trigrams on the right have two options to advance into the left Yang. The first option is 2+6+2+5=15. The second option is 6+2+2+5=15. Fifteen represents here a complete Yin number in two ways. In the "River picture" He Tu (chapter 3) 10 and 5 occupy the center and represent "earth." 10+5=15 thus represents pure Yin earth, its trigram with three Yin broken lines. Three broken lines are 2+2+2=6. 15 is also 1+5=6 and thus the description of any Yin line in the **Book of Changes** is 6. In this image of the Ba Gua steps, we can see very clearly what the Yang is doing and what the Yin can do. The Yang male/father can only cross over in one direction, but the Yin female/mother has two options to cross over.

The mother can cross underneath in one direction or she can open up and cross in two opposing directions. If we think about conception, the male has only one option. He can only give his sperm to the female. His steps go in one direction and his number is 9 (Yang/giving).

The female has two options. She can go underneath with all steps in one direction, thus aiming at giving her essence/egg to the male (option 2). On the other hand, she can open up and cross underneath and above at the same time. This allows her to receive the male sperm into her (option 1), meaning that a female can choose, by her actions, if she wants to receive the male essence or not. If she moves in one direction she behaves like the male and at this time, conception is not possible. If she opens herself up to move in two opposite directions, she behaves like a female and unification can happen, creating a new life. This is why a Yin line is a broken line. It can open up in two directions. The Yang is only one line and it can move in one direction.

The earth is the mother of the myriad things. The earth can be fertile or infertile. It depends on how receptive it is to the heaven Yang. If the earth receives the heavenly Yang, life will grow out of it. Important to understand from this image is that the male has no choice, but the female does. If a female acts as Yang, then conception is difficult, but if she acts as Yin, conception is easy. It carries meaning on many different levels and each woman should self examine and decide what more can she do to become Yin. One thing is clear according to the classics; a man needs to be a gentleman, caring, protecting and nourishing the woman. A woman does not necessarily need to be a gentleman. When we compare the images of the steps, we can also see that the male goes from one side to the other or from inside out. In contrast, the female goes to the other side and comes back. This is a clear distinction between Yin and Yang behavior. This is why, during intercourse, the male can give to the female, but the female cannot give to the male. The Yin action is to take in, while the Yang action is to give out. These Yin and Yang steps are conception and pregnancy. They are the change connecting the pre heaven (before conception/ perfect balance) to the post heaven (life/ constant change of Yin-Yang 7, 11).

The science of symbols and numbers allowing us to understand life is the tool that can help us understand Chinese medicine better and in return solve infertility more successfully. Answers to very difficult questions not answered by modern science may be answered. For example, why does a woman produce one egg per menstrual cycle, while a man produces 100 million sperm with each ejaculation? Why when a man produces so many millions of sperm only one sperm makes it to the egg? Why does 1 sperm + 1 egg make only 1 baby?

THE CULTURE'S ESSENCE

The Yellow Emperor starts off by saying: *The men of antiquity knew the Dao.* In antiquity, the vital principle of cherishing ancestry and preserving future generations was widely accepted.

Becoming a selfless nobleman, knowing nature, mathematics and medicine took place in order to preserve this principle. Whenever men of antiquity received awards from princes and emperors, they would use the award to cast bronze vessels. These vessels served as sacrificial instruments by future generations. The ancient bronze vessels, some dating as far back as 2000 B.C. contain ancient texts, allowing us a window into antiquity. Following are a few translations first published in 1899 by the Jesuit missionary Dr L. Wieger, S.J.

On the day Yi Si, in presence of the deceased grandfather, the widowed grandmother has offered, with wine and other precious items, this bronze vessel to last ten thousand years. Hoping that innumerable sons and grandsons will enjoy it forever.

During the 4th year of his reign (B.C. 768), in the 3rd month, the moon beginning to wane, on the day Xin Yu... the emperor proclaimed: 'I give master Ju ten strings of cowries (ancient money). Ju fell on his knees and thanked. Having thus been honoured and rewarded by the son of heaven, I Ju offer this amphora with a basin, to the first ancestor of my race, and place them in the ancestral temple, to be the hereditary treasure of my descendants.

The emperor having received the prime mandate, the great gift of heaven, on ascending the throne (B.C. 571) offers this precious basin, to the spirits of heaven and earth, hoping they will prevent internal wars... To last during ten thousand of generations, forever.

Chinese medicine, a medicine of antiquity, strives to preserve future generations for 10,000 years to come. Infertility treatment is in the core of Chinese medicine, preserving and creating healthy future generations. It is successful in doing so because it springs from a culture that wishes the same. A culture wishing health and vigor for its offspring.

CONCLUSION

Medicine is medicine. As I've stated previously in this book, there is no Chinese medicine or Western medicine, there is only good or bad medicine. Chen Xiuyuan said: *Medicine is in the hands of the doctor and not in the hands of the profession.*

A prospective father came to me with maturation arrest and zero sperm count. I recommended herbs, however his doctor was opposed, claiming herbs as "not being scientific" and further insisting that it might impact his hormones and make things worse. I explained to the patient that there is nothing worse than zero. However, he was worried, and for four months, commenced rigorous medical tests, preparing for sperm extraction from his testicles. At the same time, he decided to try Chinese herbs. To his excitement and the doctor's surprise, within 60 days, sperm began appearing in his semen and extraction was avoided.

Another patient, diagnosed with blood clotting disorder, suffered six miscarriages while trying different blood thinning medications to no avail. After 60 days of herbs and acupuncture, she began carrying a perfectly healthy baby to term. No blood thinning herbs were used, only herbs supporting the Yang.

The challenge of medicine is with the eyes of the doctor. In classical Chinese medicine we recognize high and low level practitioners. High level practitioners see a different method and recognize its strong points, while low level practitioners see its deficiencies. The one who sees the other's strong points can co-exist and thrive, while the one who sees the weak points will always be separated, rivaled and short lived. Western medicine has many strong points, mainly its expertise in the physical body. Chinese medicine has strong points, mainly its expertise in life. The body belongs to earth, while life belongs to heaven. If heaven and earth are separated, it is the pre heaven scenario. There is no life. However, if heaven and earth, each doing its own job, are connected, then life thrives.

Heaven needs to act like heaven and earth needs to act like earth. Heaven and earth connected together does not mean that heaven behaves like earth, it rather means that they are joined together in harmony. Chinese medicine is medicine of heaven and time. Western medicine is medicine of earth and space. When the two medicines join together it is the best that can happen to our bodies and to our lives.

I believe that the future of medicine is in the hands of high level practitioners of east and west who recognize the strong points on the other side because, in their hearts, they truly care about their patients. Medicine is here to help and heal people, to prolong lives and to insure the well-being of future generations. It must learn from the past and look to the future.

It is time to go back to classical thinking. It is time for a change. In the West, the doctor will know patients personally and treat them as if they were his own family as it used to be in the last 2000 years. In the east, practitioners will read the classics again, understand more about life and leave Western medicine for Western doctors. Joining forces so our kids can grow up healthy is the moral calling of the healer. The patient needs to know it. The doctor needs to know it. Officials and policy makers need to follow along.

Healing life is an art, while fixing the body is technology. It is like a piano and music, they are both important. The same is true with medicine. The one who can fix the muscles and bones is as important as the one who can fix the life force. For the sake of patients and future generations, both need to be available to our society. Infertility patients often talk about "window of opportunities closing down." This brings to my mind a folk song I knew as a little boy:

Open the gate, open it wide
through it there shall pass a golden thread;
mother, father, sister and brother
bride and a groom in a chariot of life.
Open the gate, open it wide
through it there shall pass a golden thread;
grandpa and grandma, uncle and aunt
grandchildren and great-grandchildren
in a chariot of strung pearls
Open the gate, open it wide

Natalie and Bob were hoping to get pregnant immediately after their wedding, but it failed to happen for a year. They decided against pursuing the path of drugs and invasive tests. Health conscious and consumers of organic foods, they were concerned about the possible effect drugs might have on their baby. Yaron says that Natalie had been told that she was infertile because her mother used a drug while she was in her womb and had promised herself not to make the same mistake with her own child. Natalie and Bob found the Hunyuan Method through a friend and after six months of herbs and acupuncture, conceived naturally. They gave birth to a healthy baby who reportedly became the smartest boy in his class!

APPENDIX A – PATIENT TESTIMONIALS

Dear Dr. Seidman,

We want to thank you for giving us the most special gift – our little daughter I.M.. After countless fertility treatments, failed IVF procedures, and tearful doctor consultations, we were about to give up on conceiving. We turned to you as a last resort, after our doctor recommended using an egg donor, which is a path we did not want to take. I was very skeptical at first at the thought of taking herbs and doing acupuncture to help my fertility. How can something so simple help me to conceive? But after only 2 months under your care, I was pregnant!! We were so surprised, and so thrilled.

Unfortunately, we found you after we had spent thousands of dollars on fertility treatments. If only we had gone to you sooner. We now have a beautiful, healthy little girl. She is now 6 weeks old, and hanging everyday. Sometimes when I look at her, I'm filled with such emotion. My husband and I are so thankful to have her in our lives. We truly believe that it was your treatments that brought us to a successful pregnancy.

Thank you so much, and good luck with your own baby to be!

Regards, C. & D.

October 2005

Dr. Seidman,

I am sorry we have not been by to visit again. We think and speak often about you – you are one of our favorite people.

Speaking of favorite people, here is another. (Look carefully...two little pearly whites have popped up!

Warmly, C.

Dear Dr Seidman,

Thank you very much for all of your help. The herbal treatments and the acupuncture helped me so much. The treatments helped me to get pregnant and I felt strong and healthy again. In February we were blessed with the birth of our healthy daughter L. She has brought us so much joy and happiness. We are so grateful to you – your kindness and care are much appreciated.

L.

Dear Dr Seidman,

There are no words to describe how grateful we are for all the help in making our dream come true! A. is a very content, happy and healthy child, much loved by her brother.
Truly, C.F.

Dear Dr. Seidman,

Our daughter, A. will turn one in August. Thank you for helping us bring her about
You probably recall that my husband was very skeptical about trying herbs, but that I had watched peers undergo what I consider invasive measures unsuccessfully. I kept hearing that, in the end, herbs and acupuncture had the best results. At age 42, I did not want to waste a whole year or more on Western medicine, only to be disappointed.
My pregnancy was typical and the delivery was without incident. A. arrived one day after the predicted date.
Again, we thank you and wish good things for others under your care.
N.B.

Dear Dr Seidman,

Thank you so much for all your help. I am very happy to report M. is growing very healthy and rapidly. She is almost 6 weeks old now. Thankfully, your herbs and acupuncture got me pregnant. Thank you again. When I am ready to try for the baby #2, I will call you again!
M.C.

Dear Dr. Seidman,

I would have never thought I would be able to get pregnant. Three years ago, I suffered from a stroke. My right side was numb and I suffered terrible back pains. Two years of physio didn't help.
Trying to get pregnant of course didn't work either. The doctors kept me on blood thinners that made it very difficult for me to get pregnant. I have started acupuncture and herbal treatment and after four months the back pains were gone and my right side felt as if I had never had a stroke.
When you asked me if I was planning to get pregnant, I was convinced that there was nothing you could do to help me. I took herbs for four more months, I got pregnant and my baby is nine months old today. My life has changed completely since I came for the first time to your office.
I am grateful forever
T.

Dear Dr. Seidman,

Almost 4 years ago I suffered a miscarriage which was devastating. My husband and I tried unsuccessfully to conceive again and after a year of trying we went to a fertility specialist.

We went thru 2 years of tests, endless needles, blood work, medications, 6 failed artificial inseminations and 2 failed IVF cycles. Every Doctor we went to said everything looked "normal" and we should keep trying different protocols. Not one Doctor could give us a reason as to why I could produce eggs but not fertilize them. One IVF cycle I produced 29 eggs and not one took. All they could tell me was because of my age it is more difficult, I was 36 years old.

Needless to say those years were filled with many tears. Tears of sorrow and frustration. A friend recommended you to me and I thought I would give a more natural course a try. I was a little skeptical to be quite honest, but I figured if nothing else, I could detoxify myself from the past years worth of infertility drugs I had taken.

From our first visit in April 2003 you told me straight on exactly why I could not get pregnant. I thought, "Finally, someone is giving me a solid reason". The beautiful part was that there were no painful needles or intrusive exams.

After 3 months of being on your prescribed herbs, and 20 days of my husband being on herbs, we conceived in August 2003. I am thrilled to tell you we gave birth in April to a beautiful healthy baby boy.

Doctor Seidman, thank you. Thank you for always answering all my questions, being straight forward with me and giving me the answers I was searching for. More importantly thank you for our son!

Sincerely, M.

Dear Dr. Seidman,

I wanted to share my story with other patients who consider your services. I have been taking herbs for 6 months, and while I did not get pregnant I went to a reproductive endocrinologist to try IVF. The RE told me at the 3rd day blood test that my FSH was high-28 so I was disqualified for the IVF. He suggested I use a donor egg. To my amazement, this same month we conceived naturally. I was sure I'll miscarry, but I am 25 weeks now and everything seems great. I am so thankful for your help, as this could have never happened without you.

D.S.

Dear Dr. Seidman,

I am writing this letter to help other women who find themselves in a position I once was. I had problems getting pregnant for 2 years. I have tried Clomaid and three artificial inseminations. Eventually I had no choice but to go through an IVF procedure. Not only I did not get pregnant, my reproductive endocrinologist advised me that a future IVF will not work, and that I should look into a Donor Egg.

You see, I have only produced one egg of poor quality and my progesterone levels were not right. I have started my herbal treatment, and even though it was a bitter tea I have never tasted before, I persisted.

Guess what? It was five months later that I found out to my amaze that I am fifth week pregnant. I found out while I was on a trip to St. Louis. I am not sure if you were able in Connecticut to hear me screaming (of joy) all the way from there.

There are only two words I can summarize my experience with: Thank You.

J.

Dear Dr Seidman,

I just wanted to send you a note to THANK YOU! for your help in bringing E. to us. There is no way for us to adequately express our appreciation. Here is a picture at 4 weeks old!

love

J. & M.

Hi Dr. Seidman,

How are you? I just took 2 pregnancy tests today and both results were positive that I am pregnant. Could the herbs be affecting the results?

I am going to get a blood test tomorrow at my OB/GYN. I am really surprised right now to say the least!

Thanks, S.B.

Dear Dr. Seidman,

I wanted to ask if the herbs could affect a pregnancy test. I drank half a cup on Wednesday night. I took the pregnancy test on Thursday night, but I didn't take the herbs that night. The test was positive. I tested again early this morning and it is positive.

Let me know what you think.

Am I really pregnant?

D.

Dear Dr. Seidman,

Hi, hope you are well. I got back my positive results & had an Ultra sound to confirm I am pregnant. You have been so amazing to me and have helped me out so much. I really appreciate everything you have done for me. Thank you so much

Sincerely, S.

Hi Dr Seidman,

I can't believe it I had yesterday only 3 follicles, and after having one acupuncture session I went in for ultrasound today and we saw 6. After a week of stimming and no response, the doctor just doesn't know where these follicles came from all of a sudden. I guess we will go to retrieval after all.

Thanks a million, D.

Dear Dr Seidman,

Your reading of my pulse was right. It turned out I am pregnant and thrilled. I couldn't believe when you said the pulse looked pregnant, but amazingly it is true.

wow

M.

Dr Seidman,

We are so grateful to you for all the help you gave us. We feel so fortunate to have our son in our lives now. Your attention and care were so appreciated. We believed in making a difference and achieving success. We hope you can meet our son soon. With great thanks

J. & S.

Dear Dr. Seidman

I had never had very regular periods, but at age 26, my periods stopped altogether. I was hoping to get pregnant in the near future and asked my OB/GYN about my chances. She referred me to a Reproductive Endocrinologist (RE) who diagnosed me with low estrogen levels. My RE recommended using injectable fertility drugs to get pregnant. I didn't see any other way, so I decided to give it a try even though my health insurance didn't cover the cost of the treatment. I went through two injectable cycles, one IUI and the other IVF, resulting in a chemical pregnancy and a miscarriage, respectively. In only a few months, I had gained 15 pounds from the hormones and spent over $15,000 with nothing but heartache as a result.

It was at this point that I read about the use of acupuncture and Chinese herbs as infertility treatments. I decided that I had nothing to lose and gave the Hunyuan center a call. I was skeptical of the Hunyuan method, but I decided to have some faith and give the herbs a chance. After a month and a half, I had light spotting and was encouraged. A little over a month later, I was pregnant. I couldn't believe it was so easy after all that we have been through. I had acupuncture treatments during my first trimester to help prevent a miscarriage, and they really helped me relax. I gave birth to a beautiful, healthy baby girl who is one of the most easygoing and happy babies I have ever seen. I can't be thankful enough for this joy.

J.

Dr Seidman,

Thank you from the bottom of our hearts for all your help and support.
K.

Dr Seidman,

An amazing thing happened W. did not get her period, and did a pregnancy test which came up with a second line indicating she may be pregnant. It was a faint line but it was definitely there and she never ever had one before, and she checks herself every month. We are going to repeat the test tomorrow.

She did not drink tea tonight and we wanted to know if she should continue with it. Please email me tomorrow. Also we wanted to continue with treatments even if she is pregnant. And need to know about your post conception programs. I look forward to your email.

Thank you for all your help.

Best Regards,

J.

Dear Dr. Seidman,

It has been an amazing two years since the birth of our beautiful baby girl, S. She is truly a blessing to our family and we are so very grateful to you for your assistance in bringing her into our lives. My husband and I were trying for over a year to get pregnant and were unsuccessful. We tried various traditional infertility options and stopped just before beginning more intensive treatments. I was fortunate enough to learn about your method through another success story patient who told me about it. I am so glad that we gave the Hunyuan Method a try before going to intramuscular injections, etc, both because I was not looking forward to the pain of those shots and because after only being on herbs for one month, we learned that we were pregnant! It was so simple, painless and natural. Not only were you able to help us get pregnant, but you also brought me to a stronger sense of health and well-being in general. I would (and have!) tell anyone in this situation to give the Hunyuan Method a try. Centuries of successful pregnancies can't be wrong! Here is a picture of our little one...thank you, thank you, thank you!

All the best, T.

Hi Dr. Seidman,

Hope all is well. Over the past two weeks, I lost track of time with scheduling an appointment. Yesterday, to our great disbelief, after being 5 days late, I took a home pregnancy test and it was positive! We are proceeding very cautiously and I am going for a blood test today. Interestingly, a blood test on Day 21 led the doctor to believe that my estrogen and progesterone were 'normal' but that I was probably not pregnant. So we are bit mystified.

Thanks so much, P.

Dr Seidman,

Words can't express my gratitude to you. I know that the acupuncture was a big help in conceiving this beautiful baby. But even more important was your caring nature. You helped me to believe that I would have a baby and taught me patience. Thank you so very much for everything. We are enjoying these early days with C. and will come by soon to visit you.

M.K.

Dr. Seidman:

Our story is a bit less complex than most of your patients, but surely others can relate. As you know, I faced issues relating to pregnancy as I had a history of miscarriages. After having a third miscarriage, my gynecologist recommended my husband and I make an appointment to discuss infertility options with an infertility clinic. At the time I was 32 years old and thought there had to be a better way. I ended up finding you by chance as I was researching options. At first, I was not too sure how you would help. But after I began to understand the Hunyuan Method I was less skeptical and trusted in your method. After six months of following your direction and taking the herbs specific for my needs, we did in fact become pregnant again. This time, however, we stayed pregnant! Our little girl, K. R., is now 10 months old. Like most that have experienced having a child, I look at her and think of how blessed we are to share our lives together. From time to time I also think of how blessed I was to find you and trust in your expertise as you helped to make this experience possible. Thank you Dr. Seidman.
C.

Hi Dr. Seidman,

I just wanted to let you know that our new little girl has arrived! Her name is P.L. and we call her P. for short. She was born on Sunday, August 26 at 7:43 p.m. and she weighed in at 6 lbs. 12 ounces. She is a delight – mom and dad are both thrilled! Thank you so much for everything that you have done for our family. I have already recommended you to other friends of mine who are struggling to build a family and if we decide that we would like a second child, we will be back!

Thank you again – my husband, P. and I are all so grateful to have had you as our doctor. Warmly, A.F.

Dr Seidman,

Once again – thank you very much for all your help and support (the second baby with Hunyuan). T.

Dear Dr Seidman,

M. is born Saturday the 29th at 2h56 am: 7 pounds and 20 inches.

So far she is in perfect health. I keep thinking "thanks to Dr Seidman".

We're so happy of her. She's alert and yet serene. And of course she's the most beautiful baby in the world!

To go on with the good health we would like to come and begin with the breastfeeding plan.

Yours, C.

It seems the fifth time was the charm! Our son J. T. was born last Tuesday, 7 lbs., 10 oz.

Thanks so much for your work with us. We greatly appreciated your effort and understanding.

So, best wishes to you and thanks.

G.K.

Hi Dr. Seidman,

I have been meaning to e-mail you lately. Hope you and your family are well and that your son is growing leaps and bounds! Our little girl surprised us and decided she wanted to come early! I will send you a picture and stop by someday soon. I can't tell how grateful we are to you. Each time she opens her beautiful eyes and looks at us, J. and I well up with joy and know that she wouldn't be here if we had not found you.

Hope to see you soon, P.B.

Hi Dr. Seidman-

Well, it happened early – I gave birth to J.W. in November. He's doing great...

I don't think I'll be leaving the house for the next few months, so I'll start again next year when we're ready to try for another one!!

Thanks again for all your help with this pregnancy. I truly believe that you are the reason I finally got pregnant and had a healthy baby boy!! You are a sensational healer. I'll send pictures soon.

A.W.

Hello Dr. Seidman,

I just wanted to send you an update – I am 17 weeks pregnant and all looks good. We had our triple screen with the nuchal ultrasound and the baby is fine. I also started feeling the baby move this week! Our due date is ~ May 28th.

Thank you again for all of your help!

Enjoy the holidays,

J.

Hi Yaron-

I just got off the phone with a friend who made an appointment with you on Saturday. Their struggle with infertility is similar to mine, but they already have 1 child. I am hopeful that you will be able to help them, because to me you are a miracle worker. Their names are A. and D. Good luck! I'm really excited they finally decided to come talk to you!

Things here are going well. Little N. is thriving and putting on good weight. Having a child is harder than I thought though, I must admit. I attached a picture of my dog and N. for you.

I'll try and stop in sometime soon with N. so you can meet your creation.

Hope things are going well.

Thanks, A.

Yaron,

We are extraordinarily grateful for your help and care, without which I am certain we wouldn't have G. He is heaven-sent! Your work is superb.

K.

Dear Dr Seidman,

We are sending you THANK YOUS! galore. Here is a picture of our two miracles that you helped bring to us. Everyone is doing well. Thank you seems such a small way to express our gratitude for walking with us through this journey. We can never fully express all that you have done for us. Your family will always be in our prayers!

Love J., M., E. and M.

Hi Dr. Seidman!

It's been a while since we last "spoke!" I hope you are doing well! Everything with me is going really well. I am writing for a couple of reasons:

(1) The biggest news of all… WE'RE PREGNANT!!!!!!!!! Yes, it's true! Can you believe it? I am in my thirteenth week, and feeling very good. I want to thank you because I think you had a lot to do with it! We conceived in early April, and I know that the effects of acupuncture/herbs can last for several months. So, THANK YOU! It is truly our dream come true! We feel so very blessed. Life seems all new now! What a wonderful, welcome surprise!

(2) I also wanted to see if acupuncture is indicated during pregnancy. If so, I would like to set up a couple of appointments by the end of the month. Would you have any appointments available? Please let me know.

And thank you, thank you, thank you once again! I look forward to seeing you soon!

All the best, D.

Dear Dr. Seidman:

As I told you this morning, I went to see the doctor today for an ultrasound. I remembered that you had said in all your successes you have never had twins before. Well, there is a first time for everything. The ultrasound showed twins today. It is still too early to say whether I will deliver twins but the doctor seemed pretty confident that both babies had strong heartbeats. Let's keep our fingers crossed and doing what we are doing.

I'll see you on Sat.

D.

I started working with Dr. Seidman and doing herbal therapy because we wanted to have one more successful pregnancy. In addition to trying to get pregnant, I had several other conditions I was dealing with. I had Chronic Lyme disease and had undergone an extensive oral and IV antibiotic treatment for a total of four years. The treatment left my digestive system very weak and I had chronic fatigue. I was also older and a neurotic nervous wreck as a result of the fertility tests and the miscarriages and I felt time was running out.

Despite it all, I persisted with the herbs, and finally, we had our little baby. I was 43 years old.

Writing this letter allows me the opportunity to share some of my life experiences with those who are going through similar challenges, and also to say thank you to Dr. Seidman for helping me accomplish great things in my life.

M.

Dr. Seidman,

I just wanted to share some great news with you. If you remember our story, we did a number of IUIs and IVFs over the past few years. They all failed and doctors did not seem to have an explanation for it. My husband and I met with you last October and by December I was pregnant. On August 11th we welcomed a beautiful very healthy happy little boy! We named him A. R. We thank you for making our dream come true. His birth was very emotional for us. We continue to tell all our friends, family members and coworkers about you and your website. We will be back to you for our next one when we are ready! We have included a picture of our miracle! Thanks again!

L. and C.

INDEX*